Lega
A Subsidiary of Pace Cor

MW00636936

LOWCOUNTRY DAYTRIPS

Plantations, Gardens, and a Natural History of the **Charleston** Region

By William P. Baldwin, III & N. Jane Iseley
Photography by Polly Walton des Francs

Palmettos and pines, the maritime forest at Hunting Island State Park.

By William P. Baldwin, III and N. Jane Iseley
Photography by Polly Walton de Francs

ISBN 978-0-933101-26-5
Library of Congress Catalog Card Number 2010938278

Edited by D.J. Bost, Ben Anderson, Jeff Griffin,
Chad Kirtland, Sarah Lindsay, Alicia Miller,
Amity Moore, and Michelle Wilco

Design | Jaimey Easler, CJE3 Graphic design
Maps | Kari Fellers

Printed in Canada

This book is dedicated to the memory of my father, William P. Baldwin.

I'd like to thank all of the friendly people I met along the way.
The staff members of the parks and other sites were always helpful, as were
the Chamber of Commerce employees I contacted. I tried to visit the library in
each community at least once, and now, more than ever, I'm certain that librarians
are the glue holding Western civilization together: a special thanks to them.
And a special thanks to the following: Clarice and Lang Foster, Bob Barker,
Janson Cox, Julie Finlayson, Genevieve Peterkin, Gurdon Tarbox, Robin Salmon,
Aurora Olivieri, George Rogers, Ben and Betsy Caldwell, Anne Bridges,
Pat Young, Dianne Belle, Cathy Townsend, Oliver Buckles, Richard Fairey,
Mary Belle, Brother Stephen, Bob Mitchell, Irvine Rutledge, George Garris,
Joe Anderson, Will Alston, Tommy Strange, Glen Stapleton, Erin Bronk, James and
Helen Maynard, Vanessa Thaxton, Rena Riddle, Cindy Cole, Betty Cotton,
Lucy Hall, June Berry, Bob Cuttino, my father's friends at Four Hole Swamp,
Bill Obrst, Peggy Harleston, Steve Hoffius, Harlan Greene, Mary Giles,
Margaretta Childs, Mark Wetherington and everyone connected with SCHS,
Mike McLaughlin, Agnes Baldwin (my mom), David Blair,
Jay Shuler, and D.J. Bost, my editor.
                                                        –William P. Baldwin, III

I'd like to thank the special people who helped with the
fact-checking and who graciously gave their time to help drive tours
and check mileage, and to the good friends who offered their support:
David and Anne Bailey, Horry and Dorothy Kerrison, Bob and Mary Dean
Richards, Richard Coen, Elinor Euliss, Virginia Griggs, Cornelia Barnwell,
and Beau Iseley. Thanks especially to the following people at Pace
Communications, Inc.: Sarah Lindsay, Carol Medford, Greg Hausler,
Sheryl Miller, Jaimey Easler, Patricia McConnell, Robert Hudson, Kit Falvey,
Kimberly Cote, Leigh Ann Klee, Dena Caulder, Martha Leonard,
Linda Smith, Laura Archer, and Bonnie McElveen-Hunter.
                                                        –N. Jane Iseley

Preface and Introduction 8

——— ◆ ———

Tour One
Ashley River | Charles Towne Landing to Magnolia Gardens 27

Tour Two
Ashley River | Middleton Place to Summerville 39

Tour Three
Mount Pleasant and Sullivan's Island 59

Tour Four
Beaufort and the Sea Islands 79

Tour Five
Awendaw to Georgetown 99

Tour Six
The Waccamaw Neck 117

Tour Seven
The Savannah River 141

Tour Eight
Four Hole Swamp to Jacksonboro 159

Tour Nine
West Shore of the Cooper River 177

Tour Ten
East Branch of the Cooper River 187

Tour Eleven
Edisto Island 203

——— ◆ ———

Additional Day Trips from Charleston 215

Index 221

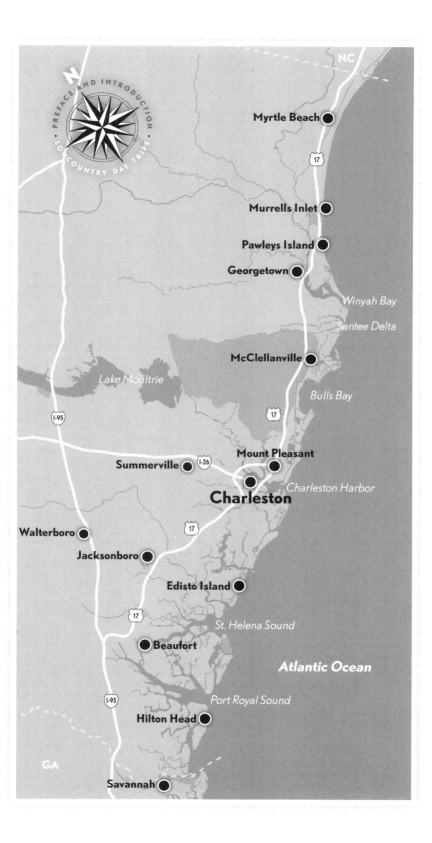

NC

Myrtle Beach

17

Murrells Inlet

Pawleys Island

Georgetown

Winyah Bay

Santee Delta

McClellanville

Lake Moultrie

Bulls Bay

I-95

17

Mount Pleasant

Summerville   I-26

Charleston   *Charleston Harbor*

Walterboro

17

Jacksonboro

Edisto Island

St. Helena Sound

17

Atlantic Ocean

Beaufort

I-95   *Port Royal Sound*

Hilton Head

GA

Savannah

PREFACE

From Murrells Inlet south to the Savannah River and inland 40 miles, the Lowcountry is, in the words of historian W.J. Cash, "unique." He felt that there had been no time between the invention of Eli Whitney's cotton gin and the Civil War for a true aristocracy to form in most of the South. But the Lowcountry was an exception—one of the few places that had been settled early enough to have "something that could be called effective settlement and societal organization." Here, there was a true gentry of indigo and rice planters with wealth, leisure, and learning, educated abroad or well tutored at home. Their sons were our statesmen; their daughters danced at grand balls, and even married European royalty. Yet the plantation system rested on a "mudsill" of forced labor, and the very ground they farmed bred malaria.

Even before the Civil War, the bloom had faded. The white population was often outnumbered 10 to one by its enslaved servants. Political power shifted away from the Lowcountry, and its residents demanded more loudly than ever to be separated from the Union. Romance, violence, death—the Civil War started here, and the aftermath of glory was not sweet. People were too poor to build new houses or even pay the taxes on the ones they owned. Rice, phosphate, cotton, half-wild cows, and hogs—eventually they all played out, and in the end, there was only the wilderness. Nothing changed and, suddenly, that has become an asset: The old buildings are "authentic"; the wilderness is "wilderness." The Lowcountry has been discovered.

Some are alarmed by this abrupt invasion of outsiders and wonder if the isolated and fragile culture can survive. I expect it can, for certain traditions of attitude and place and cultural and personal eccentricities are too firmly planted in this rich soil to be uprooted easily. So, if you're a newcomer, welcome to the Lowcountry; and if you're an old-timer, welcome anyway.

I was born here and have spent most of my life in the vicinity. Roots—I've got them. On my mother's side, one ancestor arrived from Barbados in 1670. He was a planter and deputy governor. His daughter had four husbands, and we're descended from the third. In 1694, another ancestor, a young Dutch soldier, indentured himself long enough to pay for his voyage; he became a carpenter. Others followed from France, England, Ireland, and Scotland. Among my ancestors there were at least one Indian trader, two lawyers, two doctors, two surveyors, one silversmith, one magistrate, three schoolteachers, two storekeepers, one boat captain, one minister, and one sheriff. They fought Indians and owned slaves. At least six had plantations, and yet, with the exception of the first, the deputy governor, there were none that you could point to and call aristocrats—no true gentry. They were planters; they farmed the land and lost it. Their wives raised families and went to church. "Pioneer stock," historian Cash would have called them: "The dominant trait of this mind was an intense individualism. Everywhere and invariably, his fundamental attitude is purely personal and purely self-asserting." For better or worse, I suspect such traits are inherited and occasionally have found their way into this guide.

These are called "day trips," but it usually took me longer to make them, and I'd already seen most of the sights at least once or twice. But I tracked mileage,

gathered information, and spoke with guides and naturalists. My father, William Sr., went with me about a third of the time. He came south in 1938 as a federal wildlife biologist and has worked here since as forester, land management consultant, and plantation broker. He was the naturalist on the trips we made together, and a source of much curious Lowcountry lore. My wife, Lillian, accompanied me on about a third of the trips as well. She, too, has lived her life here, and since she worked with Jane Iseley on *Plantations of the Low Country*, she could often remember the roads, places, and people better than I. Occasionally, my sister Becky would come along. She was good company and fearless on the nature trails.

To the three of them, my heartfelt thanks. When I went alone, I usually tried to pick up a local guide. Many are mentioned by name in the text, but to them, again, thank you very much.

How to Use This Book
You can drive the Lowcountry's length in five hours and its width in less than one. We chose Charleston as a central point because, geographically and historically, it is the center of the area. You don't have to use Charleston as the starting point, though; the maps and directions can be followed beginning anywhere within these bounds. These 11 trips offer a wide variety of stops—plantations, towns, museums, nature walks, churches, boat rides, fish hatcheries, forts, beaches, houses, parks, and much, much more.

The introduction is a short essay on the entire Lowcountry region and discusses its geography, history, architecture, and natural history.

A brief general description begins each trip, listing what can be visited in that particular area. I've done my best to include as entries practically anything and everything to which the public has at least limited access. You'll find phone numbers , websites, and whether there is an admission charge. This information was accurate at publication; we hope it won't have changed too much. There are so many entries that you should be able to make a day's trip out of only a portion of what's offered.

Driving instructions from Charleston begin each tour, and between each entry, further directions are given. Maps are provided not only for the highways you'll be traveling, but for some of the towns, villages, and nature walks as well.

The text for the Day Trips is a collection of entries about each site or point of interest. In each, we've tried to give a brief history, a physical description, and the entertainments offered—in short, what there is to see and do. Along the way, there's also an occasional comment on a particular spot or historical markers passed. Don't feel compelled to stop, though, especially if the battle was 200 years ago and it's a soybean field today.

If you are starting your trips from Charleston and want to return each evening, then it's suggested that you stick with the sites that interest you the most in each trip. Otherwise, if you try to see them all, your return may be very late, indeed! That's just a suggestion, though.

The idea for *Lowcountry Day Trips* wasn't original. We borrowed it from Dr. William Johnson, an intrepid Charleston doctor who, in the late 1920s, would set out on the weekends and journey into the countryside for as long as possible and record what he saw. His day started before dawn and would sometimes end at 2 a.m. You may want to follow Johnson's example, but it would probably be more enjoyable just to ramble along at your own pace and take what comes.

A Few Last Reminders
1. Unless it's the dead of winter, carry insect repellant on all trips.
2. Wherever you are, follow the safety instructions. On the nature trails, keep an
   eye out for poisonous snakes and deer hunters, and don't feed the alligators.
3. Remember that in and around churches and burial grounds, you are a
   favored guest, not a wandering tourist.

4. Many churches can be toured by appointment, even those listed as "Not open to the public." If you are particularly interested in seeing the interior of a certain church, contact someone there, and they may let you visit.

A Last, Last Reminder

This is not a genealogy, history, architecture, zoology, or botany textbook. When a man's life, a battle, a three-story building, or a forest is reduced to one sentence, there's a good chance something will get left out. The mistakes are honest ones. The facts—well, there's a remote possibility that there really isn't a 400-year-old French dwarf ghost living in the basement of that castle. And we'll never know for sure if Drunken Jack was, in fact, a "yard axe" preacher trying to slip away from his congregation for a weekend binge. Better to include a little bit of everything, though; better safe than sorry.

When to Use This Book

Deciding which way to go is easy; deciding when to go is a little trickier. It depends on how much you enjoy the company of other people. It's not likely you'll be waiting in line, but the gardens and towns like Summerville and Beaufort are particularly beautiful in the spring when the azaleas, dogwoods, and wisteria are in bloom. They're also the busiest then. If you want a more solitary visit, content yourself with the architecture and off-season plantings. Autumn foliage can be just as nice—golds, browns, and purples; even the salt marsh changes.

The beaches and towns of Georgetown and Beaufort that depend on an influx of summer visitors are most crowded then, but that is also the time when the majority of the individual tours are available and the park staff is full-time.

The same is true for weekends and holidays. These are usually the most crowded times, and you'll find a few places like the maritime culture centers closed.

Spring and autumn are usually the recommended seasons for the nature trails, but the middle of winter might be best for seeing ducks or combing the beach for fossils. Watch out for the mosquitoes and deerflies during the summer; even with insect repellent they can be unbearable.

These are decisions you'll have to make, but there should be plenty to keep you busy, no matter what time of year, week, or day you travel.

INTRODUCTION

The Lowcountry is low. In fact, in many places, it barely rises above sea level. Protective barrier islands line this 200-mile section of the South Carolina coast, and great expanses of salt marsh usually lie between the islands and the mainland. Here, bays and tidal creeks meander about, then eventually join up with an equally bewildering alignment of freshwater rivers and streams flowing out of the upcountry.

In terms of geological time, it is a new country, one only recently surrendered by an ocean that covered this area half a million years ago. Along the coast and well inland, ancient sand dunes form slightly higher sand ridges and hills. Our highways often follow their crests; the towns and villages we pass through are invariably built upon them. They, too, are islands in a sense, for vast swamplands surround them on all sides.

The European settlers were amazingly quick to understand the potential of this landscape and alter it to suit their needs. They cut, burned, diked, plowed, and built, turning whatever lay in their path into a moneymaking enterprise. In the beginning, it was wilderness, and much of it is wilderness once more. The imprint made on it is there, though faint in places, but still visible; and, of course, there are the buildings—of plantations and towns.

The Walled City

In the spring of 1670, the English settled on the west bank of the Ashley River. Their palisade and collection of cabins was called Charles Town in honor of their king, Charles II. Charles had given the great province of Carolina to the eight "Lords Proprietor" because they had helped him regain the throne. And it was the Proprietors who were financing the settling of what would become known as the Lowcountry. Ten years later, the settlers moved across the river to the present site of Charleston and built a walled city—a fortress to keep out Indians, Spanish, French, pirates, and, occasionally, each other. Gradually the city spilled beyond these confines into suburbs that at first went for blocks and now stretch for miles. From the first days of settlement, however, the adventurous and ambitious were pushing much farther into the unknown. They traveled first by river and Indian trail, then by road and even railroad, but all these routes eventually returned to Charleston.

The city's relationship with the surrounding Lowcountry would be symbiotic, a partnership, for it was from the harbor around the urban peninsula that the produce of the countryside was shipped to distant markets. In 1728, the Proprietors were ousted and, in 1782, so was the king. Much political power shifted inland then, but the city was hardly without influence. It remained the arbiter of all matters of taste and refinement. After all, the fashions and concerns of Europe were only a ship's voyage away, and Charleston was one of the wealthiest cities in North America—its wealth earned in the indigo plots and cotton and rice fields of the surrounding plantations. Great pains were taken to make sure this produce continued to come through Charleston, often at the expense of Georgetown and Beaufort, and even the distant Savannah. The plan failed, of course; other harbors were deeper, or at least more convenient.

THE SITE OF
COLLETON BASTION

THE PLAN OF
CHARLES TOWN
PREPARED BY EDWARD CRISP ABOUT 1704, GIVES THE
LOCATION OF THE SEVERAL BASTIONS

A. GRANVILLE
B. CRAVEN
C. CARTARET
D. COLLETON
E. ASHLEY
F. BLAKE
G. THE HALF MOON
H. JOHNSON'S COVE'S HALF MOON
I. THE PALISADES

OTHER PLACES
K. THE DRAWBRIDGE IN THE LINE
L. THE DRAWBRIDGE IN THE HALF MOON
M. THE PRESBYTERIAN MEETING HOUSE
N. THE ANABAPTIST MEETING HOUSE
O. THE ENGLISH CHURCH
P. THE FRENCH CHURCH
Q. THE COURT OF GUARD

PLACED BY THE CITY OF CHARLESTON
AUGUST 1940

I **H**unting Island State Park.

Cotton was being planted far inland, to the Mississippi and beyond, but on the eve of the Civil War, the city was still prosperous and so was the countryside surrounding it. In five short years, both would lie in ruins. Now, more than a century later, both are rebounding—rebounding because they have remained unchanged for so long.

Islands

There are two kinds of barrier islands. Those to the north of Charleston are called "beach-ridge"; they are formed by the action of the ocean currents and winds. Winter storms wash them down; gentler summer waves build them up. Because of the predominant inshore flow, they erode on the northern end and build on the south (until jetties interfere). Narrow and low, they are often little more than deposits of sand held in place with the help of stubborn vegetation. (Look closely and you can usually see fine sand piled around the base of these plants, one of the stages of dune formation.)

The islands to the south of Charleston are called "erosion remnant" because they are sections of the mainland that have been cut off. The soil here is richer, but these, too, are usually fronted by the same beach-ridge formation and the plants and animals to be found here are the same. It's a young country, and one that is rapidly disappearing. Twelve thousand years ago, the ocean began to rise again, and the shoreline has moved several miles west since then. You may see shrimp trawlers working where there was dry land only a century ago.

Along the wide, gently sloping beaches, you'll find a great variety of shells, flotsam, and even fossils of extinct animals and shards of pottery made by vanished Indians. Higher up, the beaches blend into the dunes where familiar sea oats grow, now protected by state law. Just beyond these, wax myrtles and the red-berried cassina begin. "Salt tolerance" is the key to understanding this maritime forest. Palmettos come next, along with cedars and live oaks draped with Spanish moss. Just inland are magnolias fighting for sunlight beneath giant loblolly pines. Deer browse on smilax here, raccoons ramble down sandy paths, and alligators rest on the banks of brackish ponds, but none of these are on constant display for visitors. The birds are more obliging; migratory and permanent, they are abundant. Especially during the winter and spring "off-season," the Sea Islands are a bird watcher's paradise.

Much of the vegetation characteristic of the area can grow and even thrive on the very edge of the ocean and creeks. But only one plant, Spartina, or marsh grass, can actually grow in the salt water, for its hollow stalk and ribbonlike leaves are a miniature desalinization processor. Only recently appreciated, the continual growth and decay of the marsh grass in conjunction with the tidal flow creates a priceless nursery ground for much seagoing life. More obvious to us are the oyster beds crowding the banks. Here fiddler crabs scurry, while in the creek itself mullet leap clear of the water as rolling porpoises pursue them. And there are more birds, of course—oyster catchers, skimmers, egrets, herons, terns, and pelicans— exotic to the visitor, a pleasure for all.

On the mainland the forest is at first much like that of the islands, but as we move up onto higher ground, the pines begin to dominate. Beneath them an occasional white splash of springtime dogwood shows. Squirrels chatter, birds call. The wildlife is as abundant, but even more elusive. Pockets of hickory and oak intrude. Then the ground drops away to swamps and river bottoms. Massive stands of bald cypress and tupelo gum once dominated here, and still do in a couple of the places we are fortunate enough to visit. Once more, alligators drift by, nostrils and eyes barely above water. Wood ducks whistle by overhead. The strange "knees" of the cypress rise from the coffee-brown water, and a wealth of natural wonder awaits the attentive viewer. This was the land before the white man came.

Aboriginal People

Ten thousand years ago, roving bands of hunters passed this way, but other than an occasional finely worked spear point, we have no evidence of their presence. About 2000 B.C., however, a revolution of sorts took place along these shores. The first pottery in North America suddenly appeared and, in association with strange ring-shaped deposits of oyster shells, suggests that the Indian population had taken the first step toward a semi-stationary, village-oriented lifestyle. A rudimentary agriculture would follow that made possible the great Mississippian culture.

By the time English settlers reached these shores, though, that culture had long since waned, and they found about a dozen small, independent tribes living here. These aboriginal people generally summered in villages close to the salt marsh and rivers. They gathered shellfish and tended gardens of corn, squash, and beans. They hunted deer, gathered acorns and hickory nuts, and took from the forest practically anything that was edible. During the winter they abandoned the coast and, breaking up into family groups, moved well inland. They lived in balance with nature, but it was a precarious balance, especially when faced with the white man's weapons and the far more deadly smallpox that the Europeans brought. Within a generation of contact, these tribes had been decimated, and within a century, they had virtually disappeared from the Lowcountry landscape. Their campsites remain, however. The middens of shell, with broken pottery and other kitchen scraps, are still sheltered by the same oaks and hickories.

Plantations

The first settlers depended on the Indians for food and protection, and almost immediately they looked to them for commercial gain as well. Deerskins bought by often-ruthless Indian traders were a major export of the colony; then, even the Indians themselves were sold. Hogs and cattle were let loose to roam freely. The forest was cut and tapped for "ship stores." Surveyors went to work setting out property boundaries, and a great variety of agricultural experiments began.

For the newcomers, land was wealth and the key to social order. That principle was written into the colony's charter. The eight Lords Proprietor intended to divide Carolina into vast, 12,000-acre baronies that would be sold or given to noble landgraves and cassiques, the colonial equivalents of earls and lords. The less fortunate would receive far less property. The plan failed, for though birth and breeding still mattered, the rigors of settlement seldom suited the lifestyle of a true country gentleman. Within a short time, though, an aristocracy of survivors had established itself, and property was still the basis of wealth and power. The land had become plantations, and the settlers were now planters.

The concept of the plantation was hardly unique to the Lowcountry. On Barbadian estates, slaves grew sugar cane, and in Virginia, tobacco. All Carolina needed was a crop. Olives, grapes, and silk were among the experimental crops, but rice proved to be the answer. Beginning in the early 1700s, inland swamps were cleared and diked—reservoirs provided the water for cultivation. Then, after the American Revolution, the rivers themselves, or at least the surrounding forest and marshes, came under cultivation—the ocean tide pushed fresh water into the fields through special water-control devices, or "trunks." We'll see remnants of the early fields and trunks.

In about 1745, indigo was introduced as an upland crop. Several planters were experimenting, but credit for the discovery usually goes to a 16-year-old Barbadian girl: Eliza Lucas. Indigo produced a dye so valuable that the English offered a bounty to keep it out of the hands of the French, but that incentive ended with the Revolution. We'll visit a vat where the dye was made.

Following the Revolution, Whitney's invention of a better cotton gin brought sudden prosperity to the inland planters, who had the land to grow short-staple cotton. At the same time, Sea Island cotton was being introduced along the coast. With a longer and finer fiber, this long-staple cotton was considerably more valuable. There was less land on which to grow it, but enough so that both cottons could make millionaires of still more Lowcountry planters. Even after the Civil War, its cultivation would continue until the boll weevils' final assault during the first part of the 20th century. Some of the land once used to grow cotton is still being used to plant vegetables, but most is overgrown. If we look carefully, though, we can sometimes spot the rows in the floor of a forest.

The planters prospered. At least most did, and for the luckiest there were the finest wines, thoroughbred horses, and handsome furniture in handsome homes. The sons had the best educations that money could buy, and the daughters, the finest prospects of a good marriage. Coachmen drove liveried carriages. The libraries were grand, the conversation, sparkling. In these homes, an 1804 visitor wrote, "you meet the polish of society, and every charm of social life; an abundance of food, convenience, and luxury."

These plantations, at least the larger ones, were little worlds unto themselves. There was a mansion for the owner, often some flanker buildings, and always a kitchen at some distance from the house. Close by were a smokehouse and creamery or icehouse, and somewhere, a privy. The overseer had a house of his own, and the slaves, a "street" of small single- or double-room cabins. In addition, there were sometimes an infirmary and praise house for the workers, workshops for carpenters and blacksmiths, stables and pasture for livestock, a rice mill or cotton gin, a winnowing house, great storage barns, and a river dock or landing. Beyond that, there were fields. Today, no plantation exists completely intact, but we get some idea at Boone Hall and an even more complete picture at Middleton Place. Bear in mind that even in the world of planters, there were greatly varying degrees of success. Some did quite well on what could more honestly be called farms, rather than plantations.

Gardens

Often, owners cared as much for the grounds surrounding a plantation mansion as they did for the house itself. The live oak avenues are familiar—they are old, but seem older. The saying goes, "An oak grows for a hundred years, lives for a hundred, and dies for a hundred." The avenue was fashionable in England and easy to come by here. Often overlooked, however, are the cedars and magnolias that were equally popular. The gardens themselves were begun along Old World lines—formal, geometric, and trimmed—but by the 1840s, camellias and azaleas were becoming common, and a more romantic approach to plants and their arrangement began. (This was also a time of revival, and many of the oak avenues date from this fairly late period.) At Magnolia and Middleton, we'll see excellent examples of both kinds of gardens; in many other places, too, fine gardens were and still are kept.

Gullah

From its very beginning, Carolina (the Lowcountry in particular) was not viewed with kind eyes—most especially when slavery was the issue. Early Quakers were offended by it and finally settled elsewhere. Bishop Asbury, "the father of American Methodism," traveled here often after the Revolution and wrote, "How much worse are the rice plantations! If a man-of-war is a 'floating hell,' these are standing ones." Similar accusations would be made by early Baptists as well, and then loudly

I **S**weetgrass basket stands entice travelers along Highway 17 North.

voiced by Northern abolitionists until war ended the institution.

If the plantations did succeed in becoming romantic little worlds unto themselves, theirs was not a romance or ease shared by all. Plantations were populated overwhelmingly by slaves—slaves who, to many masters' amazement, were not content with their station in life. The Reconstruction period following the Civil War brought chaos. Blacks, in most cases, would eventually move away or isolate themselves by choice or command in their own communities—communities that kept alive a rich African-American-Creole culture well into the 20th century.

The Gullah language (perhaps a local pronunciation of the word "Angola") is still spoken by the oldest generation, and religious and secular music draws heavily on these roots. Times change, though. In recent years, small cabins with doors and window frames painted blue to keep out the "haints" (angry ancestral spirits) have been replaced with trailers and brick veneer homes. Marsh Tacky ponies and mules have long since given way to car payments. The black population, however, still takes pride in its unique heritage. We'll see basket makers selling their wares at the roadside and, if we're lucky, hear an occasional lapse back into the old music and speech.

The Malarial Coast
Slavery wasn't the only dark cloud over the Lowcountry. Malaria, then called "country fever," was certainly another. "Miasma," or night vapor, was first thought to be its cause. Settlers quickly associated the disease with the swamps and, hence,

with rotting vegetation. Today we know that the female Anopheles mosquito transmits the disease. During the first phase of its life, the malaria parasite develops in the stomach wall of the mosquito. Later in its life cycle, the parasite releases a threadlike spore that the mosquito transfers to a warm-blooded host—in this case, human. Once in the host's bloodstream, the spore enters a blood cell, where it grows, eventually causing the cell to rupture, leaving the spore to attack another cell. Another mosquito bites the host, extracting the parasite, and the cycle continues.

What this meant for the human carrier was a succession of chills and high fever, bouts of which could recur about every three days. At the very worst, this could be accompanied by delirium, coma, and sometimes death. A strong adult might escape and even build up an immunity, but for the very young and old, it was easily fatal. It was also a leading cause of aborted pregnancies. Many planters moved inland with their families or even left the state. Those who remained did so at a considerable risk.

Summer Retreats

From its earliest days, the Lowcountry earned a well-deserved reputation as a dangerous place to live. Yellow fever, also transmitted by mosquitoes, proved even more deadly than malaria, but more urban. From 1700 on, warnings were sent out to prospective colonists that many settlers did not survive the first year's "seasoning." The problem reached epidemic proportions following the Revolution, when a particularly virulent form of the disease swept through the countryside, killing thousands. At that point, the planters began to abandon their plantations between May and November, and to abandon many of their earliest towns and villages altogether. New villages were formed, often only a few miles away. Inland, they were called pineland retreats; it was thought that the pines growing on the high sand ridges prevented the disease. Along the seashore, the credit went to the sea breeze.

Despite the grim purpose that brought these people together, the life of the summer villages was usually remembered as the happiest of times, for it gave the solitary planters a community life. Dances, picnics, horse racing, and of course, visiting, were favorite pastimes. Following the Civil War, these communities became year-round refuges for an entire displaced agrarian population. The passage of a railroad or, later, a new highway, might bend their boundaries, but many are surprisingly intact. You'll notice that, though malaria has long since been eradicated, the distribution of today's population is still dictated to an amazing degree by the flight range of the female Anopheles mosquito.

The two early towns of Beaufort and Georgetown remained safe enough from the fever to be continually occupied. Many other centers of commerce were started, but the competition from Charleston was keen, the self-sufficient plantations had little use for village-based artisans or merchants, and the coming of the malaria epidemics signaled their demise. In these two towns, however, and in the little pineland and seashore retreats that still exist, we'll catch a glimpse of a quieter, gentler way of life and see some interesting architecture as well.

Architecture—Country and Home

About 100 antebellum plantation houses still stand in the Lowcountry, and most can be visited at least once a year on tours sponsored by churches or historical societies. However, only seven are open to the public year-round, and five of these happen to be Georgian. There were three King Georges, and so practically all 18th-century architecture is Georgian. This architecture stressed symmetry: A typical dwelling was two stories with a low-pitched roof and a small central portico entry. That style would change here, for verandas were added quickly, and the original portico, if small enough, was hidden away beneath later alterations. These aren't the traditional white-columned mansions most expect. Only Hampton

Plantation fits that description, and
may have the earliest such grand
portico in the South.

Styles changed slowly here, and
Georgian architecture was never
completely abandoned, especially
its floor plans. In the earliest homes,
there were central public rooms
with drawing rooms to the side, as
in Drayton Hall, but later Georgian
houses were traditionally four rooms
over four with a central-hall dividing
each floor, an arrangement popular
up to the Civil War and afterward.

Next in America came the
Federalist period—the 30 years
following the Revolution when
the influence of England's Adam

Hampton Plantation.

brothers was felt. The Georgian façade might remain, but this period brought
delicate moldings inside and out; curved Palladian windows, and trim double
porticoes. We'll see these in Georgetown and Beaufort.

Then came the period of Classical Revival: Great Greek columns found their way
onto the fronts of many buildings, and we'll see some beautiful ones in Beaufort.
Charleston-born Robert Mills, famous as "America's first native-born architect" and
the designer of the Washington Monument, built public buildings in this style, such
as the Georgetown Court House and at least the portico of Walterboro's.

Following the Greek influence, but hardly replacing it, were the truly Romantic
revivals—a look back at past fashions and a rather loose interpretation of what
was seen. Italianate-style homes, inspired by the villas of Italy, have survived in
Beaufort. Gothic was the return to medieval England, and heavily trimmed gables
of steep roofs and arched windows identify such "cottages". Of these, only Rose
Hill survives, but we'll see plenty of the Episcopal churches built in this style.
A couple of parapeted Gothic "castles" remain as well.

Victorian is the last style we'll look at. An extension of the three revivals
that preceded, especially Gothic, the mood here was definitely away from the
early balance and conventionality of Georgian architecture. The buildings are
asymmetrical, with gingerbread trim and turrets and towers. The Victorian
period lasted from 1860 to about 1900, and we'll see it best represented in
Summerville, but also on Sullivan's Island and, to a much lesser extent,
in other communities.

Churches

When 80-year-old Governor Sayles stepped ashore here in 1670, he had left
Bermuda behind for good—a small, crowded island of dwindling resources
racked by religious factionalism. The same description could have been used
for England, the origin of many of his settlers. The same for Barbados, too, but
those settlers were all Anglican and learned the factionalism when they arrived.
Sayles saw this wilderness as a place to settle "millions" of Presbyterians. After the
revocation in 1685 of the Edict of Nantes, which had guaranteed the Huguenots
the right to private worship, French Protestants lost religious freedom, their rights
to private property, their protection under the laws, and sometimes even their
lives. And so, they came. Sometime around 1690, William Screven led a party of
Baptists down from Kittery, Maine, and his Charleston-based church established
at least five rural churches. Reverend Archibald Strobo, returning from the
failed Scotch colony near Panama, was "ship wrecked on these shores," and he
established five rural Presbyterian churches in the early 1700s. In 1706, however,

the French Huguenots allied with the Barbadian Anglicans. The resulting "Church Act" established the Church of England as the official state church and divided the colony into 10 parishes.

Others were free to continue to worship as they wished, but the Anglicans would have their churches built at the colony's expense and many of these sturdy little brick buildings still can be visited today. The Presbyterians contented themselves with simple frame meeting houses, most lost by now. Because of their opposition to slavery, the Baptists almost disappeared during the 18th century and then revived in the 19th century. This also was the time of the Methodist Revival. Their Bishop Asbury entered the state following the Revolution, mocked the Presbyterians and Anglicans for fighting over who had the highest church steeple in Charleston, and rode out into the countryside to save souls. Other "circuit riders" followed: Wherever eight or 10 would listen, the preacher erected a "brush arbor," which would be replaced with a pole cabin, and eventually with a meetinghouse; the Baptists did much the same. By the 1830s, the rural meetinghouses of Presbyterians, Baptists, and the Methodists were taking on a few of the trimmings of Greek Revival monuments. The early Anglican churches, renamed Episcopalian, were sometimes abandoned, often to be replaced by more conveniently located Gothic buildings. For the most part, all churches remained fairly small and simple. The thrust of the Protestant movement had been to return God's word, the Bible, to the people. And these small buildings, often equipped with high pulpit and sounding board, suited that purpose well. The bell towers and spires, you'll notice, often came as much later additions and sometimes not at all.

Quakers had given up on the Lowcountry early, and several other denominations had been unable to get started in the countryside. The Catholics persisted, though, and so did the Jews, and we'll visit a monastery of the first and a cemetery of the latter. All these places of God are here for us to reverently appreciate.

Battle Lines

In a sense, for much of the time, the Lowcountry was a large and ever-shifting battlefield. The early Charlestonians did well to wall their city, for the grounds beyond were uncertainly held. The Spanish in Florida provided a continuing threat and were always allied with the Indians and sometimes the French. The Yemassee Indians, whom the English had won away from the Spanish to start with, attacked the colony in 1715, and if the Cherokee had joined in, they might well have annihilated it. The Cherokee waited instead until the late 1750s to make one last passing raid through this area.

Along the coast, pirates and privateers careened their ships on the beaches, took on fresh water, and hunted wild cattle. To the planters, they traded their ill-gotten goods. They did so until Blackbeard blockaded the harbor and it was decided that things had gotten out of hand. The settlers successfully discouraged the pirates, but Charlestonians didn't get around to building real coastal defenses until the British attacked in 1775; we'll visit one of these, Fort Moultrie.

In 1780, Charles Town was flanked from the south and fell. From then on, it was British troops and Loyalists in the countryside pitted against guerrilla leaders like General Francis Marion. If it appears that Marion fought at every bridge and crossroads, it's because he did. These were usually not grand battles, just skirmishes, but they were the only American victories at the time. Cornwallis surrendered Yorktown in 1781, but the fighting here would continue for another year. More coastal defenses came with the War of 1812.

It was the Civil War, however, that was to have the greatest impact. Though the majority of heavy fighting in the area took place around Charleston Harbor, to the south, Beaufort and the Sea Islands fell the first year. And all along the coast there was continuing contact with Union army and naval forces. General William T. Sherman entered the state at the war's end and, with associated forces, burned a large path across the southern corner of our area. In isolated spots throughout,

|*St. Philips Episcopal stands sentry over Church Street, Charleston.*

there was wholesale destruction.

With the exception of Virginia, no other state has taken such a continuous pounding, so don't be surprised by the numerous references to battles won and lost, or to the many ancient forts and battle-scarred ruins that dot the countryside.

Internal Improvements

The independent nature of the planters did not lend itself to cooperative efforts, at least not constructive ones. Rivers were the earliest roads for the colonists, who traveled them by canoe, then by flats and rice schooners, and finally by steamboats. The latter, along with gasoline-powered freight boats, supplied many of these rural communities into the mid-1930s. Public commissions depended on private cooperation. Roads were usually Indian paths that had followed the high ridges of the land, but along the coast it was necessary to supplement these with additional highways, bridges, ferries, and causeways. These and short "cuts" between convenient streams were usually a combination of both public and private effort and were poorly maintained.

In 1800, a private canal company managed to connect the Santee and Cooper rivers and thus give Charleston a direct link with the inland producers. In 1818, officials established a state commission that initiated the digging of new waterways and the building of a toll road to Columbia; all soon fell into disrepair. In 1832, the first real railroad in the United States connected Charleston with the Georgia frontier. Then, Columbia, Camden, and eventually Savannah and Charlotte lines were added. In the years following the Civil War, "railroad mania" swept through and completely joined at least the inland portions of the Lowcountry.

Roads came last. If anything, they deteriorated badly after the Civil War. (It has been successfully argued that the South reverted to "a frontier state" during that time.) And Dr. William Johnson could report in 1926 that the only section of the coastal highway paved was the 29 miles between Charleston and Adams Run. The Savannah, Cooper, and Waccamaw rivers were still being crossed by ferry. The work to change this had already begun, but the infusion of federal money during the Depression made it a reality.

The Lowcountry canal was finally finished then as well. We call it the Intracoastal Waterway today, but in the beginning it was the "Inland Passage," a seemingly endless twisting of poorly connected saltwater creeks. The Army Corps of Engineers claims John C. Calhoun as its unlikely patron: In his earliest years as secretary of war, he had empowered the Corps to make such improvements, and it has pursued them with a vengeance. The waterway got most of its straight, man-made sections during the mid-1930s when rushed to completion by the threat of submarine warfare off the Lowcountry coast. Today, however, yachts compose the bulk of the waterway's traffic.

Nature Trails

Several early naturalists passed through the Lowcountry and gave accounts of what they saw: John Lawson, Mark Catesby, and William Bartram came before the Revolution. In the next century, John James Audubon and his good friend Reverend Bachman collected specimens for the former's masterpiece portfolio. It is strange to read their accounts of endless and purposeless shooting of the birds Audubon so skillfully depicted.

Most wildlife, including birds, had been a source of revenue and food from the beginning, but following the Civil War, an impoverished people put extra strain on this natural resource. Carpetbaggers reportedly wiped out most of the shore birds in Bulls Bay. It was not just outsiders who massacred, however. At a later date, shore birds perched at high tide on a tiny bank are described as being shot by cannon in the middle of the night. Egrets and herons were hunted until World War I, when fashions changed and their feathers were no longer necessary for women's hats. Ducks, too, were shot for food and sport in ever-increasing numbers. Well into the last century, it was still possible to have an illegal hundred-duck day. Such shooting finally took its toll, but the majority of the blame landed on the destruction of summer breeding grounds in the northern plains. Today the decline of other migratory bird populations is blamed on a similar destruction of winter grounds—the rain forests of South America.

In 1928, the Savannah Wildlife Refuge was established, joined three years later by Cape Romain and soon after that by the Francis Marion National Forest. Since then, the federal and state governments have increased their holdings and have been joined by a variety of other organizations, such as the Audubon Society and the Nature Conservancy.

Comparatively, then, the Lowcountry is doing well, for there is a concerted effort to conserve what wilderness remains and to preserve the wildlife in it. We find hundreds of thousands of acres held in trust for wildlife habitat and literally thousands of miles of paths, roads, and beaches that can be explored by those wishing to enjoy this natural heritage.

Modern Times

Some will argue that modern times have never come to the Lowcountry. Others think that "modern" means just this side of the antebellum period. They say "The War" when they mean the Civil War, forgetting that there have been several wars since. In 1886, an earthquake flattened much construction and sent a small tidal wave that destroyed the crops on the Sea Islands. In

1893, a great hurricane drowned thousands, left tens of thousands homeless, and marked the beginning of the end for rice planters. Phosphate mining began just after the Civil War; by hand or dredge, it was stripped from the earth south of Charleston to be pounded into fertilizer. Populist governor Ben Tillman allegedly taxed this industry out of existence in 1890, but there was already growing competition from elsewhere. By 1920, the boll weevil had finished off the cotton, and "truck crops" took its place. These vegetables, along with soybeans, are still being grown in ever-decreasing fields. For 250

I **E***disto Beach State Park and Nature Trail.*

years, the Lowcountry had been open range: Cattle were sometimes branded, and hogs sometimes had their ears notched, but both ran wild until the 1930s. A new system of mechanized logging reached the Lowcountry forests at the beginning of the 20th century, and today lumber and pulpwood are harvested even more systematically. Much once-cultivated land has reverted to forest. At least most of the small areas of virgin timber are designated as wilderness and will remain untouched.

Following the Civil War, the population quickly turned to the "creek" for food and a livelihood. Oysters and terrapin emerged as two of the earliest exports. Surprisingly, Charleston was the chief producer of shrimp in the nation in 1880, but that would have been seining and casting; a real shrimp boat wouldn't show up for another 45 years.

Modern times. When do they really begin? When does an essentially rural community become urbanized? When people commute to work? Get electric lights? Or buy a television? When no one nearby remembers your grandparents? With the Lowcountry, the process probably began with the New Deal. The Army Corps of Engineers moved a lot of dirt around, and the "Gov'ment" bought up a lot of land. You'll see that. Now it's more fashionable than ever in this conservative section to grumble about the wastefulness of the federal government up there in Washington, D.C., but Franklin Roosevelt poured millions of dollars into this area during the 1930s. He educated people, gave them health care, and gave some of them their first real jobs. His success was marginal. In 1940, South Carolina remained the most illiterate state in the Union. Even today, we rank dismally in any contest that ranks practically anything—unless it's toxic waste or voter apathy. That's the downside of a basically unchanging culture.

Our day is coming. Maybe it's already arrived. Drive around and take a look at the treasure of architecture and landscape that has been preserved. That's the upside of an unchanging culture. And keep an eye out for what our Lowcountry poet laureate, Archibald Rutledge, called "life's little extras": sunsets, wildflowers, summer breezes, birds' songs, and those intangibles that don't get ranked in national surveys. These little extras are included here at no extra charge. On the house. Be my guest. And begin.

A Note From the Publisher

1. Drive carefully. Remember, only you are on a leisurely sightseeing tour, and the rest of the world is involved in its daily rat race.

2. The number before each entry corresponds with the numbered location on each tour map.

3. Each tour begins and ends at one of three places **(see map below)**:
   a. The south side (the side away from downtown Charleston) of the Ashley River Bridge on U.S. 17.
   b. The north side (the side away from downtown Charleston) of the Arthur Ravenel Jr. Bridge on U.S. 17.
   c. At the intersection of Interstate 26 (Exit 221) and U.S. 17.

4. Before each driving instruction, there are two numbers. The first, or left-hand, number, is the cumulative mileage for the tour. The second, or right-hand, number is the mileage since the last driving instruction.
   Example:
   45.6   1.5   At the stop sign, turn....
   46.5   0.9   Turn left at the corner of....

5. All the tours in this publication were driven with the same car, but since odometers vary in accuracy, accept the mileages as approximations.

6. Because the mileages are approximations, use mileages in combination with road numbers and road and street names to arrive at your destination.

7. A digital odometer was used to clock the mileages, so no fractions smaller than tenths were available. Be aware that, as a rule, mileages may be short.

8. The cumulative mileages were recorded by adding the mileages from each instruction. As a whole, mileages may be short because all distances shorter than a tenth of a mile were lost.

STARTING POINTS from **CHARLESTON**

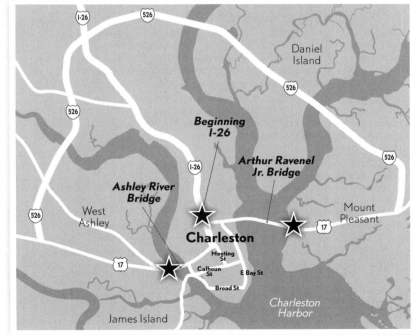

9. In South Carolina county highway numbers, such as S-10-584, are printed in white on black rectangular signs at the top of stop signs **(see right)**.

10. South Carolina intercounty highway numbers, such as S.C. 48, are posted along highways on white signs with black lettering.

11. United States highway numbers, such as U.S. 78, are posted along highways on white signs with black lettering inside a black outline of a shield.

12. Interstate 26, or I-26, signs are marked by a shield-shaped sign with a blue background and red-and-white lettering.

Identifying county highway numbers.

13. The mileages for this guidebook were driven four times, with the last tours driven in 2009. But, because of road construction in the Charleston area, be aware that there may be detours or new roads that may change your route.

14. This is a driving-tour guide. You must use your own good judgment for safe driving. Sightsee only after you have safely stopped the car.

15. The tour information presented was correct when this book went to press; every effort was made to confirm that sites were indeed open to the public and that boat and walking tours were scheduled as listed here. The publisher cannot be responsible for changes in schedules or status.

Additional Reading

A good place to start general reading about South Carolina is David Duncan Wallace's *South Carolina: A Short History*. Samuel Gaillard Stoney did the first definitive book on plantations: *Plantations of the Carolina Low Country*. I did the text for the second definitive book, *Plantations of the Low Country*. My mother, Agnes Baldwin, did the research, and Jane Iseley did the wonderful color photography. Sam Stoney's book is back in print, but Harriette Leiding's excellent *Historic Houses of South Carolina* is harder to find. You can still find Mills Lane's *Architecture of the Old South: South Carolina*. Look for E.T.H. Shaffer's *Carolina Gardens* and James Henry Rice's *Glories of the Carolina Coast* in the library. For naturalists, there are a least a dozen early books to enjoy—Lawson, Catesby, Bartram, and Audubon are all in print in one form or another. Arthur Wayne's *Birds of South Carolina* and Edward Burnham Chamberlain and Alexander Sprunt's *South Carolina Bird Life* are thorough studies. There are many field guides on the market. Audubon and Peterson both worked here; the books bearing their names are excellent for birders. You also can find guides covering everything from seashells to wildflowers—on a local, regional, or national level. Bert Bierer's *Indians and Artifacts in the Southeast* is the best handbook on Indian artifacts. Gene Waddell's *Indians of the South Carolina Low Country* contains every colonial word ever written on the Lowcountry's original tribes. Frederick Dalcho's 1820 history of the Episcopal church contains more than church history. *South Carolina: A Guide to the Palmetto State* was published in 1941 by the workers of the Federal Writers Program. It was one of my inspirations; I refer to it as the "WPA guide." My other inspiration was Dr. William Johnson, whose three bulging scrapbooks are in the South Carolina Historical Society. He's usually referred to here as "Dr. Johnson." *The South Carolina Historical Magazine* is a wonderful source of information, and *South Carolina Wildlife* magazine was an invaluable aid.

The Ashley River | Charles Towne Landing to Magnolia Gardens

TOUR ONE

THE ASHLEY RIVER | Charles Towne Landing to Magnolia Gardens
From Charleston, we cross the **Ashley River Bridge** and follow highway
S.C. 61 for about 12 scenic miles. At **Charles Towne Landing State Park**, site
of the first English settlement in 1670, we witness the "New World" as the first
arrivers might have. **Old St. Andrew's Parish Church** stands close by. A few
minutes farther along S.C. 61, we tour **Drayton Hall**, a grand Georgian mansion
and the first in America to use the distinctive Palladian portico. Just next door,
Magnolia Gardens invites us to stroll through one of America's earliest Romantic,
or informal, gardens. A world-famous tourist attraction in the early 20th century,
the plantation and garden today offer the modern visitor even more, notably the
Audubon Swamp Garden.

Charles Towne Landing State Historic Site
   1500 Old Towne Road | 843-852-4200 | *www.charlestownelanding.travel*
   Admission charged.
Old St. Andrew's Parish Church
   2604 Ashley River Road | 843-766-1541 | *www.oldstandrews.org*
   Grounds open daily.
Drayton Hall
   3380 Ashley River Road | 843-766-0188 | *www.draytonhall.org*
   Admission charged.
Magnolia Plantation and Gardens / Audubon Swamp Garden
   3550 Ashley River Road | 843-571-1266 | *www.magnoliaplantation.com*
   Admission charged.

BEGIN TOUR
0.0   0.0   *Take U.S. 17 South out of Charleston. Begin clocking*
                    mileage at the south side of the Ashley River Bridge.

❶ ASHLEY RIVER BRIDGE, c. 1926
Travelers crossed the Ashley River here by ferry until 1803. General P.G.T.
Beauregard burned the original bridge when he learned that Sherman had
entered the state. Ferry service resumed until 1885, when a toll bridge was built:
5 cents for walkers and 10 cents for horse-drawn vehicles. The current structure
opened in 1926 as a memorial to soldiers killed in the Great War. (After the
next war, it was a memorial for both.) Brand-new, the bridge was billed as "the
handsomest and widest in the South" and an important link in the new Atlantic
Coast Highway, the "all paved road from Quebec to Florida."

How the Ashley River Got Its Name
The Ashley and Cooper rivers were both named for one of the Lords Proprietor,
the Earl of Shaftesbury, otherwise known as Anthony Ashley Cooper. Described
as short and ugly and having a surgical drainage tube permanently implanted in
his side, His Lordship still had a reputation as a notorious rake. His patron,
King Charles II, once referred to him as "the biggest whoremonger in England."

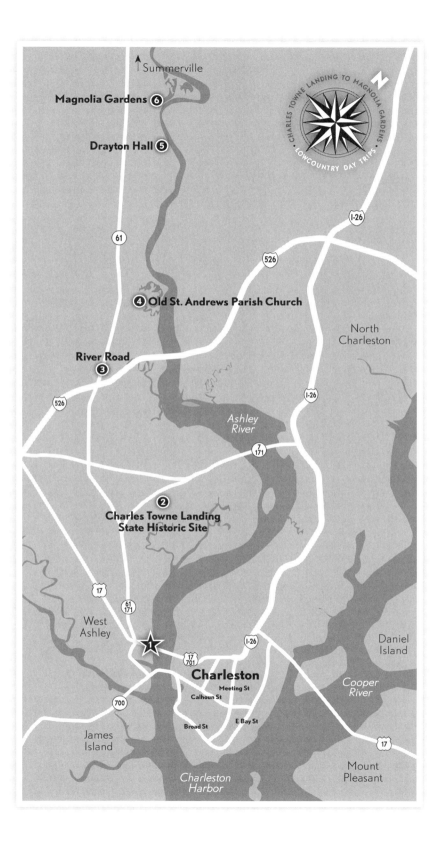

More noteworthy was the almost Machiavellian political career of this early defender of English democracy and "father of the Habeas Corpus Act." Though he'd been given his share of Carolina as a royal gift, for a time he ran the colony from a cell in the Tower of London.

200 ft **200** ft	*Veer right onto S.C. 61 North / St. Andrews Blvd.*
2.0 **2.0**	*Veer right onto S.C. 171 / Old Towne Road.*
2.9 **0.9**	*Turn right into entrance gate of Charles Towne Landing State Park.*

History of Charles Towne Landing

The first permanent English settlers endured a stormy ocean voyage. Of the three ships that set out, two had to be replaced in mid-passage—only the *Carolina* survived. However, these proved to be fortunate accidents. Along the way, the settlers chanced upon their "marooned" Indian interpreter and negotiator, young Dr. Henry Woodward, and picked up a new governor, 80-year-old Bermuda administrator William Sayles.

The choice of a town site proved equally fortunate. Their Proprietor sponsors had planned to settle them at Port Royal. However, the chief of the Kiawah Indians, wanting protection for his tribe, warned that this area was open to attack from both the warring Westoes and the Spanish. Governor Sayles heeded the Kiawah recommendation and instead chose this peninsula well up the Ashley River. About 150 settlers came ashore here in April 1670. They called their town Albemarle Point in honor of the Proprietors, who renamed it Charles Towne in honor of the king.

A fair number of letters and documents have survived from this period, so we know something of the hopes and needs of the settlers, their political squabbles, and even their personalities. Surprisingly, we know very little about the actual town and adjoining settlements. Apparently, as their first project, the settlers erected a palisade across the 10-acre tip of the point; trenches, moats, embankments, and "seaven great Gunns" soon supplemented the fortification. In September of that same year, the Spanish enemy and its Indian allies attacked, but were repelled at some distance by the colonists and their own Indian compatriots.

In the summer of 1672, the settlers divided an 80-acre tract just beyond the palisade into 62 building lots, each with a 10-acre garden plot nearby. From the beginning, the houses here were crude. Governor Sayles was allotted "a mansion," but later, subsequent Governor West described the ones he built only as "convenient." Experiments in agriculture came quickly, and the Proprietors encouraged craftsmen to immigrate. Cattle, hogs, sheep, and horses arrived soon after humans, and the cattle quickly provided a good source of income. Rosin, timber, and deerskins traded from the Indians were the first exports. Barbados was a chief trading partner, and Barbadians looking for new land became eager immigrants.

Even as Charles Towne was being divided into lots, authorities were planning another settlement. Governor Sayles was ill and would live less than a year, but he had the foresight to set aside 600 acres of Oyster Point (now Charleston) for a future town and fort. Plans for this new port town continued, and in 1680, the government officially moved across the river to a new Charles Towne. This spot between the Ashley and Cooper rivers was an immediate success—it grew from four houses to 100 in just two years. The original settlement was quickly deserted and ended as Old Towne Plantation—owned by the Waring family until 1969.

| **3.6** **0.7** | *State historic site parking lot.* |

❷ CHARLES TOWNE LANDING STATE HISTORIC SITE, c. 1670
Open to public.

Opened as part of the state's tricentennial celebration, this park gives visitors an idea of what the first arrivers would have seen and felt in 1670. For $1, we pick up a map at the entrance for a self-guided tour. I've visited here in the winter when there weren't a dozen people in sight, but on a midsummer tour the park can be filled with visitors—mostly families.

The History Trail travels about 1.5 miles roundtrip from the Visitor Center, which opened in 2006. It winds past the Legare-Waring House, a site overrun with weddings, receptions, and other celebrations. The house is open for tours in January, February, July, and August, but really there's little to see inside except the interior architecture of 1840 and a very few pieces of period furnishings. The trail then wends to the edge of the palisade and an archaeology exhibit, where work continues today. Weather permitting, staff archaeologists

The *Adventure*
*This 53-foot-long vessel would have been used only for coastal trading. The replica is a favorite attraction, especially for children. And since the vessels of passage were hardly bigger than this one, the **Adventure** gives us some idea of the hardships of ocean crossing. An interpreter works daily with visitors, especially youngsters, showing them what it was like to operate the ship.*

spend their days in the field, uncovering and cataloging artifacts. Inside the palisade, we're standing in the original settlement area, circa 1670-80.

Before leaving England, Joseph West (the second governor) had been instructed to carry along "cotton seed, Indigo seed, Ginger roots ...Canes...Ollive setts...and upon arrival build a right house for self and servants and then plant corn, beans, peacse, turnips, carretts, and Potatoes." He also was instructed to build a fence for the cattle that would soon be sent down from Virginia. A selection from this first experimental farm is grown today, but ironically both indigo and cotton were crops of the future, and the colonists were soon relying on Indian corn to keep from starving.

There are no definite records, but historian H.A.M. Smith suggests that the first settlers built cabins with poles or axe-hewn beams. The park staff, pointing to the presence of a trestle saw and carpenters among the settlers, suggest otherwise: Construction from the beginning was at least as advanced as half-timber construction. In fact, timbers and sawn planks were an early export.

From the beginning, all sorts of artisans were encouraged to come, and some did. Still, a 1682 instruction advises newcomers to bring along clothing, shoes, ammunition, hardware, nails, and sails. Since the records are so scanty, the stocks we see are probably a guess, but a good one.

From here, it's a short walk to the *Adventure*, a replica of the ketch settlers used for trading, before looping past the Horry-Lucas site, a statue of Kiawah Indian "Cassique," a Native American ceremonial center, and the Animal Forest.

At the Animal Forest, we see some of the species the settlers encountered. (The bison and puma may have been smaller varieties.) To the Indians here, the animals were sacred brothers with whom they shared the wilderness. I've gone back to the early records for accounts of the animals: John Henry Logan's *History of the Upper Country of South Carolina* (1700), Mark Catesby's *The Natural History of*

Carolina, Florida and the Bahama Islands (1731), and *Carolina* (1862) by Thomas Ashe, for whom fireflies and hummingbirds were the true marvels.
You can also read the modern information inside the park.

The Animal Forest covers about 20 acres of Lowcountry wilderness. The half-mile trail is an easy up-and-back walk that often brushes against the marsh and proceeds past the following exhibits:

Shore bird aviary | The pelican, naturalist John Lawson writes, has a pouch to hold its prey. "Web-footed, like a Goose, and shap'd like a Duck. The food is never eaten but they make Tobacco pouches of his maw." Of herons, he writes: "They were the same as in England. Plentiful…White Herns… are as white as Milk, and fly very slowly." Aptly put.

Black bears | Logan says that for the Indians the black bear was an "essential of their domestic and religious life," providing perfume, oil for skin and hair, insect repellant, and a preferred food. The only carnivore eaten by the Indians, Lawson says, "equalizes, if not excells any Meat I ever eat in Europe."

Deer | Indians upheld deer as the most sacred animal, and next to combat, the number of deer slain by a brave was the best measure of his success. They killed millions for their skins alone, and Logan complains that the carcass was often left to rot. Lawson points out several differences between the English deer and our "Fallow-Deer," and calls them "one of the best commodities Carolina affords."

Elk | Logan says that the Indians valued the elk for its horn and skin; it was one of the first animals to disappear from the colony.

Bison | For the Indians, the buffalo was "the Bull of the Gods." Even in Carolina, Logan says, they were stalked and stampeded as on the western plains. "A bunch on his back" is how Lawson describes the bison, and he says few remained in 1700.

Wild turkeys | Wild turkeys were baited with maize into pens by the Indians or decoyed with tame turkeys. Lawson claims to have seen 500 in one flock, and notes that eight hungry men get two meals from one bird. He correctly points out that the head of the wild variety was one color.

Bobcats | Quite different from bobcats of Europe, notes Lawson, they are large, fierce, and nimble, with a "Tail that does not exceed four Inches," and can overpower swine and occasionally deer by leaping onto their backs from trees. "That he can conquer, he destroys," says Lawson.

Puma | The panther, or puma, was the "Cat of God" for the Indians. Children of the first Americans slept on its skin, says Logan. There were only a few left in the state in 1859, and today, there aren't any. "Greatest enemy of the planter," writes Lawson of the puma. In 1695, the colonial government demanded that every Indian bowman bring in yearly one wolf, one tiger, one bearskin, or two wild cat skins. The Indian was to be whipped if he failed, but soon a bounty replaced this directive, and these predators were on the way out.

Otters | This animal didn't surprise; the same as in Europe, Lawson says. "I shall insist no farther on that Creature. Their Furs, if black, are valuable."

And we'll insist no more on Charles Towne Landing State Historic Site. It is a nice place to spend much of the day and fun for children especially.

3.6	**0.0**	*Retrace to main gate of Charles Towne Landing.*
4.3	**0.7**	*Turn right onto S.C. 171 / Old Town Road and move into left lane.*
4.6	**0.3**	*Turn left onto Sumar Street, which is hard to see.*
4.6	**1** blk	*Turn left onto S.C. 7 South / Sam Rittenburg Blvd.*
6.1	**1.5**	*Turn right onto S.C. 61 North / Ashley River Road.*
6.5	**0.4**	*Veer right, continue on S.C. 61 North / Ashley River Road. Ignore the brown informational signs that say "To Plantations and Gardens," which indicate the other route.*

| *Live oaks drape Highway 61, The River Road.*

❸ RIVER ROAD

Highway 61 was once the "River Road." Most of these river systems had river roads—Indian trails and wagon paths that were widened to link plantations originally reached by water. This road has been a matter of controversy because the giant oaks crowding its edges proved a danger to the ever-increasing traffic. It appears that in this section, at least, the trees have lost the battle. It's not such a new problem, though, for E.T.H. Shaffer, author of *Carolina Gardens*, quotes a 1721 statute stating that the road commission would deliberately leave "such trees standing on or near the line of such road or path." Anyone cutting within 10 feet of the path paid a fine of 20 shillings per tree. The pound is up. Somebody owes about 75 cents an oak.

9.0   2.5   *Turn right into parking lot of Old St. Andrew's Parish Church.*

❹ OLD ST. ANDREW'S PARISH CHURCH, c. 1706
Open to public.
St. Andrew's Parish was one of the 10 created by the Church Act of 1706. This cruciform church, a rare style in the Lowcountry, was constructed in that same year, making it the state's oldest. Over the west door, early brick masons and wardens likely inscribed "Superv. 1706 J.F.-T.R."

Thanks to a $1.5 million restoration completed in time to celebrate the church's tricentennial in 2006, the church looks much as it did in 1706. The nave to our left is the original building; the transepts (wings) and the chancel (for priest and altar) are a 1723 addition. If you're able to peek inside, note the reredos above the altar. These printings of the Ten Commandments and the Lord's Prayer also date from

1723. Also notice the marble baptismal font; its base is of three carved pelicans, the symbol of the Anglican Society for the Propagation of the Gospel.

A 1764 fire partly destroyed the building, and with the repairs, the window behind the altar was enclosed. To cover the cost, the church sold pews to the congregation; those too poor to pay worshipped from the balcony. Like most other Anglican churches, this one fell on hard times after the Revolution, but vestryman William Bull repaired it in 1855, and Reverend Grimke-Drayton of nearby Magnolia Plantation kept the little congregation together until his death in 1891. The Colonial Dames repaired the building again in 1933, but services didn't resume until 1948.

The ancient graveyard is pretty, with many stones crowding close to the structure to increase the chances of a heavenly reward. Off to the left, one stone bears the account of Thomas Nairn, "brutally murdered by the Indians." Nairn was among the boldest Indian traders. Traveling to the Mississippi, he sent back to his supporters thoughtful reports sprinkled with Biblical and classical allusions. He planned to use Indian allies to forcibly take the Mississippi Valley from the French. The United States purchased the valley more than a century later. In the first moments of the Yemassee uprising, Indians captured Nairn, stuck him full of lightwood splinters, and slowly burned him to death for two days. Contrary to tradition, this is not his grave. His son is buried here, and the account of his murder is on his wife's stone.

9.0   **0.0**   *From church parking lot, turn right onto S.C. 61 North / Ashley River Road.*

Scenic Highway 61
This section of S.C. 61 is designated a scenic highway, and though the oaks aren't quite so large as those we just passed, this part is well canopied. When the leaves fall, we can see that some of the low places are still marked by the eroded ridges of rice-field dikes. In other spots, note the mounded earth left behind when phosphate was mined here after the Civil War.

From the very earliest days of settlement, this was plantation country. At first, any crop attempted by a planter was considered a plantation—10 acres or 1,000—but the meaning changed quickly, especially in this area. Runneymede, Ashley Wood, Soldiers Retreat, Archdale, MacBeth, and Millbrook: Shaffer says 35 mansions graced these banks before 1800—most surrounded by great groves and avenues, gardens and terraces, and fields planted in rice. These were probably the finest estates in the Lowcountry, but it's sometimes debated whether after the settlement years they continued as working plantations. Much of the money was being made in rice fields elsewhere and these were largely baronial estates. The debate goes on, but in 1865, Union troops moved up the river and burned almost all the houses.

11.6 **2.6**   *Turn right into Drayton Hall entrance.*

❺ DRAYTON HALL, c. 1738
Open to public.
Drayton Hall is considered among the finest examples of Georgian Palladian architecture in America. "Georgian" refers roughly to most 18th-century English design. "Palladian" refers to the 16th-century Italian architect Andrea Palladio, who, influenced by early Greek and Roman buildings, used columned porticoes and other classical elements in domestic architecture. This, then, was the current style of the English country house at the time, but here the mansion is set down on

what only a generation before had been the American frontier.

The National Trust for Historic Preservation owns this 126-acre property; every hour one of their guides provides an extensive and thorough tour of the museum house. The state owns an adjoining 500 acres, left as a natural buffer from encroaching development.

John Drayton began his house in 1738 and finished it four years later. "Mr. Drayton's Palace on the Ashley" was a description of that time. There is no known architect, but several details, including one of the massive Georgian overmantels, have been linked to pattern books. Master

Drayton Hall.

builders worked from these books, and a really good one sometimes allowed the owner to bypass the architect.

The tour guide spends a lot of time dispelling illusions about how life was lived in the house over the years—*Gone With the Wind* illusions as well as more justified ones. The entry was a public room that adjoined the stairwell; the second story holds the main ballroom. Residents entertained here, and withdrew to the side rooms for privacy—withdrawing rooms, hence "drawing rooms." Over the years, the uses of the rooms would change. In early days dining was haphazard; there was no set dining room. Tables were set out in the most comfortable location. Furniture was pushed against the wall when not in use, thus the phrase "straightening the room."

The ceilings were reported at the time to be unfashionably low: The first floor is only 12 feet high and the second, a mere 14. One drawing room ceiling sports a hand-carved plaster carving—perhaps the only one surviving in America from this period. The interior decoration, in general, can be described as massive, balanced, and elaborate. Intricate carvings of mahogany and poplar are particularly distinctive. In some spaces, Drayton Hall has received only one coat of paint since it was built, so there are no thick layers of paint to disguise the details. In fact, relatively few changes have been made. Larger paned windows went in when the originals blew out during a hurricane in the Federal era. Neoclassical mantels were inserted in that period as well. Victorian wood ceilings on the second floor, and shingles on the roof pediment were added later. The freed slaves burned the newel post for firewood, and perhaps removed the false doors, thinking they held secrets. Miss Charlotte Drayton lived here through much of the 20th century without electricity or plumbing, so there was none of that to remove in a search for authenticity.

Drayton Hall was once as famous for its garden as for its mansion, but few plantings remain. Of the 30 support buildings that stood here, only two remain. One, a solid little brick building, was once a seven-seat privy. On the landfront, we see the brick foundation of the two flankers, one perhaps served as a kitchen and the other as a laundry. The walk to the river is short and pleasant.

It was said of the builder, "Such was his character, he lived in riches—but without public esteem. He died in a tavern, but without public commiseration." The guide adds that upon Drayton's death, his fourth wife, a 20-year-old bride, Rebecca, used the estate to provide for six of her slaves. She retired to Charles Town, lived past 80, and left what remained to her grandchildren. The Draytons were an interesting and illustrious family then and in later years. The house survives now, it's said, because the resident Drayton convinced Union troops that it was a smallpox or yellow fever hospital. In the years following the Civil War, phosphate mining allowed it to remain in the family's hands.

Perseverance and a great deal of luck have kept Drayton Hall standing over the years. The mansion is far more fragile than its stately appearance suggests, and the National Trust is simply trying to maintain an authentic treasure.

| 11.6 | 0.0 | *Retrace driveway and turn right onto S.C. 61 North / Ashley River Road.* |
| 12.1 | 0.5 | *Turn right into entrance of Magnolia Plantation and its Gardens.* |

❻ MAGNOLIA PLANTATION AND GARDENS / AUDUBON SWAMP GARDEN
Open to public.

To tour the original garden, use the map-brochure given upon entering and follow the numbered path signs on foot. The unusual house also is open to the public. The rockers on the porch provide the perfect place to sit a spell and think about what life there might have been like. A 15-minute film in the Orientation Theater gives a nice overview, as do the Nature Tram and Boat Tour.

The House
The Drayton family started on this site, not next door at Drayton Hall. Thomas, the father of Drayton Hall builder John, arrived from Barbados in 1679. He built a mansion that accidentally burned, and the Union burned its replacement. The current house, parts of which are pre-Revolutionary, was the family's hunting lodge that originally stood on another site. Workers dismantled the lodge and floated it here in 1873; it now sits on the foundation of the previous structure. The Victorian details and the curious square water tower were added then. The stucco, phosphate-lime finish went on after an earthquake in 1886.

The Garden
Today the plantation's garden spreads out informally about the house and meanders along the river for some distance. In fact, Magnolia is famous for its "informal garden." Originally, this was all the dream of Reverend John Grimke-Drayton. A hunting accident killed his brother and unexpectedly left the young theology student heir to the family fortune. He completed his degree, married a Philadelphian bride, and settled here. His church was Old St. Andrew's, mentioned earlier.

Grimke-Drayton laid out his garden in the Romantic or informal style then popular in England. Before this, geometry and strict pattern had ruled, but now landscaping allowed for more personal expression and placed a greater value on existing forest. In 1843, Grimke-Drayton imported *Camellia japonicas*, and five years later, *Azalea indica*. In 1851, tuberculosis caused him to retire for a while and he gave his project his full attention. "Dig in the soil" was the prescription—what we might call therapy today.

The Civil War brought ruin. Grimke-Drayton sold much of his property and leased the rest for a time to a phosphate company. (He hated what they did so much that he forbade a reoccurrence in his will.) He managed to save his garden, and in 1870 he opened it to the public. Visitors came up the river by paddle-wheel steamboat, and the reviews were unanimous. Baedeker's travel guide listed it with only two other American attractions—the Grand Canyon and Niagara Falls.

Today, arrows direct us down paths that twist and turn through a variety of botanical wonders. Ornate little white bridges arch across narrow black-water lagoons. Two hundred and fifty varieties of azaleas bloom in spring—the traditional time for visiting and still the most dazzling. A great variety of camellias and the extensive plantings of other shrubs, however, are gradually shifting to a more year-round display of color. In addition, small, specialized areas within the larger garden add interest as well as beauty.

The biblical garden near the path's beginning delights both gardeners and biblical scholars. What really grew in the Holy Lands in ancient times? Was Eve's apple really an apricot? Or a quince? Were the lilies of the field narcissus? Did Judas hang himself from a Judas tree? Some of these questions can't be answered, but in this unique little spot, almonds, roses, papyrus, pomegranate, oleander, date palm, and even cedars of Lebanon grow. Farther along, we come upon a maze copied from the time of Henry VIII. And there's an herb garden from the days of colonial Carolina. Most plantations had one, and in fact, it's now believed there was no prejudice against having vegetables, herbs, and flowers all together in the earliest gardens. Author Ashe says that in 1682, Carolina gardens already contained vegetables and herbs as well as "Rose, Tulip, Carnation, and Lily." At the center of Magnolia, at the heart of Drayton's larger creation, lies a small patch of cultivation called "Flowerdale." It may date back to the 1680s and be the inspiration for the rest of the garden.

I **M**agnolia Plantation.

Other Attractions

The entire 500 acres is a wildlife refuge. I visited the petting zoo, talked to the goats, and petted the miniature horses. No law against that, but a sign warns, "Not responsible for articles nibbled."

Magnolia is well known to birders. Together my wife and I took the Audubon nature walk and stopped at the slave cemetery. Influenced by his abolitionist aunts, the famous Grimke sisters, Drayton referred to his slaves as his "black roses" and broke the law by teaching them to read and write. We finished up the walk through a reserve where islands of thick vegetation float. My wife identified four bantam chickens that had wandered down from a nearby cabin. I was proud of the several bitterns I spotted until I read the Audubon notice on the way out declaring something to the effect that bitterns at that time of year were "as thick as pigeons."

We had a good time. But Owen Wister gets the last word. In his novel *Lady Baltimore* he wrote: "I have seen gardens, many gardens, in England, in France, in Italy…but no horticulture that I have seen devised by mortal man approaches the unearthly enchantment of the azaleas at Magnolia."

12.1	**0.0**	*Return to S.C. 61 / Ashley River Road and turn left.*
21.7	**9.6**	*Arrive at junction of S.C. 61 South and U.S. 17 North.*
21.7	**0.0**	*Continue straight on U.S. 17 North.*
22.1	**0.4**	*Arrive at south side of Ashley River Bridge.*

END TOUR

Ashley River | Middleton Place to Summerville

TOUR TWO

ASHLEY RIVER | Middleton Place to Summerville
We begin this day on the Ashley River by driving up scenic S.C. 61 to **Middleton Place**. A century older than the one at Magnolia, the tremendous garden here is laid out along more formal lines. We tour the house and grounds, where plantation craftsmen work. A few miles ahead, we leave S.C. 61, cross the Ashley River, and arrive at **Colonial Dorchester State Historic Site**. Once the site of a 1697 town, today only a fort, church ruins, and part of a log wharf remain. After a right turn to **Summerville**, aka "Flower Town in the Pines," we'll catch springtime azaleas in bloom and take a look at the town's distinctive architecture during a leisurely drive.

Middleton Place
　　4300 Ashley River Road | 843-556-6020 | *www.middletonplace.org*
　　Admission charged.
Colonial Dorchester State Historic Site
　　300 State Park Road | 843-873-1740
　　www.southcarolinaparks.com/park-finder/state-park/725.aspx
　　Admission charged.
Summerville
　　843-873-8535 or 866-875-8535 | *www.visitsummerville.com*

BEGIN TOUR

0.0	**0.0**	*From Charleston, take U.S. 17 South and begin clocking mileage at south side of Ashley River Bridge.*
200 ft	**200** ft	*Veer right onto S.C. 61 North / Ashley River Road.*
2.0	**2.0**	*Veer left, continue on S.C. 61 North / Ashley River Road.*
3.8	**1.8**	*Stay in right lane and follow 61-N.*
13.4	**9.6**	*Turn right into entrance gate of Middleton Place.*

❶ MIDDLETON PLACE, c. 1741
Open to public.
More than just a world-famous formal garden, Middleton presents slices of authentic plantation life. The house tour offers an overall picture of family and plantation history, as well as a lesson in interior design of the time. In the plantation stableyards, plantation craftsmen ply their skills, explain rice planting, and emphasize black culture. Guided kayak tours introduce the black-water cypress swamp or the Ashley River, while carriage rides trot visitors around the plantation in the same fashion as the Middletons in the 18th century. In short, Middleton presents as complete a look at plantation life as you're going to find anywhere in the Lowcountry.

A Very Short History of the Middleton Family
The first Henry Middleton acquired this property in 1741 as part of his wife's dowry. He added the flankers to the existing house and began the formal garden.

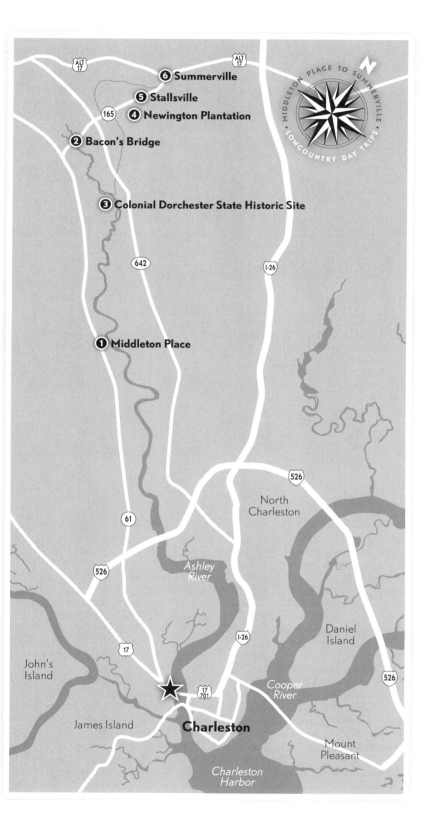

MIDDLETON PLACE TO SUMMERVILLE · LOWCOUNTRY DAY TRIPS

N

ALT 17
ALT 17
6 Summerville
5 Stallsville
165
4 Newington Plantation
2 Bacon's Bridge
3 Colonial Dorchester State Historic Site
642
I-26
1 Middleton Place
526
North Charleston
61
526
Ashley River
17
I-26
Daniel Island
John's Island
526
Cooper River
17 701
James Island
Charleston
Mount Pleasant
Charleston Harbor

I *Middleton Place.*

Tradition says that it took 100 slaves almost a decade just to complete the terraces and walks, artificial lakes, and vistas we see today. Henry was a president of the First Continental Congress, and his son Arthur signed the Declaration of Independence. Arthur's son Henry (who would be governor and minister to Russia) was an avid botanist. Assisted by friend André Michaux, who held a botanical garden in the area for the French government, this second Henry experimented with exotic and domestic plants and added much to the garden. His son William may have made the single most important contribution to the garden, however— the azalea. Instead, he's mostly remembered as the signer of the Ordinance of Secession and the custodian of ruin. The family held on until 1975, when Middleton was taken over by a nonprofit foundation and public trust.

The Garden

Developed in 1741, Middleton's garden is laid out in a formal geometrical design popular in Europe at the time. Armed with a brochure-map acquired at the entrance, we follow low-lying signs that correspond to the brochure and lead us through the maze-like tour. Just beyond the parking lot, we come upon a long, rectangular lake. Turtles sun on the far shore, and to our left, white swans float on the black water. The lake marks the back leg of a gigantic triangle; soon, we're walking up another leg, through a forest of great camellias and grand magnolias. To the right, sheep graze and there's a distant view of what remains of the house. A couple of sharp turns bring us to the rubble of the pre-1741 original that the Union burned. "The Quake" of 1886 brought down all the walls except those of the right flanker, a 1755 bachelors' quarters, which was rebuilt in a more Jacobean style than the original. Standing in what was once the center of the house, we get an excellent view of the river and the tremendous butterfly lakes in front. Notice that the axis of the landscaping from the River Road to the river ran straight through the center of the house. A right turn leads to the remaining wing.

The House Tour

The house is actually the renovated 1755 flanker. When it became a house-museum, family members donated and loaned museum-quality heirlooms, so it was possible to re-create a portion of the vanished whole. On the ground floor hang portraits of various family members by Benjamin West, Thomas Sully, and other artists. Fine furnishings outfit a dining room and a music room, while elsewhere exhibits include silver "marrow spoons" and piles of worthless Confederate money.

Of equal interest, the second floor contains two rooms, each dressed for a season. The winter bedroom lies opposite a summer bedroom. Come summer, occupants removed the headboard, relocated the bed to the center of the room, and dropped a mosquito net. Also upstairs, a library holds a nice collection of first editions, including an Audubon book and one by Mark Catesby. A children's room up here showcases fine furnishings and antiquated toys.

Plantation Stableyards

At the stableyards, you'll find several carriages of varying models, plus shops and stables. Usually at least three craftspeople are on hand, reenacting the self-sufficient ways of the early plantations. On this day, spinners, weavers, and a potter demonstrate their skills. Just beyond, a guinea hen pecks about, and a squirrel

More on Middleton Place
Blacksmith | *On the plantation, the smith would have been a jack-of-all-trades, but contrary to the popular view, he wouldn't have shoed horses. Horses went unshod because they traveled in the woods or on dirt roads, and they wore boots of leather and wood in the boggy fields.* **The Quake |** *In August 1886, an earthquake that measured an estimated 7.2 on the Richter scale shook the East Coast. Large fissures opened in the Lowcountry. Geysers shot water 15 feet into the air. "The Quake" leveled homes throughout South Carolina and rang church bells in New York.*
Ongoing Archaeology | *Archaeologists continue to work at Middleton Place, uncovering bits of history. Visitors to the park can often observe them working.*

eats corn from the center of a grindstone. There's a cooper and carpenter's shop where everything from barrels to fine furniture is made, as well as a candle shop and tannery. We see planking and shingle splitting, and food grown with the aid of hoe, plow, and scythe.

The blacksmith, who happens to be a young woman, explains that it's "black" for the color of iron and "smithing" for smiting: "blacksmithing." By the Civil War, there was no longer a need for self-sufficiency, since goods were imported.

Next, head toward the river and the Spring House Chapel, where stored jars once cooled in the natural spring water. Upstairs, the Plantation Chapel holds an interpretive panel that explains plantation chapels and tells how William Middleton enlarged the spring house. From here, we see one gigantic wing of the butterfly lake spreading to the right; ahead, displays in a small rice mill interpret rice culture. E.T.H. Shaffer, author of *Carolina Gardens*, notes that this is the only waterwheel rice mill that he knows of being driven by water from a decorative pond. He describes Middleton further: "Camellias of winter and the azaleas of spring, the roses of summer, and the magnolias blossoming are the major notes. Blending with these are the minor: heatherbell, hawthorn, lotus, iris, and 1,000 more. The formal terraces and lakes at varied levels may recall better-known European gardens, but the live oaks and Spanish moss weave a spell that is of a New World and an Old South."

13.4	**0.0**	*From Middleton Place parking lot return to S.C. 61 North / Ashley River Road and turn right.*
17.9	**4.5**	*Veer right onto S.C. 165.*
18.7	**0.8**	*Cross second bridge, which is the location of the old Bacon's Bridge.*

❷ BACON'S BRIDGE

Dorchester settler Michael Bacon kept a bridge here across the Ashley River not long after 1700. The crossing remained important, as many did, during the Revolution. Revolutionary War commander Francis Marion posted a guard here and skirmished with the British. Dr. William Johnson, who compiled tons of history in scrapbooks now held by the South Carolina Historical Society, points out "Marion's oak" that the men camped beneath, and a little farther along the "Tory oak," where Americans hanged one of the opposition. A road widening may have claimed the trees, or they may be part of a grove high and to our left. At the beginning of the 20th century, Summerville youngsters used Bacon's Bridge as a favorite swimming hole, while churches and the community enjoyed it for picnics.

18.7	**0.0**	*Continue on S.C. 165.*
19.3	**0.6**	*At stoplight, turn right onto S.C. 642 East / Old Dorchester Road.*
21.1	**1.8**	*Turn right on Dorchester State Park Road / S-18-373.*
21.3	**0.2**	*Entrance gates into Colonial Dorchester State Historic Site.*

❸ COLONIAL DORCHESTER STATE HISTORIC SITE, c. 1697
Open to public.

Information kiosks, exhibits, maps and markers help interpret the history of this historic site. It began when Congregationalists moving south from Dorchester, Massachusetts, founded South Carolina's Dorchester at the end of the 17th century. They came to "settell the gospel" here; not such an easy task, for their ship was "neer run under water ye stormy wind being so boistrous." This intrepid band of Puritans divided the surrounding 4,000 acres into 40- to 50-acre farm plots, but here at Dorchester, following New England patterns, they laid a common, a mill site, and a "place of trade."

Ironically, according to noted historian Judge H.A.M. Smith, Congregationalists claimed they were settling an Indian frontier. With some indignation, he pointed out that the 1696 founders had spent their nights in neighboring plantations. Bacon had bought his bridge from an earlier arrival. And finally, the Congregationalists had built their church not by the river, but beside a well-established public road—"the Broad Path."

Nevertheless, the spot was a good one, considered very healthy in those early days. (Several proposals were made to move the government here from Charles Towne during the summer months.) Its location at the headwaters of the Ashley River made it ideal for Indian trading and transport of forest and farm produce to the port. The relocated Northerners built a church and lined the bluff with stores (the wharf of one still shows at low tide). They sent their kids to a free school and participated in weekly market days, fairs, and militia drills. The town prospered until the 1750s, when some Congregationalists moved to Georgia. Still, enough citizens remained for the town to be the third largest in the colony at the time of the Revolution.

In about 1720, an Anglican church was built and the remaining tower added in 1751 (It once boasted four bells). The British burned the building uring the Revolutionary War. Notice the gravestone of James Postell, for they sharpened their sabers on it. Although partly restored after the Revolution, the church was abandoned. Soon after, a local shepherd sheltered his flock here.

After the Revolution, Dorchester declined. Bishop Asbury reported in 1788, "I passed Dorchester where there are remains of what appears to have been once a considerable town."

21.3 0.0 *Return to park gates and continue straight on Dorchester State Park Road / S-18-373.*
21.5 0.2 *At stop sign, turn left onto S.C. 642 West / Bacon Bridge Road.*
23.3 1.8 *At second stoplight, turn right onto S.C. 165 West / Bacon Bridge Road.*

The Road to Summerville
We're getting close to home now. Nearly 50 years ago this bottomland was a wilderness dissected not by streets, but by ancient rice-field dikes and ditches. They've canalled the area since then and planted houses.

24.5 1.2 *On right, pass by Newington Road.*

❹ NEWINGTON PLANTATION
At the top of the hill on the right, a small sign announces Newington Road—one of the earliest of Summerville's many subdivisions. I moved to the end of that lane when I was 12 in 1955 and stayed through high school.

Newington Plantation, for which our road was named, occupied most of the land beginning at Bacon's Bridge and extending into the edge of Old Summerville. The 3,000-acre land grant was given in 1680 to Daniel Axtell, whose wife passed it on to her daughter, the wife of landgrave Joseph Blake. Blake's father had been a celebrated admiral under Cromwell's rule, but when the Restoration came, Charles II disinterred the seaman's body from Westminster Abbey. This sacrilege, so the story goes, sent Joseph off to Carolina. His son Joseph (Axtell's grandson) was one of the wealthiest men in the colony and built a tremendous mansion here.

The "House of a Hundred Windows" it was called, and Eliza Lucas said in 1742, it "seems designed by Nature for pious Meditation and Friendly Converse." Naturalist and author Mark Catesby wrote at about the same time of the largest rattlesnake he had ever seen, "about eight feet in length, weighing between eight and nine pounds. This monster was gliding into the house of Colonel Blake of Carolina."

Some ruins remain, but they're off to our left. Judging by Judge Smith's maps, our Newington Road was a little off the mark, and I may have been living on the less promising and less poetic Barren Heath Plantation.

24.5 0.0   *Continue on S.C. 165 West / Bacon Bridge Road.*
24.9 0.4   *Pass through Stallsville.*

❺ STALLSVILLE

The small pineland village of Stallsville claimed the area's first post office. Today, several antebellum dwellings still stand hidden away. Old Trolley Road joins on the right. It's a pretty straight shot to the old Dorchester area—originally, this was to have been a trolley connection for commuters to Charleston, but it was abandoned and finally paved.

25.7 0.8   *Cross Sawmill Branch, as S.C. 165 becomes Summerville's Carolina Avenue.*

Across Sawmill Branch, Summerville's history really begins.

25.7 0.0   *Continue on S.C. 165 / Carolina Avenue.*
26.0 0.3   *At second stoplight, known as "Five Points" intersection, turn right onto U.S. 17A North / South Main Street.*
27.1 1.1   *Turn right onto East Doty Avenue, which runs parallel to railroad tracks.*
27.2 1 blk   *Turn right into Chamber of Commerce parking lot.*

Summerville's History

In 1707, this area was sawmill land, and the old dam that held the water that powered the mill wasn't obliterated until workers improved the area's drainage in the 1880s. We know that planters were moving in this direction, but neither they nor the mill seem to have interfered with the pines growing on these high sandy ridges. The occupants of Dorchester, searching for fever-free summer homes, deserted that town and started another here.

Old Summerville's streets wind about, following the paths of cows and wagons. The pleasures of its early days proved to be picnics with dancing, visiting, and whist instead of poker. Citizens attended church in their homes or in the Lecture Hall until around 1830, when Episcopalians and Presbyterians got buildings.

Then, in 1832, the train "The Best Friend of Charleston" puffed in, and the new railroad company laid out New Summerville. It didn't experience much growth at first, but by the mid 1840s, year-round residents, businesses, and a post office had come to town.

From the beginning, the community considered the pines sacred. As elsewhere, they believed that the trees somehow kept out malaria. In 1847, however, the railroad company cut trees in New Summerville for fuel and ties. The outraged citizens incorporated the town as a legal way of halting further cutting. Yellow fever epidemics beginning in 1852 brought an influx of visitors from Charleston, and six years later a regular commuter train to the city brought a real estate boom. The Civil War ended that, but the Union Army allowed the citizens to remain armed and, led by the Episcopal rector, they protected their property from marauders.

As was often the case, planters either chose not to return to their plantations or lost them to bankruptcy, and they and their children took refuge here. Still basically rural and family oriented, the little town with its railroad depot transformed into a commercial center for the surviving agriculture and new lumber industry. Commuting to Charleston and summer visiting resumed. After much disagreement, the town was adequately ditched and drained. Most residents enjoyed a modest prosperity.

Then in 1886, the Great Quake derailed the train and twisted the tracks. Every chimney in town toppled. Porches collapsed and some houses fell from their foundations. It left a demoralized citizenry camping in their yards.

Yet Summerville was about to be discovered. In 1889, the Congress of Physicians meeting in Paris named it one of the two best places in the world for victims of lung diseases. Suddenly, wealthy visitors rushed to Summerville. Inns, boardinghouses, and rooms to let thrived. And, there were many new permanent residents who, once they visited the place, couldn't bear to leave. New houses and churches went up everywhere. A new business district and town hall were built on the spot laid out 50 years earlier by the railroad's civil engineer. Soon after, electricity and telephones went into service. Dr. Charles Shepherd was experimenting with tea farming, but that venture proved more successful as a charity. In the mid-20s, they drilled for oil: "Spent $10,000 and found a pint." For those not dependent on visitors, commuting, or keeping shop, the well-established lumber and brick-making business provided employment. (You'll notice no brick homes built in the years immediately after the quake, though.)

The Crash of 1929 hurt the inn businesses, but the town survived the Depression. The war that followed changed people's ideas about how money was made. In the 1950s, industries found homes to the north of town. And the inns closed just as Summerville was being discovered by suburbanites, who would live not in the community but in an ever-widening circle around it. The original town is still there, and it's relatively quiet once you're off the main street.

TOUR 2 **SUMMERVILLE**

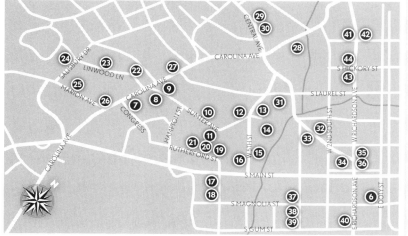

Before We Start

Somewhere along the line, Summerville acquired the moniker "The Flower Town in the Pines," and it still lives up to that name. Incidentally, the pines aren't exactly original. They may have come only about 10,000 years ago when nomadic Indians moved through, burning the indigenous hardwood forest as they hunted. The azaleas were brought here starting in the 1840s. In the spring, especially on Sunday afternoons, outside visitors have traditionally driven through, and now there's a weeklong azalea festival, the Flowertown Festival, celebrating the blooms. Dogwoods and wisteria should ask for equal billing, but so should the houses.

Victorian Houses

Summerville is unique in the Lowcountry in that it alone experienced a genuine post-Civil War prosperity. Elsewhere, we find communities where a handful of large Victorian houses were built by a few well-to-do citizens. On Sullivan's Island we see a holiday version of this style, but only Summerville experienced a steady influx of money and newcomers (mostly Northern). Old houses were repaired unless completely destroyed by the quake, and new ones were built in the latest style.

Victorian architecture in this county generally dates from about 1860 to 1900. Its character depends heavily on the Gothic (a romanticized English cottage or castle) and Italianate (a romanticized Italian villa) styles that were introduced here in the 1840s. Victorian, however, carried these already highly romanticized interpretations to new extremes and borrowed from Greek Revival as well. In short, it was an experiment in beautiful excess that was foreign to most of the South in those still beleaguered times. Most often, these buildings have an asymmetrical façade, with steep-pitched and multi-gabled roofs. Siding is a collaboration of shingle and board, interrupted by large-paned windows, and decorated with much delicate and ornate trim. Depending on the combination of these characteristics, Victorian can be divided roughly into half a dozen styles, but we'll be seeing only Queen Anne, the Second Empire or Mansard, and Folk Victorian. This last style technically can cover many of the dwellings, but it's usually applied to traditional styles that display a spindle-trimmed porch and gingerbread roof trim. That definition doesn't quite do justice to these unique, elaborate, raised cottages, so even as we move into the Victorian era, we'll stay with the catchall "Summerville style."

➎ 106 EAST DOTY AVENUE, This Whole House, c. 1890
Open to public.

The railroad first owned the house, which once held the Greater Summerville Chamber of Commerce but is now occupied by This Whole House, a tea room and antiques shop.

27.2	**0.0**	*From Chamber of Commerce parking lot, turn right onto East Doty Avenue.*
27.2	**50** ft	*Turn right onto South Magnolia Street.*
27.3	**1** blk	*At stop sigh, turn right onto East Richardson Avenue.*
27.4	**1** blk	*At stoplight, turn left onto South Main Street.*
28.4	**1** blk	*At the second stoplight, turn right onto West Carolina Avenue.*

Once called the Great Thoroughfare, and later Main Street, Carolina Avenue traveled through the center of "Old Summerville." It's fairly narrow and well traveled, so watch the traffic. Also, if you're interested in fine old houses surrounded by pines and azaleas, it's impossible to make a wrong turn in this area. The path we're following is just one suggestion.

28.6	**2** blks	*First house on right just beyond Congress Avenue is 201 West Carolina Avenue.*

❼ 201 WEST CAROLINA AVENUE,
c. 1858
Not open to public.
Formerly the Town Hall, and now
home to the Summerville Preservation
Society, this simple Greek Revival
structure with four square "country
columns" replaced an 1838
"Village Hall."

Summerville Preservation Society.

28.7	**1** blk	*Take first right onto Sumter Avenue.*
28.8	Same blk	*Second house on right, 423 Sumter Avenue.*

❽ 423 SUMTER AVENUE, c. 1820
Not open to public.
The Summerville Preservation Society includes this street on its walking tour,
and you might enjoy parking here and walking at least the next 10 entries.
There are many fine old residences on it. Two Gelzer brothers built three houses
in a row here. Known as one of the "back-to-front" homes, this one used to face
another street no longer in existence. The railroad obliterated that roadway
in 1832, sending business elsewhere.

28.8 0.0   *Across street, on left, is site of Carolina Inn.*

❾ CAROLINA INN SITE
Not open to public.
The tremendous Carolina Inn still stood here almost 70 years ago. The 1915
building had been turned into apartments and a swimming pool was added, but
it was finally replaced by a couple of new residences. In 1855, this site hosted an
earlier inn, the Summerville House—a lodging that boasted a 10-pin alley and
billiards room, wide piazzas, spacious parlors, and airy chambers. The clientele
in that day usually rode the train from Charleston.

29.0 1 blk   *On left is 302 Sumter Avenue.*

❿ 302 SUMTER AVENUE, c. 1896
Not open to public.
We used to call this "the House of Seven Gables." This type of Victorian architecture is often given the name "Queen Anne." Note the turret, pagoda, rounded
porch, widow's walk, several steep-roofed gables, ornamentation, and finely
turned porch supports. Well-known Charleston architect Albert Simons said it
was one of the finest houses in town.

29.0 1 blk *On right in curve is 223 Sumter Avenue.*

⓫ 223 SUMTER AVENUE, c. 1850s
Not open to public.
Likely built sometime just before the Civil War, this home features
Classical Revival details that embellish its "Summerville style." Because of the
high ceilings, wide halls, and good ventilation, the influence of West Indies
architecture has been suggested, but by this late date, those were standard
features of most Lowcountry homes. By the end of the 19th century, Victorian

gingerbread had been added to the porches and roof trim of many well-ventilated houses, including those of the Caribbean, Summerville, and many other places. Three trees in the backyard are called "faith, hope, and charity."

29.1 Same blk *On left with iron fence is 208 Sumter Avenue.*

⑫ 208 SUMTER AVENUE, The Elizabeth Arden House, c. 1891
Not open to public.

Barbadian arrival Samuel Lord built this large Victorian home in 1891, which locals sometimes called "the Pirate House." First used as a boarding school for "Northern Young Ladies," it later became known as "the Elizabeth Arden House" after the cosmetics executive who bought it for a winter home in 1938.

29.1 ¼ blk *Arrive at stop sign at corner of Sumter Avenue, Pressley, and West 5th South streets. It looks as if Sumter Avenue will run into First Baptist Church.*

29.1 0.0 *Turn into parking lot on the right side of First Baptist Church. The far right side of the parking lot is actually part of Pressley Street / S-18-171. Continue on Pressley Street.*

⑬ FIRST BAPTIST CHURCH, post-Civil War
Not open to public.

The First Baptist Church has a modern brick façade, but the structure is probably more than a century old. Black Baptist pastor Anthony Alston came up from Charleston and started preaching beneath a brush arbor down the street where the large Catholic church stands. Alston served for 43 years.

29.2 ½ blk *On right is Wesley United Methodist Church.*

⑭ PRESSLEY STREET / S-18-171,
Wesley United Methodist Church, post-Civil War
Not open to public.

Another black congregation built this beautiful little Victorian church hidden away on the lane running beside the Baptist church. (The pathway is also called Pike Hole Path, perhaps because there was good fishing in the stream at the bottom.) The walls of the 1870s building have since been bricked in, but the remaining ornate gable and steeple attest to the skill of these churchgoing artisans.

29.2 0.0 *Make a U-turn onto other side of Pressley Street / S-18-171.*

29.3 ½ blk *At stop sign, turn left onto West 5th South Street.*

29.4 ½ blk *Second house on left is 127 West 5th South Street.*

⑮ 127 WEST 5TH SOUTH STREET, Teacherage, c. 1882
Not open to public.

Note the cupola at the top. The center of the house has an octagonal room lit by an 18-foot skylight that also helped ventilation. The school board housed single teachers here, but later sold the residence to author Paul Hyde Bonner. (He's probably best known for *Aged in the Woods*.) Since Queen Victoria was around for the last two-thirds of the 19th century, it can be called Victorian architecture, but judging by the distinctive small gable on the piazza roof and bracketed eaves, this is a late Italianate building.

29.4 0.0 *Across street on right is The Squirrel Inn.*

⑯ 116 WEST 5TH SOUTH STREET,
The Squirrel Inn, c. 1913
Not open to public.
Miss Raven Lewis built this inn, and
the Sutter sisters operated it for many
years. Ironically, real success didn't
come until the 1940s when the larger
inns were failing. Author Bonner
stayed here, used the inn in one of
his novels, and moved in across the
street. Since converted to condo-
miniums with a closed front porch,
the inn no longer shares what made
it special—the rockers, guests, and
original façade. Across the street,
the community center and the azalea-
filled town park host the Flowertown
Festival and Sculpture in the South
each spring.

I *St. Paul's Reformed Episcopal Church.*

29.5	½ blk	At stop sign, turn right onto South Main Street / U.S.17A.
29.6	1 blk	Turn left onto East 6th South Street / S-18-224.
		On right, facing South Main Street, is 705 South Main Street.

⑰ 705 SOUTH MAIN STREET, early 1900s
Not open to public.
The ballroom of this residence measured 3,000 square feet. Note the "broken"
pediment above the door and the substantial columns. We've moved out of the
Victorian era and into the Colonial Revival period, but the surrounding veranda
of an even earlier architecture remains. For years the Pinewood School, it is now
the Cummins Theological Seminary and the headquarters of the Diocese of the
Southeast of the Reformed Episcopal Church.

| **29.6** | ½ blk | On right is St. Paul's Reformed Episcopal Church. |

⑱ ST. PAUL'S REFORMED EPISCOPAL CHURCH, c. 1883
Not open to public.
The seminary moved St. Paul's Reformed Episcopal Church, formerly known as
Bishop Pengelley Memorial Chapel, to the back of 705 South Main Street. The
distinctive little Gothic chapel was built in 1883 to serve "underprivileged whites"
and also served as an infirmary during the Civil War.

29.6	0.0	Make a U-turn and return to South Main Street /
		U.S.17A.
29.7	½ blk	At stop sign, cross South Main Street continuing
		on West 6th South Street.
29.8	1 blk	Turn left onto Rutherford Street.
29.8	Same blk	First house on right is 102 Rutherford Street.

⑲ 102 RUTHERFORD STREET, c. 1886
Not open to public.
The next three houses are strikingly different examples of post-Civil War
construction, all of which could technically be called Victorian. The first,
102 Rutherford Street, is high off the ground, with an almost classical trim
and dormer windows. It is closest to what we call Summerville style—cottage
architecture refined, decorated, and expanded.

29.8 Same blk   *Next house on right is 108 Rutherford Street.*

⑳ 108 RUTHERFORD STREET, c. 1871
Not open to public.
The design of the next house is one we encounter here a little less often.
A Christian merchant built it in about 1871 as a summer residence (My parents
lived in this one for years). The veranda surrounded the house completely at one
time, and the ceilings are 14 feet high. That's all ceiling—no second story. The only
concessions to style are the small scalloped vergeboards (end rafters) and the
double chamfered porch columns.

29.8 Same blk   *Next house on right is 114 Rutherford Street.*

㉑ 114 RUTHERFORD STREET, c. 1888
Not open to public.
Distinctly and typically Second Empire Victorian, this house is symmetrical with
a mansard roof, bay windows, and French doors and window. But porches still
surround it on three sides, and the ceilings are 14 feet high. While other styles
looked to medieval England or old Italy, this romantic vision was French-inspired.
François Mansard of mansard roof fame was a 17th-century architect whose style
was revived during the reign of Emperor Napoleon III—the Second Empire.
This was the "modern architecture" of the day.

29.9 **1** blk   *At stop sign, turn right onto Hampton Street / S-18-74.*
30.2 **2** blks   *At stop sign, turn left onto Sumter Avenue.*
30.3 **1** blk   *At stop sign, turn left on West Carolina Avenue and*
                        make an immediate right onto Linwood Lane / S-18-522.
30.4 First blk   *First house on right is 112 Linwood Lane.*

㉒ 112 LINWOOD LANE, **The Rectory**, c. 1860
Not open to public.
Co-editor of *Beth's Pineland Village* and my high school English teacher, Clarice
Foster writes that houses sometimes went by names instead of street number, but
that's not so unusual in this case because it's "The Rectory." The church sold some
of its silver and with the proceeds bought this little summer cottage around 1870.

30.5 ½ blk   *Fifth house on right is 126 Linwood Lane.*

㉓ 126 LINWOOD LANE, **Out of Plumb**, pre-1838
Not open to public.
This cottage is called "Out of Plumb" with good reason: It can claim not a single
square or level corner. No exact date for construction is known, but it's listed in
Hutchinson's 1838 history, so both old age and a hurricane in 1888 contributed
to the name. It's said that one of the owners could never bake a flat cake; one side
always baked higher than the other. My cousin Effie Wilder and her husband, Frank,
lived in this house for years. (She co-authored *Pawleys Island—A Living Legend*.)

30.6 ½ blk   *At stop sign, look across Salisbury Drive*
                   to left for Pine Forest Inn gates.

㉔ PINE FOREST INN SITE
Not open to public.
This was the entrance to the old inn that no longer remains. President Circle
occupies much of the inn site today, but I can remember at least a substantial
portion of the old building. Gradually collapsing, it was still filled with
molding furnishings from that bygone era.

30.6 **0.0**   *Turn left onto Salisbury Drive.*
30.7 **1** blk   *At stop sign, turn left onto Marion Avenue / S-18-172.*
30.8 **½** blk   *On left is 128 Marion Avenue.*

㉕ 128 MARION AVENUE, **Cuthbert House**, c. 1825
Not open to public.
Look to your left for the old, square, two-story house surrounded by a veranda.
The Cuthbert family lived here for more than a century. When the house was
built in 1825, cottages with second-story bedrooms under the eaves were the
predominant summer-house style, so this was a cut above its neighbors.
Still, the house is plain and simple, especially when compared to its finely
spindled Victorian neighbor at 116 Marion Avenue.

30.9   **½** blk   *On left is 100 Marion Avenue.*

㉖ 100 MARION AVENUE, c. 1890s
Not open to public.
"Moved back, turned around, and set down," says editor Clarice (whom I've
resisted calling Foster or "Miss Foster") of this villa, and so it was. Once 5½ feet
off the ground and right on the street corner, it was relocated and handsomely
restored in the 1950s. Margaret Kwist, author of *Porch Rocker Recollections*, says
the house served as a gambling casino and as a retreat for nuns.

31.0   End of blk   *At stop sign, turn left onto West Carolina Avenue.*
31.2   **2½** blks   *Turn left into St. Paul's Church parking lot.*

㉗ 316 WEST CAROLINA AVENUE, St. Paul's Church, c. 1857
Not open to public.
The Dorchester congregation migrated here and built the first church on
this site in about the 1830s. They outgrew that building and replaced it nearly
10 years later with this similar one—a little larger and better finished. Weathered
gravestones and azaleas crowd in on every side. It's a handsome village church
with simple portico and pediment, great arched windows, and bell tower. But
Clarice points out that the portico is Greek Revival, the windows Federal, and
the bell tower Gothic. "Eclectic" is what we call that in the tour-book business.
A monument to the Confederate dead sits beside the steps. Inside, heavy
columns once supported a balcony, but now they uphold only a barreled ceiling.
I was confirmed in this church.

31.2   **0.0**   *From St. Paul's Church parking lot, continue around*
                  St. Paul's white clapboard Sunday-school building on
                  one-way drive.
31.3   **1** blk   *At end of drive, turn left onto S-18-209.*
31.4   **½** blk   *At stop sign, turn left onto West Carolina Avenue.*
31.8   **4** blks   *Go straight through the light and cross Central Avenue.*
31.9   **½** blk   *On right is 517 West Carolina Avenue. Heavy traffic—be careful.*

㉘ 517 WEST CAROLINA AVENUE, c. 1808
Not open to public.
Built in 1808 by Joseph Waring, this summer cottage is probably the second-
oldest house in town.

31.9   **½** blk   *Turn left onto Dorchester Avenue / S-18-766.*
32.2   **1** blk   *At stop sign, turn left onto Old Postern Road.*
32.3   **1** blk   *At stop sign, turn left onto Central Avenue.*
32.4   First blk   *Fourth house on left is 516 Central Avenue.*

㉙ **516 CENTRAL AVENUE, The Allen House**, c. 1849
Not open to public.
Once upon a time, "Miss Maria" Allen taught school here and had her students perform skits on the lawn. Her son Glennie Allen wrote popular fiction in the servants' quarters. Art gallery curator Agnes Jacobs lived here, and her brother Samuel Gaillard, well known for his watercolors and silk-screens of Lowcountry scenes, used to live here.

32.4 Same blk *On left, next door, is 510 Central Avenue.*

㉚ **510 CENTRAL AVENUE**, c. 1880s
Not open to public.
We've seen that mansard roof before on Rutherford Street, but here's a more symmetrical Victorian beauty.

32.7 2 blks *At intersection of Central Avenue and South Laurel Street on right is the Summerville Presbyterian Church.*

㉛ **CORNER OF CENTRAL AVENUE and SOUTH LAUREL STREET, Summerville Presbyterian Church**, c. 1895
Not open to public.
A.J. Braid, the same contractor who built the Pine Forest Inn and the Elizabeth Arden House, also built this church. Asymmetrical façade, contiguous windows, and some minor trim work—these sedate and pleasing adaptations of Victorian motifs transform a large white meetinghouse.

32.8 1 blk *On left is Epiphany Episcopal Church.*

㉜ **212 CENTRAL AVENUE, Epiphany Episcopal Church**, c. 1894
Not open to public.
This handsomely built little Victorian church was started sometime before 1894. A memorial in the churchyard honors Miss Catherine Springs, a well-educated black seamstress who was instrumental in founding the church.

32.8 0.0 *Across street is Timrod Library.*

㉝ **217 CENTRAL AVENUE, Timrod Library**, c. 1915
Open to public.

The town of Dorchester had a lending library that was eventually divided between those colonists heading for Georgia and those who stayed. The last of this collection was reportedly carried throughout the area in a cowhide bag by mule, before being finally divided after the Revolution. Heir apparent but a century later, Summerville's Chautauqua Reading Circle evolved into the privately operated Timrod Literary and Library Association. It took possession of this new building in 1915. Today, more than 30,000 volumes line the shelves here. The library's rocking chairs make a perfect place to sit and read for a spell.

The Timrod Library, Summerville.

32.9 **1** blk *Turn right onto West 2nd Street and park.*

This segment and the next are best done on foot.

32.9 0.0 *On right is 143-145 Central Avenue.*

㉞ 143-145 CENTRAL AVENUE, Tupper's Pharmacy, early 1900s
This business district is now closed to vehicle traffic.
About seven years after a fire swept this block in 1895, construction began on
Tupper's Pharmacy. Most of the other buildings were built at about the same
time. The drugstore closed in 1955, but its building and those nearby have been
revitalized with art galleries, restaurants, boutiques, and gift shops. Gaillard's
painting studio was here, as was a bookstore.

32.9 0.0 *Turn around and return to the stop sign, turn right.*
33.0 1 blk *Turn right onto West Richardson Avenue, and, again, park
somewhere along the street and walk.*

㉟ 127 WEST RICHARDSON AVENUE, Mr. Cauthen's Mercantile, c. 1890s
Open to public.
On the left, nationally recognized People, Places & Quilts quilting store was once
Mr. Cauthen's Mercantile. It was another generation when he sold coffins and
hardware, and his wife ran a needlecraft business, but you could still "ask Mr.
Cauthen" for hardware up until the 1980s.

33.0 0.0 *At stop sign, turn right onto West Richardson Avenue.*

Business District
The business district was well established as you see it by 1900. Beyond Guerin's
Pharmacy, a line of 1890s stores faces the town square. At the far end, the metal
decoration at the top of the Sires Building indicates that the post office was once
here. A good friend of the town, philanthropist Saul Alexander, owned the building
for some time, and then Barshays Department Store occupied it. Today, it houses
retail shops. To our right, a modern town hall overlooks the square, just as the
railroad's engineer predicted it would in 1832.

**㊱ 140 OLD MAIN STREET on corner of WEST RICHARDSON AVENUE,
Guerin's Pharmacy**, c. 1871
Open to public.
The nephew of Guerin's assistant runs
Guerin's Pharmacy, South Carolina's
oldest operating pharmacy. It holds an
antique apothecary and is one of the
few places you can get a homemade
hot dog and a real cherry coke.

33.1 100 ft *Cross Main Street.
(You're now on
East Richardson
Street.)*

We've crossed into "New Summerville." The streets are straight, and
though there are sometimes fewer
trees, people made up for that by
naming the roads after them. Those

Guerin's Pharmacy, Summerville.

streets on this side of the tracks are "South," the opposite, "North." We can't leave town without a drive down South Magnolia.

33.2 **1** blk　*At stop sign, turn right onto South Magnolia Street / S-18-208.*
33.5 **2** blks　*On right is 400 South Magnolia Street.*

㊲ 400 SOUTH MAGNOLIA STREET, c. 1899
Not open to public.
The house at 400 South Magnolia Street is built in the Queen Anne style. Beth McIntosh, author of *Beth's Pineland Village*, called this one a "valentine picture."

33.5 **0.0**　*Across street on left is 401 South Magnolia Street.*

㊳ 401 SOUTH MAGNOLIA STREET, c. 1860-1870
Not open to public.
The house at 401 South Magnolia Street is perhaps 20 years older than the house at 400 South Magnolia Street and more in the Summerville style, so they are a good comparison.

33.5 *Same blk* 　On left is 405 South Magnolia Street.

㊳ 405 SOUTH MAGNOLIA STREET, late 19th century
Not open to public.
This Queen Anne beauty was moved from South Main Street.

33.6 End of blk *Turn left onto East 4th Street / S-18-354.*
33.7 **1** blk　*At stop sign, turn left onto South Gum Street.*
33.9 **2½** blks　On left is 210 South Gum Street.

㊵ 210 SOUTH GUM STREET, c. 1910
Not open to public.
This house is in the very late Victorian style, but it's impressive.

33.9 ½ blk　*At stop sign, turn left onto East Richardson Avenue.*

If you have time and wish to see more Summerville architecture, proceed into the West End neighborhood.

The West End
The West End developed in the 1890s when Summerville was in its commuter heyday. A railroad executive, not wanting to walk from the nearby public station, had his own personal stop built here where he lived—"the West End."

34.6 **7** blks　*At corner of West Richardson Avenue and South Palmetto Street, on left far corner facing South Palmetto Street, is 200 South Palmetto Street.*

㊶ 200 SOUTH PALMETTO STREET, Linwood, c. 1883
Not open to public.
On the corner of West Richardson Avenue and South Palmetto Street stands Linwood. It, too, is a gingerbread-trimmed version of the Summerville style. Julia Drayton Hastie built it as a summer home in about 1883. She was the daughter of Magnolia Gardens' founder, Reverend John Grimke-Drayton. Clarice says that Grimke-Drayton spent much time here, and he died in this house.

34.6 **0.0**   *Across street on right is 603 West Richardson Avenue.*

㊷ 603 WEST RICHARDSON AVENUE, White Gables, c. 1890s
Not open to public.
White Gables was one of the smaller of the 1890s inns and now, like the others, is a private residence.

34.7	**1** blk	*Turn left onto West Carolina Avenue.*
34.9	**1** blk	*Go through the s-curve and turn left. This is West 2nd Street / S-18-122, although there aren't any signs to tell you.*
35.0	**2** blks	*Turn left onto South Hickory Street, also unmarked.*
35.1	¾ blk	*On right is 201 South Hickory Street.*

㊸ 201 SOUTH HICKORY STREET, Judge Smith House, c. late 1880s
Not open to public.
This large Victorian belonged to Judge Smith. Genealogists and historians are familiar with the judge's work, but he also designed this house—very up-to-date for the time—and was the botanist responsible for the exotic shrubbery surrounding it.

35.1 **0.0**   *Across street on left is 202 South Hickory Street.*

㊹ 202 SOUTH HICKORY STREET, c. 1880s
Not open to public.
Directly across Hickory Street, another nice Victorian—high off the ground—features a front porch and dormer windows of the Summerville style. Plenty of equally fine houses and beautiful gardens are on the opposite side of the tracks, and many more on this side, too, but I'm calling it a day, or at least a day trip.

35.1	**0.0**	*To return to Charleston, continue on South Hickory Street.*
35.2	**1** blk	*Cross railroad tracks and turn right onto West Luke Avenue / S-18-183.*
35.6	**4** blks	*At stop sign, turn left onto North Main Street / U.S. 17 North.*
37.4	**1.8**	*Turn right onto I-26 East.*
60.0	**32.6**	*End of I-26 in downtown Charleston.*

END TOUR

Mount Pleasant and Sullivan's Island

TOUR THREE

MOUNT PLEASANT and SULLIVAN'S ISLAND

We stay fairly close to Charleston for this trip. Just across the Cooper River spreads **Patriots Point**, the world's largest naval and maritime museum. Close by, we stroll through an almost unchanged portion of **Mount Pleasant's old village**.
A short drive north brings us to **Christ Church**, one of the state's oldest churches, and while in the neighborhood, we can shop for **sweetgrass baskets**. **Boone Hall**, an authentic antebellum plantation, lies just off U.S. 17. Across the creek, **Palmetto Islands** offers a wonderful spot to picnic and an exceptional nature walk. On nearby **Sullivan's Island**, we admire several Victorian beach houses and conclude our day at **Fort Moultrie**, a colonial fort used until World War II that is now a national park.

Patriots Point Naval and Maritime Museum
40 Patriots Point Road | 866-831-1720 | 843-884-2727, *www.patriotspoint.org*
Admission charged.

Mount Pleasant
800-774-0006 | *www.townofmountpleasant.com*

Mount Pleasant Presbyterian Church
302 Hibben Steet | 843-884-4612 | *www.mppc.net*
Churchyard open daily.

Christ Episcopal Church
2304 Highway 17 North | 843-884-9090 | *www.christch.org*
Churchyard open daily.

Sweetgrass Basket Stands
Open daily.

Boone Hall Plantation
1235 Long Point Road | 843-884-4371 | *www.boonehallplantation.com*
Admission charged.

Palmetto Islands County Park
444 Needlerush Parkway | 843-884-0832 | *www.ccprc.com*
Admission charged.

Charles Pinckney National Historic Site
1254 Long Point Road | 843-881-5516 | *www.nps.gov/chpi/index.htm*
Admission: Free.

Sullivan's Island
www.sullivansisland-sc.com

Fort Moultrie
1214 Middle Street | 843-883-3123
www.nps.gov/fosu/historyculture/fort_moultrie.htm
Admission charged.

BEGIN TOUR
0.0   0.0   *From Charleston, take U.S. 17 North across Arthur Ravenel*
Jr. Bridge. Begin clocking mileage at the north (away
from downtown Charleston) side of bridge.

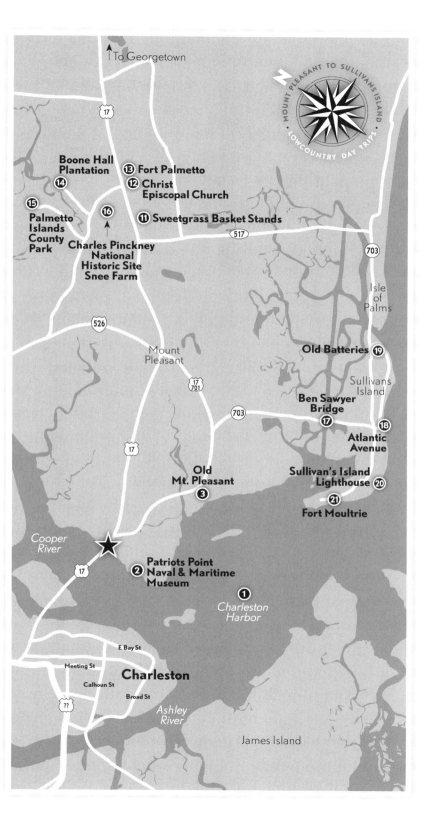

To Georgetown

17

MOUNT PLEASANT TO SULLIVANS ISLAND · LOWCOUNTRY DAY TRIPS

Boone Hall
Plantation

⑬ Fort Palmetto

⑭

⑫ Christ
Episcopal Church

⑮

⑯

Palmetto
Islands
County
Park

Charles Pinckney
National
Historic Site
Snee Farm

⑪ Sweetgrass Basket Stands

517

703

Isle
of
Palms

526

Mount
Pleasant

Old Batteries ⑲

Sullivans
Island

17
701

Ben Sawyer
Bridge

⑰

703

⑱

17

Atlantic
Avenue

Old
Mt. Pleasant

③

Sullivan's Island
Lighthouse ⑳

㉑

Fort Moultrie

Cooper
River

★

17

② Patriots Point
Naval & Maritime
Museum

①

Charleston
Harbor

E Bay St

Meeting St

Charleston

Calhoun St

Broad St

??

Ashley
River

James Island

The Arthur Ravenel Jr. Bridge
This cable-stayed bridge, first opened in 2005, spans the Cooper River and connects Charleston to Mount Pleasant. The main span stretches 1,546 feet, placing it among the world's longest for this type of bridge. This bridge replaced two obsolete truss bridges that had been built in 1929 and 1966. The Ravenel Bridge bustles between 5 and 6 p.m., so do your best to avoid crossing it during this hour.

❶ CHARLESTON HARBOR
We start the morning by crossing Charleston Harbor over the Arthur Ravenel Jr. Bridge. Although still sometimes called the Cooper River Bridge, it is in fact a different traverse.

On our left, the former colonial ferry landing and shipyard Hobcaw Point juts into the water. Beyond it, the white cranes of Wando Terminal unload containerships, placing containers onto trucks for immediate transport. Farther afield, the distant white arch of the Mark Clark Expressway connects Mount Pleasant with North Charleston and the rest of the state.

At the foot of the Ravenel Bridge, Mount Pleasant completed a multi-million dollar Waterfront Memorial Park in 2009. The park offers access to the harbor and bridge. A popular pedestrian and bicycle path, accessible from the park, offers views of the city and harbor.

To the right, the Maritime Museum harbors the carrier *Yorktown* and other impressive vessels. People sometimes call this entire area Hog Island, but the actual Hog Island was a spit at the far end of this area. The small island near the carrier, known first as Shute's Folly, holds Castle Pinckney: It's said that Shute tried to duplicate the garden on Hog Island only to have it wash away. In the War of 1812, a fort (the second on the site) was built and named for General Charles Cotesworth Pinckney, who helped successfully defend Charleston during the Revolutionary War.

Just as it did in its early days, Charleston Harbor bustles with boats. During the colonial period, Charles Towne was a major port—a rival to New York and Boston. By the early 1800s, however, ships of the day were too large to enter and there was a serious slump in commerce. There's plenty of traffic today, though—banana boats, tugs, Coast Guard patrols, dredges, sailboats, crabbers, tour boats, containerships, and the many vessels passing to and from the naval base upriver. Most of the harbor's famous naval battles were fought around distant Fort Sumter and Sullivan's Island. We'll get a closer look at these by the end of the day.

0.0	**0.0**	*As you cross the bridge, follow the right-hand lane marked Coleman Boulevard/Sullivan's Island onto S.C. Hwy. 703.*
0.5	**0.5**	*Turn right at first stoplight onto Patriots Point Blvd.*
1.1	**0.6**	*Turn right into Patriots Point parking lot.*

❷ PATRIOTS POINT NAVAL AND MARITIME MUSEUM, c. 1975
Open to public.
Although we get a good glimpse of the complex as we cross the Cooper River, it's not until we're here that we appreciate the size of the ships, and the carrier in particular. The 888-foot *Yorktown*, the centerpiece of the museum, was once a

small town and airfield combined: During World War II she carried 90 aircraft and almost 3,500 men. Today, she carries planes for display only, and she's crewed for the most part by fellow visitors. The small printed guide and map that come with our ticket include a list of safety precautions. Signs direct us up the steps to the hangar deck and an information booth.

To your right, screens loop the hour-long, Academy Award-winning documentary, *The Fighting Lady*, which shows actual battle scenes shot on the *Yorktown*. These visuals help us populate the ship in our imagination and fully appreciate its contribution to the American's Pacific war effort. Clips from the film also enhance appropriate exhibits throughout the museum.

A Japanese submarine sank the first carrier *Yorktown* in 1942, but the keel for this one had already been laid by then. In the spring of 1943, she went to sea under the command of Captain "Jocko" Clark. She carried 36 fighter planes for long-range defense, and 36 dive-bombers and 18 torpedo

Aircraft Aboard the *Yorktown*

T*he **Yorktown** showcases a variety of aircraft. The flight deck displays planes from Vietnam to the War on Terror, including radar-equipped submarine trackers. The hangar holds a B-25, like those Colonel Doolittle led on a successful bombing run of Tokyo in 1942, and one Navy trainer. Also on display are the Corsair and the Hell Cat—the two most successful World War II fighter planes.*

bombers for attack, all of which would be put to good use. The *Yorktown* would spearhead the Fast Carrier Task Force that eventually defeated the Japanese Navy. On September 16, 1945, with the war over, she entered Tokyo Bay. In 1950 she was modified to carry jets, but reached Korea just after the war ended. Converted next to an antisubmarine carrier, she served off the coast of Vietnam (1965-68). Coming home in time to recover the Apollo 8 astronauts, she was decommissioned in 1970 and arrived in Charleston in 1975. Exhibits detail this long, distinguished, and varied career as we walk the many decks. Interactive exhibits within the onboard National Medal of Honor Museum share information about recipients from the Civil War to the War on Terror. Take a moment to search your last name to see if any of your ancestors have received this highest of military honors.

We explore the remainder of the ship by following six self-guided tours marked by arrows. Unless you're a Navy veteran, the miles of maze-like corridors can be confusing. The flight deck is three decks up, and seven decks up is the bridge—favorites for most visitors. The bridge provides a good view of Charleston Harbor, and powerful binoculars to aid the truly curious.

Below the hangar deck, four other tours take us through a continuing labyrinth of living quarters and work areas, many of which have been turned into mini-museums and memorials. The engine room lies at the very bottom. A sign here announces that "one of the unheralded triumphs of the Navy and the young American men was being able to teach, and learn, what every pipe, every valve, every piece of equipment did and its relationship to the engineering plant as a whole." It's a triumph bordering on a miracle. A quick look at this close and complicated world of super-steam and we're ready to seek the sunshine and the sea breeze of the decks above.

In addition to the *Yorktown*, several other vessels were retired to Patriots Point. The submarine *Clamagore* delivers an unforgettable experience. A little longer than a football field, she's hardly wider than the aisle we walk down. Entering on the stern, we step into a cramped and strange Jules Verne world where about 80 officers and men once lived and worked. Twenty-two bunks crowd the aft torpedo room that we enter, and ahead, generators, air conditioners, freshwater evaporators, engines, toilets, sonar, and more bunks are all scrambled together in a baffling combination. Sadly for all those fans of the movie *Run Silent, Run Deep*, there's no safe way to access the conning tower, so there's no periscope to peer through. We travel the length of the *Clamagore* and are reassured at the exit by a small plaque: "There are only two kinds of ships—submarines and targets."

The destroyer *Laffey*, one of the most celebrated ships of World War II, typically resides at Patriots Point, but was undergoing restoration off-site at the time of this book's update, and officials were uncertain when she would return. Commissioned in February 1944, the destroyer assisted the Normandy invasion. Sent to the Pacific, she participated in several operations. On April 16, 1945, 22 kamikazes and bombers attacked the ship. In the 70-minute battle that followed, she shot down nine and assisted in downing two more, but was hit by five of the suicide squad and by three bombs as well. It was the strongest air attack on any single ship during the war, and it left the *Laffey* on fire, sinking, and with a third of her crew dead or wounded. But she survived. "The ship that wouldn't die" eventually made it back to the Pacific coast under her own power and wasn't decommissioned until 1975. She earned National Historic Landmark status in 1986.

Patriots Point entertains thousands of visitors a year, allows youths to camp overnight on the carrier, and is a departure port for tours going to Fort Sumter. We could stay all day, but let's give our sea legs a rest and look at something a little older—and surrounded by grass and trees.

1.1	**0.0**	*Turn left out of Patriots Point parking lot and retrace your route to the first stoplight at S.C. Hwy 703 North.*
1.7	**0.6**	*At stoplight, turn right onto S.C. Hwy. 703 North/North Coleman Blvd.*
2.6	**0.9**	*After third stoplight, cross Shem Creek Bridge.*

TOUR 3 **OLD MOUNT PLEASANT**

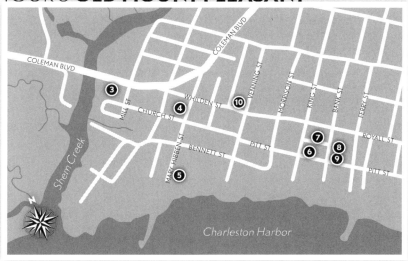

| *Shrimp boats line the shores of Shem Creek.*

❸ OLD MOUNT PLEASANT

Before entering the old village, we must cross Shem Creek (originally the Sewee Indians' Shem ee). Now crowded with fishing boats and shrimp trawlers and lined with seafood restaurants, Shem Creek boasted an even more exotic fleet a century ago. Portuguese and Spanish fishing smacks anchored here, and the creek supported a thriving oyster and terrapin business as well.

In 1793, rice mill inventor Johnathan Lucas owned a mill here; the village that grew up around it was called Lucasville until it joined Mount Pleasant in 1872. Since then, Mount Pleasant has grown tremendously, but the old village remains tucked away in one corner. Actual settlement of this area began in 1680 with the arrival of Irish soldier Florence O'Sullivan. Of dubious moral character and questionable ability and loyalty, he was nonetheless given "a great gun" and entrusted with the defense of this section of the harbor. Old Woman's Point, probably a corruption of an Indian name, Oldwanus, shows on the maps of that day, but the arrival of more settlers brought the designation of Haddrell's Point. Jonathan Scott promoted the area as a healthy spot, thanks to its high bluff and sea breeze. He laid out a typical English village and was advertising lots there as early as 1766. "Extadinay (sic) good Water...A pure Air and South aspect without the least Marsh on front...the best Oysters and Salt Water Fish in the Province," Scott wrote, recommending it as a place of retreat "in times when contagious disease rage in town." The disease was probably yellow fever, but planters would soon be looking for an escape from malaria as well. Other entrepreneurs followed suit during the next century, and in 1858, the results were joined together as Mount Pleasant.

Once over the Shem Creek Bridge, we enter the old village on Whilden Street. The area is primarily residential, but tourists are welcome. We'll turn right onto Hibben Street and park at the Presbyterian church to keep our intrusion to a minimum.

2.8	**0.2**	*At second stoplight, veer right onto*
		Whilden Street.
2.8	**2** blks	*Turn right onto Hibben Street.*
2.9	**1** blk	*On right is Mount Pleasant Presbyterian Church.*

Pause and walk this tour of Mount Pleasant if the weather permits.
The streets are narrow, so it is best seen on foot.

❹ 302 HIBBEN STREET, Mount Pleasant Presbyterian Church, c. 1854
Not open to public.
The oldest in the community, this church was built by a congregation that migrated here not from Charleston but from a few miles to the north of Mount Pleasant. Before 1700, a group of New England Congregationalists was shipwrecked on the Outer Banks of North Carolina. Rescued, they settled up the coast about 15 miles, and their descendants eventually came here to summer and then to live year-round. They built a chapel in 1827, now a private residence. In 1847, they constructed this simple meetinghouse. It's well cared for now, but during the Civil War, the roof was bombed. It was used briefly as a Confederate hospital, and at the war's end it was used as a schoolhouse for newly freed slaves.

> **2.9**   **50** ft   *Look right as you cross Church Street.*

Look down Church Street to Shem Creek. The Old King's Highway once ended near here at Hibben Ferry landing, but today options for waterfront dining and drinking abounds.

> **2.9**   **0.0**   *Continue on Hibben Street.*
> **3.2**   **1½** blks   *On left is 111 Hibben Street.*

❺ 111 HIBBEN STREET, The Hibben House, c. 1759
Not open to public.
This is the back entry we're looking at, disguised now by the addition of great Victorian columns, but the simple two-story house with the hip roof is still clearly evident. Jacob Motte built this Mount Pleasant plantation. Local lore claims that in 1775, Colonel Moultrie erected a quick rampart in the front yard, fired on two British men-of-war, and successfully drove them from Charleston Harbor. He went on almost immediately to defend the more famous Fort Moultrie on Sullivan's Island, but he returned here to visit as a prisoner of war. So did Cornwallis, who was using this as a headquarters. James Hibben purchased the plantation in 1803 and divided it into lots.

> **3.2**   **0.0**   *Continue to end of Hibben Street.*
> **3.2**   **½** blk   *At end of street at the Cooper River, make a U-turn.*
> **3.3**   **1** blk   *At stop sign, turn right onto Bennett Street.*
> **3.5**   **1** blk   *Turn left on Venning Street.*
> **3.6**   **1** blk   *At stop sign, turn right onto Pitt Street.*

This narrow thoroughfare leads us through what was the business section before the Revolutionary War.

> **3.7**   **2** blks   *Turn left onto King Street. Immediately on right,*
>   *facing Pitt Street, is The Darby Building.*

❻ 302 PITT STREET, The Darby Building, c. 1884
Built as a county courthouse when the village was a part of Berkeley County, this yellow building was soon converted into a Lutheran seminary. From 1916 to 1963, it was a Baptist church, but now it is back in government service as the arts center of the Mount Pleasant Department of Recreation.

> **3.7**   **1** blk   *Behind The Darby Building, turn right onto Carr Street.*
> **3.8**   **½** blk   *On left is Confederate Cemetery.*

❼ MONUMENT TO WAR OF 1812

This small graveyard contains the only memorial in the Southeast to the casualties of the War of 1812. See the marker for additional information.

3.8   ½ blk   *At stop sign, look across Bank Street to Old Town Hall.*

Patjens' Post Office on Pitt Street.

❽ 309 BANK STREET,
now a Police Substation, but formerly Old Town Hall, c. 1890
Not open to public.
This one-story frame building served as the old Town Hall. It originally stood 50 yards northwest, facing Pitt Street, near the yellow Darby Building we just saw.

3.8   **0.0**   *At stop sign, turn right onto Bank Street.*
3.8   ½ blk   *At stop sign, look to left at small wooden building.*

❾ CORNER OF PITT and BANK STREETS, **Patjens' Post Office**, c. 1880
Not open to public.
This building originally stood at the corner of Rivers Lane and Church Street. The Mount Pleasant Post Office occupied it in the late 1890s and early 1900s under the management of Postmaster John Patjens. The building was moved to this location in 1971. The Alhambra Garden Club restored it then, and again in 2001. If time permits, you can continue down Pitt Street toward the old Pitt Street Bridge that extended to Sullivan's Island. It's now a recreation area near Alhambra Hall. Here, Charles Jugnot and Oliver Hillard, owners of Mount Pleasant Ferry Company, developed a picnic ground in a grove of live oaks, called Hort's Grove. They built the first Alhambra as a summer retreat and dance hall overlooking Charleston Harbor. The town maintains the present building, built in 1937, as a multipurpose recreational facility.

If you are driving this tour, from the corner of Pitt and Bank streets:

3.9   **0.0**   *Turn left onto Pitt Street.*
4.0   **1** blk   *Turn left onto Ferry Street.*
4.1   **1** blk   *Turn left onto Royall Street. At third block, Royall Street becomes Whilden Street.*
4.4   **4** blks   *On right is St. Andrew's Episcopal Church.*

❿ 440 WHILDEN STREET, **St. Andrew's Episcopal Church**, c. 1857
Not open to public.
Bishop Theodore Dehon built the first church on this site in 1835. The congregation outgrew the old building; they held the first service in this new Gothic building on Christmas Day, 1857.

4.4   **0.0**   *Continue on Whilden Street.*
4.5   **3** blks   *Turn right onto Hibben Street.*

If you are walking this tour:

0.0	**0.0**	*At stop sign, turn right onto Pitt Street.*
0.0	**3** blks	*Veer right and continue straight onto Church Street.*
0.0	**2** blks	*Return to parked car near Hibben Street and Presbyterian church.*
4.5	**0.0**	*Turn car around and retrace Hibben Street to stop sign at corner of Coleman Blvd. Join driving tour here.*

The village has seen what many of the older residents would consider more than its fair share of changes. The broad sandy beach that ran for more than a mile muddied when the harbor jetties were built. The construction of the Cooper River bridges brought residents crowding in on every side and a further subdivision of even the older section. There's still a hint of the place recalled in Miss Petie McIver's *History of Mount Pleasant*, however, so I'll let her reminiscence be the last word.

"To the villagers, their hometown was pronounced 'Mumplesson,' a creek was a 'crick,' a terrapin was a 'cooter,' and any long-legged white bird was a 'crane.' Andirons were 'dog irons,' a wharf was a 'waff,' eggplant was 'guinea squash,' lima beans were 'sibby beans,' tomatoes were 'tomattus.' Everyone said 'cyar,' 'gyarden,' and 'pam' (the resort was the 'Oil of Pams') and called their parents 'Ma' and 'Pa.'"

4.6	**0.1**	*At stop sign, turn right onto Coleman Blvd.*
5.4	**0.8**	*Turn left onto W 526.*
7.6	**2.2**	*Exit 30, 17 North (Sweetgrass Basketmakers Highway) at Georgetown exit.*
9.6	**2.0**	At interesection of 17 North and Isle of Palms Connector, begin looking for roadside basket stands along 17 North.

⑪ SWEETGRASS BASKET STANDS

Area basket weavers practice a trade that originated in Africa more than three centuries ago. Dozens of such vendors once lined Old Georgetown Road. Today, most stands have moved to Hwy. 17. The first of these early slave-made baskets—broad, shallow "fanners"—were used to fan the chaff from harvested rice. The women used rush, split oak, and palmetto. When rice cultivation ended around 1900, basket making became more delicate and decorative. Sweetgrass, sometimes accented with pine straw, became the "bundle" to be woven in place with a "binder" of narrow palmetto. A Charleston bookstore owner marketed the work of Mount Pleasant area basket makers, or "sewers," through the mail. Then, with the completion of the Cooper River Bridge in 1929, weavers at roadside stands began selling directly to tourists. Hours of careful craftsmanship are required to make the simplest basket—and many are far from simple. It's hard to imagine a better Lowcountry souvenir or a better buy. Pieces identical to the ones for sale here have shown in museums all around America.

10.6	**1.0**	Continue on 17 North. *On right is Christ Church. Just past church, turn right onto Old Georgetown Highway and then immediately turn right into church parking lot.*

⑫ CHRIST EPISCOPAL CHURCH, c. 1706
Grounds open to public.

Christ Church was one of the original 10 parishes laid out by the Church Act of 1706. A wooden building erected at that time burned in 1725; the following year construction began on this brick church replacement. At that time, parishioners were described as "sober, industrious, and regular attendants of public worship." This was not, however, a particularly prosperous region, boasting

Sweetgrass baskets feature skilled craftsmanship and deatiled artistry.

few wealthy planters other than the nearby Boone family. The congregation struggled to maintain services. The British burned the building. Once rebuilt, the church lost members to its own Mount Pleasant Chapel. Union troops gutted the building. Grazing cattle knocked over tombstones, and the hubs of passing wagons wore a groove in the roadside corner of the structure. In 1873, church members gathered and agreed to repair and restore the church. In 1874, it was restored and consecrated for the first time.

There have been numerous changes to the little church over the years. At an early date, the pews were rearranged, and the side doors became windows. The cupola was added with the new roof after the Revolution, and was later replaced. The boxed eaves and rear addition were added in the 20th century. Extensively restored, the little brick building was probably the vestry, but tradition says it was built to shelter waiting coachmen from rain and cold.

10.6 0.0   *From church parking lot, look 20 feet to where Old Georgetown Road crosses the mounds of Fort Palmetto on both sides of the road.*

⓭ FORT PALMETTO and THE CONFEDERATE LINES, c. 1861
Behind the basket stand 50 yards north and just across the King's Highway
from the church, a tiny section of Palmetto Fort, to which the Confederate
Lines ran, remains. The defensive earthen mounds once stretched across this
neck of land and were meant to defend Charleston from invasion during the
Civil War. My great-great-grandfather supervised the fort's construction,
and Robert E. Lee congratulated him on a job well done, but the fort was
manned for only one day. When the city was evacuated, these last-minute
defenders slipped off across the Wando River. Union troops advancing from
Bulls Bay stepped through the redoubt of sharpened logs and branches and
bivouacked here for the night.

10.6	**0.0**	*From Christ Church parking lot,*
		turn left onto Old Georgetown Road.
10.7	**0.1**	*Cross 17 North, heading back toward Charleston.*
		Proceed 0.1 mile.
11.2	**0.5**	*Turn right onto Long Point Road.*
11.9	**0.7**	*Turn right into entrance of Boone Hall Plantation.*

⓮ BOONE HALL PLANTATION, c. 1681
Open to public.
Billed as "the most photographed plantation in America," the great white-
columned Boone Hall house and formal garden wait at the end of a long avenue
of majestic oaks. With the possible exception of Tara, probably no other plantation
has succeeded so well in capturing the public imagination.

Though there is some disagreement about how much of the house is
reconstruction rather than restoration, hostesses dressed in antebellum costume
give an enjoyable tour of the premises. General Washington might not have sat at
the dining-room table, but there's no denying that Patrick Swayze did. And, there's
a small display of plantation artifacts that have been uncovered over the years.

The grounds and outbuildings tell the history of continuing use since the
arrival of the first English settlers. Major John Boone sailed aboard the *Carolina*
and settled on this spot in 1681. An Indian trader, he was closely linked with the
resident Sewee tribe. His purchase of Indian slaves from the Sewees, combined
with his dealings with pirates, got him expelled from the colonial assembly
three times. The transition to a more staid and responsible citizenship was

rapid. John's son Thomas was a
distinguished servant of state and
church. He died in 1749 and may
be buried here beside the avenue of
oaks, which he first planted. John's
daughter was the grandmother
of two of South Carolina's most
noted statesmen, John and
Edward Rutledge.

The slave cabins, listed in the
National Register of Historic Places,
are of particular interest since few
such "streets" remain. Built to shelter
the house servants, the brick walls
and tile roofs were a luxury, but the
dirt floors, sashless windows, and
wide hearths to facilitate cooking

Avenue of oaks at Boone Hall Plantation. were the norm for such quarters.

Note the use of blue "glazers"—brick singed in the kiln—in the cabin wall and the especially elaborate decoration of the nearby round smokehouse.

In 1817, the Horlbeck family of Charleston bought the property. Best remembered for the construction of the Exchange Building, these master builders of Charleston operated a brickworks here and ran an extensive cotton plantation. The slave cabins date from 1790-1810. About the house were "miles of pasture upon which fine stock is raised....the gin houses, stables, barn and dozens of little cottages where the several hundred

|**S**lave cabins at Boone Hall Plantation.

slaves have their home—not in a negro quarter but dotted about over the country," says one account.

The scattered cottages are gone, the remaining gin house is a gift shop and restaurant. The 1890 commissary-chapel now contains restrooms and tourist information. Fine horses, kept in another generation of stables and barns, still graze here. A tradition of pecan trees remains, in keeping with the ones the Horlbecks planted in 1904, when Boone Hall boasted the world's largest pecan grove; today the plantation grows strawberries, tomatoes, and other u-pick fruits and vegetables.

Beyond the farthest of the remaining quarters, an ancient wharf known as The Cotton Dock appears to have been used well into modern times. Wapeckercon Creek, on which it sits, circles around the far side of the main house, and a road that can be walked or driven leads to a small black-water pond where dozens of egrets sometimes nest.

Boone Hall serves as a thoroughly entertaining and non-academic beginning for those unfamiliar with the plantations of the Lowcountry. For the more serious-minded, enough original support buildings remain to satisfy. For all, there are open grounds to stroll and, of course, a valuable photographic opportunity.

11.9	**0.0**	*Retrace to Boone Hall entrance gate and turn right onto Long Point Road.*
12.3	**0.4**	*Turn right onto Neederush Parkway.*
13.6	**1.3**	*Arrive at Palmetto Islands County Park entrance.*

⑮ PALMETTO ISLANDS COUNTY PARK
Open to public.

This park may be the best bargain in the area. Despite losing many trees to Hurricane Hugo, Palmetto Park remains a jewel. There are picnic areas, playgrounds, paddleboats, bicycles, the small Splash Island waterpark, and a snack bar. On the weekends, especially during the summer, the park can get hectic. During weekday mornings (and all day during the winter), it can be a surprisingly quiet retreat. Scenic paths and boardwalks lace all the low palmetto-and-pine-crowded islands; maps are given out at the entrance. The areas at the western end (to the right of the entry) are the farthest off the beaten path, and after parking, we can begin immediately on the marsh trail that leads along the edge of Boone Hall Creek. Here, oyster beds show at low tide, crab-pot floats bob in the channel, and egrets and ospreys seem to be constant companions.

| Charles Pinckney house at Snee Farm.

There are plaques along the boardwalk of Nature Island to identify the more familiar flora and fauna, but for the most part we're left on our own to enjoy and observe. In recent years, the park designated three acres as a dog park, which gives your traveling canines a place to roam off-leash.

13.6	**0.0**	*From park gate, retrace to Long Point Road.*
14.9	**1.3**	*Turn left onto Long Point Road.*
15.4	**0.5**	*On right is Charles Pinckney National Historic Site.*

⑯ CHARLES PINCKNEY NATIONAL HISTORIC SITE,
c. 1990, **and SNEE FARM**, predates 1695
Open to public.
Don't expect to see a plantation house or formal gardens at this historic site. All that remains from Snee Farm, which Charles Pinckney inherited from his father in 1782, is 28 acres and a traditional Tidewater cottage, built in the 1820s of native cypress and pine. The cottage, however, stands on the site of the Pinckney plantation house, and is well worth a visit for its compact and extremely informative exhibits. In addition to numerous artifacts and a good visual narrative of Lowcountry archaeology, the exhibits highlight the life of Pinckney, one of the major contributors to our country's Constitution and four-time state governor. Pinckney's country estate was the favorite of his seven plantations, and it's where he invited George Washington to breakfast with him in May 1791.

16.0	**0.6**	*At light, turn right onto U.S. 17 South.*
17.3	**1.3**	*Pass 526 N. Charleston exit.*
18.8	**1.5**	*Take E 526 exit on right.*
20.5	**1.7**	*At stoplight, turn left onto S.C. 703 North / Ben Sawyer Blvd.*
22.3	**1.8**	*Cross Ben Sawyer Bridge to Sullivan's Island.*

⑰ BEN SAWYER BRIDGE, c. 1945
This bridge carries us over the Intracoastal Waterway. In 1945, it replaced the old trolley line bridge that we spy on the far right, extending from Pitt Street in Old Mount Pleasant. Off to our distant left, we can see the Isle of Palms connector bridge. It's the other way off (or onto) the island, via the Isle of Palms, connecting S.C. Highway 703 with S.C. Highway 517.

A History of Sullivan's Island
"This island is a singular one. It consists of little else than the sea sand, and is about three miles long. Its breadth at no point exceeds a quarter of a mile. It is separated from the mainland by a scarcely perceptible creek oozing its way through a wilderness of reeds and slime." The creek has been dredged to a navigable depth now, but this description from Edgar Allan Poe's "The Gold Bug" is otherwise fitting. Poe found the setting for his gothic tales of pirates' buried treasure while he was stationed here as a young man at Fort Moultrie.

| *Palmettos, the South Carolina state tree, at sunset.*

He calls the architecture "miserable frame buildings, tenanted during summer by the fugitives from Charleston dust and fever." But beauty is in the eye of the beholder; architect Robert Mills described it as appearing "like a city, floating upon the bosom of the wide waters, and glittering in the sunbeams."

The domestic history of the island begins in 1791. Charleston citizens in need of a place to escape the city's yellow fever epidemics rented half-acre lots for a penny a year. By 1800, streets had been laid out, Sunday gambling forbidden, and the pesthouse closed.

In 1817, the community was incorporated as Moultrieville, with its first election held in the pesthouse, now converted to an Episcopal chapel. By then, the city's fever epidemics were so frequent that it was decided that the much-used refuge would require a police force and a school, and that only permanent buildings should be built on the lots. In 1826, Mills reported 200 houses in the village, two churches, and several excellent hotels. It was not a perfect world, however, for resident William Craft reported at about the same time that "an hour's idleness may obtain you a curlew, and having blistered your fingers you may catch a sheephead. The island air rusts metals, destroys shoeleather, and inspires verse making."

Actually, there were a few more serious problems: Hurricanes, like one in 1822, did considerable damage despite the fact that many of the houses were built on pilings, and the entire northern end was left abandoned because of the prevalence of malaria, or "myrtle fever." And of course, there was the Civil War, which left most of the locale flattened. Despite this, the community slowly grew. Ferries connected it with the city except during wartime, when makeshift bridges were built. But in 1898, the development of Isle of Palms as a resort brought with it the construction of a trolley line that crossed over from Mount Pleasant and ran the entire length of the island. (The "Station" street names are the old trolley stops.) In 1926, the islanders adapted the system to automobile traffic and the modern world began its assault in earnest.

Hurricane Hugo inundated the island, and the destruction was extensive. Today, it's hard to see any remnants of the hurricane's effects, though the memory of it remains vivid with islanders. Just ask one of them about the storm, if you want proof.

22.3 0.9   *At third stop sign, turn left on Atlantic Avenue.*

⑱ ATLANTIC AVENUE

Once upon a time, this was beachfront dotted with Victorian architecture and unusual fortifications. Between Station 20 and 28, a good concentration of turn-of-the-century cottages still stands. Once a bit shabby, almost all of the cottages have been restored to their former glory. Many of the buildings ramble across small, mimosa-crowded lots, with porches surrounding curious square and octagonal turrets at the corners. As a rule, at least one small wing has been added by each generation, so there's no danger of falling out of fashion. Sadly, Hurricane Hugo carried away a number of these old beauties, but fans of Victorian architecture will enjoy this street and many others inland and to the south. (Watch along Middle Street as you drive toward Fort Moultrie.) The northern end of the island contains newer homes, but many of these, like the newer houses throughout, are "tin roof" construction and blend in easily with the old.

23.2 0.9 *At dead end of Atlantic Avenue, turn right onto Station 28½ .*
23.3 0.1 *Proceed one-half block, take the next left onto Brownell Blvd.,*
          where you'll see batteries tastefully converted into homes.
23.7 0.4 *At end of block, turn left onto Station 31.*

⑲ BATTERIES

Five tremendous batteries dating from the Spanish American War to World War II dot the town. Some have been converted into homes. One is the island library. The largest, Battery Capron or Mortar Battery, towers above the island playground. At the north end there's a good view of the ocean at Breach Inlet, but a note of caution: There's no swimming or even wading here—the inlet's currents have drowned many.

24.9 0.2 *Turn left onto Middle Street.*
25.6 1.7 *Look to the left at Station 18½ for U.S. Coast Guard*
          Station and Lighthouse.

⑳ SULLIVAN'S ISLAND LIGHTHOUSE, c. 1961

Not open to public.
The old U.S. Life Boat Service buildings constructed in 1890 still stand at the base of the 1961 lighthouse. It replaced the Morris Island Lighthouse, which was located on the far side of the harbor. At 161 feet above sea level and with 3 million candlepower, the light was the most powerful in the United States when it was built. Because of heat problems, the oxide carbon lights were replaced with a cooler system, which became automated in 1977. Boasting the only elevator and the first triangular construction, the lighthouse can be seen from 15 miles at sea.

26.3 0.7 *Turn right into parking lot of Fort Moultrie Visitors' Center*

I**Sullivan's Island Lighthouse.**

㉑ **FORT MOULTRIE,**
c. 1776 (with later additions in 1798 and 1809)

In the first years of colonization, the notorious Florence O'Sullivan maintained a lookout here (hence the name Sullivan's Island). For almost a century, that would be the only military function of the island. Any large draft ship wishing to enter Charleston Harbor, however, had to round the shoal, which would later be the site of Fort Sumter. South Carolina's Revolutionary War government quickly utilized this strategic position. "An immense pen" of spongy palmetto logs banked with sand was erected and placed under the command of Colonel William Moultrie.

Six weeks before the signing of the Declaration of Independence, the British fleet arrived and, confident of victory, crossed the Charleston Bar. American forces responded with grave concern; most felt the more reliable line of defense would be at Haddrell's Point (Mount Pleasant). "Those ships…will knock it down in half an hour!" a critic said of the fort. "We will lay behind the ruins and prevent their men from landing," Colonel Moultrie replied. Such drastic measures were not required, though. Nine men-of-war with about 260 guns faced off against only 31 cannons and 400 men inside the fort. In the furious day-long exchange that followed,

Fort Moultrie's Famous Faces

A *surprising number of celebrities have passed through the fort's sally port. Osceola, the Seminole Indian war leader, is buried here. Archaeologists are certain of that, because the remains have no head. The attending physician carried it off, supposedly for scientific reasons, but reportedly hung it on his children's bedpost to frighten them. Edgar Allan Poe was stationed here and used the setting in his writing. Abner Doubleday served here under Major Robert Anderson. Once when he was moved to nearby Fort Sumter, Doubleday took aim and fired a Union cannonball into the Moultrie House Hotel. General William T. Sherman was stationed here. Some say that's why he spared Charleston on his march. George C. Marshall was in charge at Fort Moultrie in 1933, and promised, "I'm going places."*

the British suffered numerous casualties and lost one ship before retreating. Charleston would not fall for another three years. And Moultrie earned his name on the serviceable structure.

That fort was abandoned soon after the Revolution and fell victim to hurricanes and scavengers searching for building material. A hurricane destroyed a second fort, but in 1809, a new brick structure was finished. The National Park Service maintains this construction today.

When we enter Fort Moultrie, the restoration allows us to virtually walk through time. To our left rises the World War II Harbor Entrance Control Post tower. Moving right, we come in turn to the fortification and cannons of the post-Spanish American War, post-Civil War, Civil War, and post-1809 construction. Though the fort continued to serve as a principal means of costal defense throughout this period, actual combat occurred only during the Civil War. Major Anderson crossed over to Fort Sumter, and Southern forces, which aided in the bombardment of Anderson's new stronghold, occupied Fort Moultrie. Fort Moultrie remained a key to the harbor's defense, keeping the blockading forces at bay, especially the menacing new ironclads, and guarding Charleston's center

Fort Moultrie's Other Amenities

Bird Watching | *Observe several species near the open fields and dunes in front of the fort, and along worn paths to the beach.*

Scenic Views | *From the Park Service building's observation deck, you can look across the harbor to well-known Fort Sumter.*

Celebrity Sites | *Osceola's grave lies just to the right of the sally port. Behind the Park Service building on the back side of the island is the relocated grave of General Moultrie, and beyond that, a large concrete dock that gives a good view of Poe's "slime and reeds."*

Sunken Ships | *Beneath the offshore waves rest the remains of unsuccessful blockade-runners that ran aground when capture proved inevitable. The sands also conceal the sunken hulls of the Union's "stone blockade."*

Charleston Jetties | *These two-mile-long strips of black rock protruding from the waves are the work of Quincy Adams Gillmore, who served here in the Corps of Engineers during the Civil War and returned in 1878 to begin the 17-year-long project. Gillmore's plan was only one educated guess, but it proved correct. The two curved underwater sections of the jetties, beginning here and on the opposite Morris Island, allow the incoming tide to pass over, but funnel the outgoing tide in a scouring path through the channel between the visible rocks. The side effects have been more controversial: It appears that since the jetties' completion, Sullivan's Island has grown considerably, but Morris Island and Folly Beach to the south have eroded, and Mount Pleasant has lost its beach. However, you won't find a better place than this to watch the great variety of oceangoing vessels that pass through the jetties in a steady stream.*

Morris Island Light | *Keepers burned pitch as a signal from the earliest days, and in 1767, they built the first lighthouse. The one standing today replaced the earlier version in 1870—the 264 pilings driven into rock beneath it allowed it to withstand hurricanes and earthquakes, and finally, the washing away of the island.*

MOUNT PLEASANT and SULLIVAN'S ISLAND **77**

line of defense. The fort was not abandoned until the city was evacuated in 1865.

In the years that followed, Moultrie was continually upgraded as cannons became more powerful and the concepts of coastal defense changed. Guns that disappeared from view when not being fired and the spreading of the batteries throughout the island were the last of these innovations. By the conclusion of World War II, it was obvious that ships and planes could handle the defense of mainland America.

Don't forget to go home eventually. As local islander and historian W.W. Wannamaker, Jr., warns, "It's a nice place to visit, but I would not want to live anywhere else."

Fort Moultrie Tours

The park service offers tours of Fort Moultrie in spring and summer. Tours begin in the Park Service building across the street from the fort. A movie introduces the fort, and guided tours are conducted three times daily. A detailed brochure also allows you to explore on your own. On the roof, an observation platform provides a good view of the surroundings.

26.8 0.0		*To return to Charleston from Fort Moultrie Visitors' Center parking lot, turn left onto Middle Street.*
28.0 1.2		*Turn left onto Station 22½.*
28.0 1 blk		*Junction of S.C. 703 South; continue straight on Ben Sawyer Blvd.*
30.7 2.7		*At second stoplight, Ben Sawyer Blvd. becomes S.C. 703 South Business.*
31.9 1.2		*Cross Shem Creek Bridge.*
33.3 1.4		*Arrive at base of Cooper River Bridge and junction of U.S. 17 South.*

END TOUR

Beaufort and the Sea Islands

TOUR FOUR

BEAUFORT and the SEA ISLANDS
We begin by heading south on U.S. 17 to visit the ancient and beautiful ruins of **Sheldon Church**. From there, a short drive toward the coast brings us to **Beaufort**, the second-oldest town in the state. Its architecture, especially from the Federalist and Greek Revival periods, easily rivals that of Charleston, and we'll spend most of the day wandering the quiet streets. Next we cross over the Beaufort River to the once-isolated **Sea Island of St. Helena** and visit **Penn Center**, a place that encapsulates the area's black history. The trip ends beside the ocean at **Hunting Island State Park**, a facility that includes a museum, historic lighthouse, nature trails, fishing pier, and, of course, miles of beaches. To fit this tour into one day, start early and enjoy your day in the Lowcountry.

Sheldon Church
  Sheldon Church Road, near the intersection of Highways 21 & 235
Beaufort Visitors Bureau
  713 Craven Street | 843-525-8500 | *www.beaufortsc.org*
Beaufort National Cemetery
  1601 Boundary Street | 843-524-3925
  www.cem.va.gov/cems/nchp/beaufort.asp
Henry C. Chambers Waterfront Park
  Bay Street roughly between Cartaret and New Castle streets
  843-525-7070
The George Parsons Elliott House
  1001 Bay Street
The John Mark Verdier House Museum
  801 Bay Street | 843-379-6335 | *www.historicbeaufort.org*
  Admission charged.
Baptist Church of Beaufort
  600 Charles Street | 843-524-3197 | *www.bcob.org*
St. Helena's Episcopal Church
  505 Church Street | 843-522-1712 | *www.sthelenas1712.org*
Penn Center
  16 Penn Center Circle West | 843-838-2432 | *www. penncenter.com*
  Admission charged.
Hunting Island State Park
  255 Sea Island Parkway | 843-838-2011 | *www.huntingisland.com*
  Admission charged.
Getting There
  Though we travel U.S. 17 South on several other tours, we'll use this one to mention the historical markers passed and the other points of interest.

BEGIN TOUR
0.0   0.0   *From Charleston, take U.S. 17 South. Begin clocking mileage from south side of Ashley River Bridge.*
9.5   9.5   *Red Top Community.*

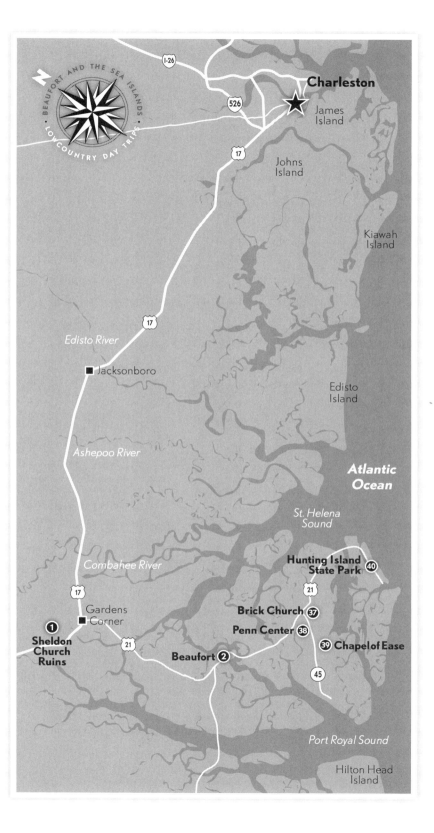

Red Top was a boom town in the phosphate mining days, but the little community has since calmed down.

10.3	**0.8**	*Cross Rantowles Creek.*
10.3	**80** ft	*On right, William Washington Historical Marker.*

William Washington, a cousin of the first president, fought the British under Tarleton at Rantowles Bridge and is buried nearby.

13.2	**2.9**	*On right is the former Tea Farm, now part of Caw Caw Interpretive Center.*
13.6	**0.4**	*Turn into the parking lot for Caw Caw Interpretive Center on the right.*
13.6	**1.4**	*Return to U.S. 17 South and turn right.*
15.0	**1.4**	*On your right in the curve is a section of the old Jacksonboro to Charleston road, which was replaced by U.S. 17.*
22.6	**7.6**	*To the left of the highway, note railroad tracks.*

The **Rail Line** running parallel to the highway was completed on the eve of the Civil War, and the Union spent most of the war trying to capture it.

28.7	**6.1**	*Cross Edisto River.*
29.1	**0.4**	*On the right is the parking lot for the Edisto Nature Trail. It—along with the town of Jacksonboro—is featured in Tour 8 (page 159).*
29.1	**0.0**	*Continue on U.S. 17 South.*
29.2	**0.1**	*On right, in fenced-in pasture, is location of old capitol building.*
35.1	**5.9**	*Cross Ashepoo River.*
35.2	**0.1**	*On left, historical marker for Edmundbury Chapel of Ease.*

The **Edmundbury Chapel of Ease** was named for landgrave Edmund Bellinger. A chapel built here in 1758 collapsed by 1810. Then, Union troops burned its replacement.

36.2	**1.0**	*On left is turnoff for Bear Island.*

The **Bear Island Wildlife Management Area** holds 12,021 acres, about 3,700 acres of which are former rice fields. They draw ducks, eagles and more, but it's a day's trip in itself. (Please see "Additional Day Trips From Charleston" on page 218 for details.)

43.7	**7.5**	*Cross Cumbahee River Delta.*

The road slices through the **Delta Rice Fields**, where indentions and rises reveal the path of old canals and dikes. Now this area is well known for duck hunting and fishing. Neighboring ACE Basin, named for the Ashepoo, Cumbahee, and Edisto rivers, consists of 350,000 acres of river basin land (both state and privately owned) protected by conservation easements.

45.0	**1.3**	*Cross Cumbahee River.*
51.1	**6.2**	*Turn right onto Old Sheldon Church Road / S-7-21.*
52.7	**1.5**	*Pull off onto right-hand side of road and park near Sheldon Church ruins.*

❶ SHELDON CHURCH RUINS,
c. 1757
Open daily.

Sheldon Church ruins.

Built under the direction of Governor William Bull, Sheldon Church was considered at the time "the second best church in the province and by many esteemed a more beautiful building than St. Philips." On the Sabbath, the Bull family entertained the entire congregation ("seldom less than 60 or 70 carriages") at their nearby Sheldon Plantation. Sadly, first the British, then later Sherman burned the original church and its replacements. So what's left? Some of the finest holy ruins.

Note the six engaged columns running down each wall, for these represent the earliest attempt in America to emulate a Greek temple. The small holes in the walls are "put-log holes," which once held the scaffolding for the bricklayers. Repeated burnings have caused the plugs to pop out. Note the brickwork too. The blue glazers forming a diamond pattern beneath the portico on the rear wall spell out the date of construction, but are staggered on the sides as decoration. The cut bricks at about head height in the attached columns, known as "hogs in the wall," suggest that at one point stucco may have covered the columns.

A dozen early tombs dot the grounds; the majority belong to the Bull family and their descendants. Their family coat of arms, now badly worn, adorns one gravestone—an armed sword above the figure of a bull and the motto, "God is cortues," which translates, "God is gracious."

52.7	**0.0**	*Turn around and retrace Old Sheldon Church Road / S-7-21 to U.S. 17.*
54.2	**1.5**	*Turn left onto U.S. 17 North / U.S. 21 South.*
54.5	**0.3**	*Veer right onto U.S. 21 South.*
59.0	**4.5**	*Cross Whale Branch River.*
64.8	**5.8**	*On left is entrance to Marine Corps Air Station.*
66.1	**1.3**	*Continue straight, but to right is S.C. 280 South, which leads to Parris Island Marine Base, where there is a museum.*
68.5	**2.4**	*Turn left into Beaufort National Cemetery.*

❷ BEAUFORT

In 1520, the Spanish explored the area. Captain Jean Ribaut with his small band of French Huguenots followed in 1562, but their settlement ended in disaster. Attempting to sail back to France in a homemade boat, the few surviving adventurers were forced to cannibalism. The Spanish returned in 1566, and for 20 years maintained a fort and mission. When they left, they still considered it part of their domain. In 1663, William Hilton explored the area for the English Lords Proprietor, giving a glowing account to his employers. To posterity, he left the island name "Hilton Head." This Port Royal locale became England's official destination in 1670, but because of hostile Indians, the English chose Charles Town instead. A party of Scots settled here in 1685, but the Spanish destroyed their Stuart Town the following year. In 1711, two of the colony's most ambitious Indian traders, Thomas Nairne and "Tuscarora Jack" Barnwell, urged the construction of a town here once more. Four years later, the Yemassee, instigated by the Spanish, killed most of the region's settlers and burned this infant community. Luckily, most of Beaufort's occupants escaped to a ship in the harbor. The Indians continued to raid the area for another dozen years; nevertheless, residents rebuilt the town almost immediately. Indigo production, shipbuilding, and rice planting replaced Indian trading, and prosperity followed.

In the years after the Civil War, citizens earned a living from phosphate and cotton. Gradually, the community revived. The hurricane of 1893 swept through the area, though, killing thousands on the Sea Islands, and by 1919, the boll weevil had brought economic disaster to the region. As elsewhere, truck farming and seafood harvesting took up the slack, and the payroll from the nearby Marine base infused much-needed revenue. Today, resort communities occupy former plantations throughout the Sea Islands.

❸ BEAUFORT NATIONAL CEMETERY, c. 1863
Open to public.
Though the world remembers Abraham Lincoln's address dedicating the Gettysburg Cemetery, many don't realize that nine other national cemeteries existed. In 1862, Beaufort fell to the Union, and the following year this plot was set aside. Bodies were brought in from local battlefields and the town's own hospitals, as well as from all along the Southern Seaboard. Ironically, fever killed most, not bullets. Usually a name and a place—Illinois, Indiana, New York, Ohio—mark the small stones radiating from the entry, but some are more anonymous—"U.S.A. soldier," or just "U.S.A." At the end of the Civil War, the site held about 3,789 graves; today, almost 7,000 veterans from America's other conflicts join them. Just beyond the center rows, note the distant monument to the Union—a memorial unique to the Lowcountry, and perhaps to the entire South. Interestingly, Beaufort does not have one for the Confederates.

TOUR 4 **BEAUFORT**

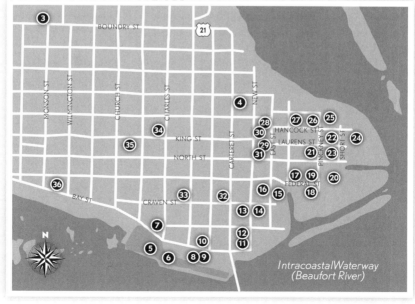

*Intracoastal Waterway
(Beaufort River)*

68.5 0.0   *Return to cemetery entrance; turn left onto*
Boundary Street / U.S. 21 South Business.
69.0 **10** blks   *At dead end, bear right onto Carteret Street /*
U.S. 21 South Business.

As you drive down Carteret Street, the scenery gradually shifts from aluminum and concrete to tabby, brick, and wood.

69.2 **3** blks   *On left is The Old Beaufort College.*

❹ 800 CARTERET STREET, The Old Beaufort College Building, c. 1857
Open to public.
Nowadays, the Office of the Chancellor and Academic Affairs offices of the University of South Carolina use this unusual Greek Revival building. The original college started as a preparatory school in 1795 and moved to these new quarters in 1857. After the Civil War, the Freedman's Bureau used it, then a private school, and then a public one before the current tenants.

69.6 **7** blks   *Turn right onto Bay Street.*
69.8 **3** blks   *Continue to Downtown Marina.*

❺ 1006 BAY STREET, Downtown Marina
Shops, restaurants, and dozens of moored boats fill Beaufort's colorful Downtown Marina. It's worth a stop to just poke around, grab a bite to eat, and appreciate the block's historic architecture. Though it's possible to drive around town from here, park your car and walk as much as possible.

69.8 0.0   *Adjacent to the marina and next to the water spreads*
Henry C. Chambers Waterfront Park.

❻ HENRY C. CHAMBERS WATERFRONT PARK
This six-acre waterfront park provides a brief history of the area cast in brass. For the less studious, there's a seawall promenade, as well as picnic tables, a playground, and even porch swings.

69.8 0.0   *Walk across Bay Street from the marina and waterfront*
park to Elliott House.

❼ 1001 BAY STREET, The George Parsons Elliott House, c. 1840
Open to public.
This Greek Revival mansion is a good example of "Beaufort style" architecture. Built by Elliott on the eve of the Civil War, it was occupied by one of the community's richest men, Dr. W.J. Jenkins. The Army confiscated it and used it as an Army hospital, eventually selling it for taxes. A century later, the Bank of Beaufort purchased the home and arranged for it to become a house museum operated by The Beaufort Historical Foundation. The floor plan is traditional Georgian, with a central hallway containing a fine staircase. Opulence abounds in the ceiling's gilded cornices and moldings and Italian marble mantels. The exceptionally fine furniture reflects the period when Dr. Jenkins shared the house with his wife and eight daughters. Architecture enthusiasts appreciate the home's exterior as well, notably the fanlight door and original iron banister and, of course, the massive columns, which are a hallmark of the Beaufort style.

69.8 0.0   *After visiting Elliott House, cross the street and*
turn left on Bay Street. Enter business district.

Beaufort Style

As in Charleston, the architecture of Beaufort developed as a result of the city's climate and surroundings. The resulting Beaufort style refers to free-standing houses on relatively large lots, on high foundations, that face into the southerly breeze. The floor plan is often T-shaped, with a wing off the back, and two small projections off the side to bring the breeze into the rear rooms. Giant porticoes on the front often eclipse the shallow, hipped roof. The design incorporates elements from Georgian, Colonial, or Greek Revival. Most houses featured double piazzas, although some changes have been made. The Elliott house (above), for example, began with only one piazza. Owners added the second-story porch in about 1900. The impulse to conform to the Beaufort style has been so tempting that owners of Federalist, Italianate, and Victorian buildings have completely refaced them.

70.0 1 blk *On right is the John Cross Tavern.*

❽ **808-812 BAY STREET,**
formerly the John Cross Tavern
Open to public.
There's no exact date for its original establishment, but until it became a retail store, the John Cross Tavern had been around for a very long while (or at least the name and site have). Pirates frequented the popular meeting place, and some say the infamous Blackbeard imbibed here. Methodist founder John Wesley spent the night here in 1735. Biographer Parson Weems, the man who invented the story of George Washington and the cherry tree, died in one of the upstairs rooms. A variety of businesses now occupy the historic building.

70.0 Same blk *Next door, on right, is 802–806 Bay Street.*

❾ **802-806 BAY STREET,**
Saltus House, c. 1795
Not open to public.
Once home to a thriving shipyard, the three-story building also saw service as a customhouse and commissary before becoming a department store. Today it has been broken into a variety of shops.

70.0 Same blk *On left of Bay Street and across the street is 801 Bay Street.*

❿ **801 BAY STREET, The John Mark Verdier House**
(The Lafayette Building), c. 1804,
Open to public.
The son of Purrysburg Huguenot immigrants, builder John Mark Verdier was a prosperous Beaufort merchant. (He later moved to Charleston and went bankrupt.) The Union used the house as a headquarters during the Civil War, and in later years it served as a fish market, icehouse, law office, and barbershop. In 1942, the structure was condemned, but the Marquis de Lafayette, on his tour of the South, briefly addressed the citizens from the portico, so "The Committee to Save the Lafayette Building" did just that. Historic Beaufort Foundation took over in 1968, eventually restoring and furnishing the home.

The Verdier house's double portico has been altered slightly since 1865, but take a good look anyway. This look appears elsewhere in the Lowcountry, but in Beaufort the style becomes a more delicate, but still perfectly proportioned portico. These porticoes are almost as distinctively Beaufort as the double piazzas. Inside, note the woodwork, the graceful stair, and the familiar Federalist Venetian or Palladian window. Upstairs, there's one strangely rustic bedroom. The second-story drawing room features elaborate Adam Brothers mantels.

70.0 0.0 *After visiting the John Mark Verdier House, continue on Bay Street.*

70.1 1 blk *Cross over Carteret Street, and on right is The Point.*

John Mark Verdier House, Beaufort.

The Point

An area thick with moss-draped oaks, flowering shrubs, and grand old homes, Black's Point became Sams Point after the family that settled on nearby Dawtah Island. The first, William Sams, was a Tory seeking a "healthier climate," but he arrived in time to plant Sea Island cotton. His two sons grew rich and proliferated, and the family built fine town houses. It's just "The Point" now, though; the "Sams" has been dropped. The earliest house dates from c. 1810.

70.1 Same blk *Last house on left is 601 Bay Street.*

⑪ 601 BAY STREET, Lewis Reeve Sams House, c. 1852
Private residence.
During a fire in 1907, workers in a nearby cotton gin formed a bucket brigade to save this particularly fine example of the Beaufort style, built by Lewis Reeve Sams. Note the marble entry stairs and the use of Doric and Ionic columns rather than the single pillar, soon to be popular.

70.1 0.0 *At end of Bay Street, turn left onto New Street.*
70.1 1 blk *On the left is 214 New Street.*

⑫ 214 NEW STREET, The Thomas Hepworth House, c. 1750
Not open to public.
This is the oldest house in town. Note the massive chimney. It appears to have four flues but is actually only one. In addition to its architectural interest, this little house holds an intriguing social history; rumors claim Eli Whitney's cotton gin was demonstrated inside. Called "the Temple of the Sun," the home was at one time associated with the Masonic order and also shows up as "the Republican headquarters."

70.2 1 blk *On left is 310 New Street.*

⑬ 310 NEW STREET, The Berners Barnwell Sams House, c. 1818
Not open to public.
Another Sams house, but an earlier generation—actually Dr. Berners Sams' slaves—built this one in 1818. The original was only one room deep and had a parapet around the roof. It was used as a hospital for freed slaves during the Civil War.

70.2 Same blk *Turn right on Craven Street.*
70.2 1st blk *On right, see Rainbow Row / 506-510 Craven Street.*

⑭ 506-510 CRAVEN STREET, Victorian Row, c. 1870 to early 1900s
Not open to public.
These Victorian homes feature ornate gingerbread, towers, and turrets—
all worthy of praise and attention. Since they're painted different colors,
the neighborhood is sometimes referred to as "Rainbow Row."

> **70.3** **1** blk *Turn left on East Street. On right facing Craven Street
> is 411 Craven Street.*

⑮ 411 CRAVEN STREET, The Castle, c. 1859
Not open to public.
Observers have described this intriguing home as Italianate, Greek Revival,
even Medieval—thanks to six massive hexagonal columns, a five-foot parapet,
and great chimneys that are all coated with a mottled stucco that shifts from
pink to tan to gray, depending on the day's mood. Yes, it's the perfect castle for
a ghost; in this case, it's a dwarf who arrived more than four centuries ago with
French Protestant Jean Ribaut. The builder, Dr. Joseph Johnson, saw the wee man
enter the basement one day. Later, his gardener said that the little man lived there.
Others would see him pass from the creek edge into the house, but nowadays, only
children can spot him.

> **70.3** ½ blk *On left is 412 East Street. The street number—
> difficult to see—is on the gate.*

⑯ 412 EAST STREET, The Henry Farmer House, c. 1810
Not open to public.
Still within the bounds of the Federal period, builder Farmer included a traditionally
proportioned portico (far wider than that of the Verdier house) that embraces two
side windows as well as the doors. The next owner, widow Charlotte Beadon, married
her lawyer, Dr. Thomas Fuller, and together the couple traveled through Europe
gathering exotic plants for the garden.

> **70.3** **0.0** *At end of block, turn right on Federal Street / S-7-165.*
> **70.4** **2** blks *On left is 315 Federal Street.*

⑰ 315 FEDERAL STREET, The John Blythewood House (Cassina),
c. early 1800s.
Not open to public.
A former slave of Margaret Blythewood (daughter of builder John), Mary Belle
bought this Beaufort-style house in 1863. It still belonged to black owners when
the 1893 storm brought floodwaters up to the front porch. Boatloads of refugees
from the islands stepped directly onto the porch to refuge inside.

> **70.4** Same blk *Last house on right is 302 Federal Street.*

⑱ 302 FEDERAL STREET, The William Fripp House (Tidewater), c. 1830
Not open to public.
The Fripp family had lived in the area for more than a century when William, a
wealthy St. Helena planter, built his traditional summer home, Tidewater, in 1830.

> **70.4** **0.0** *Across Federal Street is 303 Federal Street.*

⑲ 303 FEDERAL STREET, The James Rhett House, c. 1885
Not open to public.
Something of an architectural novelty, James Rhett's home was reportedly built in
his effort to win the hand of a woman who demanded the finest house in Beaufort.

He intended to make the house two rooms deep, but ran out of money and built what you see. It's called "Rhett's Folly," a reference apparently to both love and architecture.

70.4 0.0   *At end of Federal Street is Marshlands (501 Pinckney Street).*

⑳ 501 Pinckney Street,
The James Robert Verdier House (Marshlands), c. 1814
Not open to public.
With the exception of the single encircling veranda showing Barbadian influence, Marshlands is typically Federal in design. Its builder? Dr. James Verdier, known for his work with yellow fever patients.

70.4 0.0   *Turn left onto Pinckney Street.*
70.5 2 blks   *On left is 604 Pinckney Street.*

㉑ 604 PINCKNEY STREET,
The Edward Means House, c. 1857
Not open to public.
Colonel Means' house is one of few brick homes and also one of the few entered from the east, or street, end. An occupying Yankee reporter wrote, "The splendor of the houses and furniture and the beauty of the place have been exaggerated, but the house of Col. Edward Means would be called handsome in any town in the North."

70.5 0.0   *Turn right on Laurens Street.*
70.5 1 blk   *On left is 201 Laurens Street.*

㉒ 201 LAURENS STREET,
The Berners Barnwell Sams House, c. 1852
Not open to public.
This second home built by Dr. Berners Barnwell Sams is a far cry from his modest first one on New Street. The large open square in front of the columned, Greek Revival brick home, known as "the Front Green," is actually part of the property. The doctor's son recalls that carriages favored this turn in the evening; for sport, he and his brother would catch on behind and drop off in front of their father's office. But they were finally caught. "The next carriage that drove by was not troubled by outriders. Here were right and wrong. Father was right and we were wrong."

70.6 1 blk   *Second house on right is 100 Laurens Street.*

㉓ 100 LAURENS STREET,
The Paul Hamilton House (The Oaks), c. 1856
Not open to public.
At the corner of Laurens and Short streets, obscured by lots of oaks, stands the handsome Paul Hamilton House. It is one of several Italianate houses in the neighborhood. Note the decorative brackets beneath the eaves and compounded columns of this romanticized Italian villa.

At the end of the war, Hamilton was given three days to go to Charleston and raise the money to redeem the house. When the sale took place on the second day instead, irate neighbors led by a Northern merchant bought it for Hamilton. "We shook hands with the Northerner that night," Hamilton's daughter wrote, "though up to that time we had said we would never shake hands with any Yankee."

70.6 Same blk   *At end of Laurens Street on left is 1 Laurens Street.*

㉔ 1 LAURENS STREET, The Edgar Fripp House, c. 1856
Not open to public.
Edgar Fripp's home started out as an Italianate villa and even boasted Romantic
turrets and wings. Badly damaged in the hurricane of 1893, however, it was
reconstructed as you see it now. This one, too, was about to be sold out of the
family at the war's end, but a Frenchman seeing the owner in tears bought it for
him, kissed him on both cheeks, and departed. True story; it's documented.

70.6	**0.0**	*Turn around and return one block to Short Street.*
70.6	**1** blk	*Turn right onto Short Street.*
70.7	**1** blk	*At stop sign, turn left on Hancock Street.*
70.7	**½** blk	*On right is 207 Hancock Street.*

㉕ 207 HANCOCK STREET, The Elizabeth Hext House, c. 1810
Not open to public.
Set well back from the road, this little two-story house was once considered to be "in
the country." Elizabeth, an only child of the pioneer builders, married a grandson of
"Tuscarora Jack" Barnwell, William Sams. They started the local Sams dynasty, but
this house went out of the family's hands when the Union sold it for taxes.

70.7	**1** blk	*On corner of Hancock and Pinckney streets,* *on right, is 804 Pinckney Street.*

㉖ 804 PINCKNEY STREET, The Johnson House, c. 1855
Not open to public.
Similar to the home of Edward Means in that the entrance is to the side,
Dr. John Johnson's home is slightly smaller and made of painted brick. Johnson's
brother-in-law, Franklin Talbird, a builder, constructed both houses. In 1873,
the doctor wrote a good reminiscence, quoting in hindsight, "Thrice happy the
farmers, did they but know their own blessings."

70.8	Same blk	*On right is 313 Hancock Street.*

㉗ 313 HANCOCK STREET, Talbird-Sams House, c. 1810
Not open to public.
According to local lore, Henry Talbird sold his home to a Sams, who sold it back to
a Talbird. The house is unusual because the second story is only one room wide.

70.8	**1** blk	*Facing you at the dead end of Hancock Street* *is 708 East Street.*

㉘ 708 EAST STREET, The Tree House, date unknown
Not open to public.
Legend has it that this house was cut in half when it was moved here so that it could
slip in beside the giant oak. Famous slave pilot Robert Smalls' family moved it in
1910; it's still called the "Tree House."

70.8	**0.0**	*Turn left onto East Street.*
70.8	**1** blk	*Turn right onto Prince Street.*
70.8	Same blk	*First house on left is 502 Prince Street / S-7-110.*

㉙ 502 PRINCE STREET, Pretty Penny, c. 1885
Not open to public.
Builder George Doane had a lumberyard that allowed him to put only the
choicest woods into his Victorian dwelling. The low lot was filled with palmetto logs
before construction began. "Pretty Penny"—well built and well named.

70.9 Same blk *On right is*
511 Prince Street.

㉚ 511 PRINCE STREET,
McKee-Smalls House, c. 1834
Not open to public.
Though the exterior and interior trim
of Henry McKee's home suggest a
continuing line to the earlier Federalist
period, the 12-foot ceiling and great
windows suggest Greek Revival
proportions. It's a house with a history
of unusual occupants. Robert Smalls
was born a slave in a cabin behind the
house and, for service to the Union,
would earn the money to buy this
house at a tax sale. The DeTreville
family, which had lost the house,
carried the suit to regain it all the way
to the Supreme Court and lost.

70.9 0.0 *Turn left on*
New Street.
On left is 601
New Street.

㉛ 601 NEW STREET,
First African Baptist Church,
c. 1886.
Not open to public.
Even before the Civil War, many
blacks met in their own little "praise
houses" or "praise churches."

70.9 0.0 *Continue on*
New Street.
71.1 2 blks *Turn right onto*
Craven Street.
71.2 2 blks *On right is the*
Beaufort Arsenal,
now the Beaufort
Visitor Center, at
713 Craven Street.

The First African American Church (top)
and The Tabernacle Baptist Church,
home to the grave of Robert Smalls. At
23, slave Robert Smalls daringly piloted
a Confederate ship loaded with his family
across Civil War lines to Union freedom.
He went on to empower blacks on both sides,
start a school, serve as a Congressman and
U.S. Collector of Customs. He later owned
the home in which he had been a slave.

㉜ 713 CRAVEN STREET, **Beaufort Arsenal**, c. 1852
Beaufort Visitor Center
An 1852 face-lift gave this building an appropriately Gothic fortress façade.
It has since been renovated by the Historic Beaufort Foundation.

71.2 0.0 *Continue on Craven Street.*
71.3 2 blks *On right is 907 Craven Street.*

㉝ 911 CRAVEN STREET, **The Tabernacle Baptist Church**, c. 1894
Grounds open to public.
Supposedly, a temporary schism in the Baptist congregation caused an earlier
church to be built on this site sometime before the Civil War, but the split

healed quickly and it became a meetinghouse and lecture room. At the war's end, 500 black members of the congregation withdrew and bought the church. The storm of 1893 caused severe damage, but the congregation rebuilt the building close to the original style. Robert Smalls' grave is here. He's honored additionally with a bust and plaque.

71.3 ½ blk   *Turn right onto Charles Street.*
71.4 **2** blks   *Turn left onto King Street.*
71.4 20 ft   *Turn left into the Baptist Church of Beaufort's parking lot.*

Beaufort and the Revivals
Resident William Grayson reported in the years following the Revolution that in Beaufort "religion was very little regarded…Sunday was a day of boat racing, foot racing, drinking, and fighting." There were exceptions, of course, but the town needed the revivals that passed this way like "comets." The first, he recalls, was followed by the terrible hurricane of 1804, which swept away the old barbecue house that had been the scene of much merriment. The grandest revival of all was held in 1832, when Reverend Daniel Baker, a Savannah Presbyterian, preached with such fervor that "the hardest natures were softened. Ancient quarrels were reconciled. The lion and the lamb lay down together." Six members of one law firm gave up their practices to become priests and preachers.

㉞ 600 CHARLES STREET, Baptist Church of Beaufort, c. 1844
Open to public.
Prior to the construction of what many consider to be among the finest Baptist churches in America, the First Baptist Church in Charleston had established a mission in nearby Euchaw. It served a tiny Beaufort congregation until an official church organized here in 1804, the foundation of which remains. A converted lawyer, Reverend Richard Fuller, oversaw the construction of the new building. Midway through, a sudden need for more funds sent him soliciting and won him the not-so-holy title of "the prince of beggars." It was for a good cause.

Fuller may have tapped Robert Mills' plans for Charleston Baptist Church, though he made some major changes: the attic story doesn't exist, and part of the portico area is enclosed. The resulting Greek Revival was the first building in the area to use the massive columns, considered a bold departure at the time. The addition of a grand steeple in the mid-20th century made the structure less a pagan temple and more a proper church. Inside, finely worked Doric columns support a three-sided balcony once used by the slave membership. High above, a cove ceiling features plaster rosettes—the finest such decoration in Beaufort.

During the Civil War, black soldiers used the church as a hospital, constructing a temporary walkway between the side balconies. The communion table had been carried off to Charleston and the pews scattered, but all this was retrieved. A black deacon hid the communion silver to keep it safe. Following the war, the black membership had dropped from 3,557 to 3; the white from 182 to 20. Nevertheless, the church survived and is growing still.

71.4 **0.0**   *From the Baptist Church parking lot,*
                    turn left onto King Street.
71.5 **2** blks   *Turn left onto Church Street.*
71.5 ½ blk   *On left is St. Helena's Episcopal Church.*

㉟ 501 CHURCH STREET, St. Helena's Episcopal Church, c. 1724, 1842
Open to public.
This substantial church began in 1724 as a small 30-by-40-foot brick building on the very edge of the frontier. By 1712, the parish of St. Helena had been laid out, and Presbyterian and Anabaptist ministers had already come and gone. That same year,

Reverend William Guy took over the parish; he was the only man of God about—a fortunate one, for he escaped the attacking Yemassee. In the century following, church historian Frederick Dalco reports a high turnover of priests, poor health, and death as the usual causes of change. The Wesley brothers visited in 1736, but as with the Baptists, it was Dr. Baker's revival of 1832 that poured new life into the Episcopal efforts. By then parishioners had enlarged the building and added a great 118-foot steeple. Further additions were made in 1842.

During the Civil War the church became a hospital. Workers stripped away the pews and galleries, and hung a second story inside between the galleries. They used tombstones as operating tables. At the war's end, they removed the tottering steeple with its London clock; the present Christopher Wren-like replacement wasn't erected until 1942. Gradually the building has been restored inside and out.

71.5	**0.0**	*Continue on Church Street.*
71.6	½ blk	*Turn right onto North Street.*
71.8	**3** blks	*Turn left on Monson Street.*
71.8	**1** blk	*Turn left on Bay Street.*

❸❻ 1411-1103 BAY STREET, **Bay Street Residences**, c. 1800 to 1920 **Not open to public**.
From the outside, this three-block-long collection of nine houses offers an interesting commentary on the Beaufort style, or styles. The first, **1411 Bay Street**, was a Victorian house remade completely into a Beaufort-style mansion. The next, **1405 Bay Street**, replaced its slender columns and double piazzas with these grander columns. The third, **400 Wilmington Street**, is unchanged, but note the front door. It's fake. The front windows open as doors, but the real entry is on the side, so the house doesn't get a Bay Street address. The next, **1307 Bay Street**, is a rather modest home built in 1883 by a Connecticut foot soldier who decided to stay. Stephen Bull had a small cottage here at **1305 Bay Street**, but this big house dates from 1920. This pre-Revolutionary home at **1301 Bay Street** was said to have been moved here from St. Helena Island in 1850. The rector of Sheldon Church, Charles Leverett, reclaimed it after the Civil War. The tabby manse at **1211 Bay Street** is next—a graceful Federal-style building, similar in feel to the Verdier house, but made completely of tabby. Thomas Fuller built it in c. 1805, and Baptist lawyer convert Reverend Richard Fuller lived here. It's said that he gave one last party for his friends at this home before renouncing worldly ways. Robert Means, merchant and planter, built the home at **1207 Bay Street** in 1810. The classical columns were added in the 20th century. Built in 1810, the John Cuthbert House at **1203 Bay Street** has been given additional porches and bay windows. Tradition says the family sawed the house in half and relocated it from an "unhealthy" location. The home at **1103 Bay Street** got a substantial face-lift in the 1900s. William Elliott—sportsman, poet, politician, and essayist—lived here. One of the few to oppose secession, he still kept the respect of his fellow citizens.

72.8	**1.0**	*Turn right onto Carteret Street / U.S. 21 South Business.*
76.5	**3.7**	*Cross the bridge onto St. Helena Island.*

St. Helena Island
Like Edisto, St. Helena was in many ways a world unto itself. Not 40 years after Columbus's discovery, the Spanish dropped by and named it. The settlers on the Carolina voted not to settle on it, but the English soon returned to run cattle here. Next, they planted indigo, and finally, cotton, which made them suddenly rich. In 1815, St. Helena's citizens, assuming they were the only island of the name in

existence, protested to the British government when they heard that Napoleon was to be exiled to St. Helena. Other outsiders came instead, and on January 16, 1865, the southern tip of St. Helena, now divided into 3,000 lots of the new "City of Port Royal," went on sale. This utopian get-rich-quick project went nowhere, but a few who were not land speculators or soldiers or dreamers intended to give practical aid to the newly freed slaves.

78.7	**2.2**	*Turn right onto Martin Luther King, Jr. Drive /*
		S-7-45 at Frogmore.
79.1	**0.4**	*On left is Brick Baptist Church.*

㊲ BRICK CHURCH, c. 1855
Not open to public.
"Good Billy Fripp" built this church for the few white and many black Baptists on the island. His freed slaves didn't recall him as being particularly good to them. They took possession of the church in 1862, and it's still in the hands of their descendants and others.

79.1	**0.0**	*Continue on S-7-45.*
79.2	**0.1**	*Watch carefully for the entrance to the parking lot at*
		Penn Center, about 60 feet before historical marker.

㊳ PENN CENTER, c. 1862
Open to public.
In response to the United States government's capturing of the Sea Islands in 1861, Philadelphia Quakers set up the Port Royal Relief Society and sent two teachers to educate the former slaves. Laura Towne and Ellen Murray arrived

Penn Center, St. Helena Island, *an early school for former slaves.*

Students built most of the structures at the Penn Center.

on the island in 1862 and were joined later by the first black teacher, Charlotte Forten. Together, they instructed and provided health care for newly freed slaves. First, they held classes on a nearby plantation, then in the Baptist church across the street. In 1864, a small prefab schoolhouse was set up on the present site. All that remains of that first school is the bell tower and a model of the Liberty Bell it held.

Other buildings date from the 20th century, when Penn School became an industrial and agricultural school, teaching not only reading and writing but also homemaking, midwifery, carpentry, blacksmithing, basketry, farming, and more. In fact, the students built most of these structures.

A cultural center and museum welcomes visitors and scholars. Enjoy oral histories and photographs in the archives, and farm implements and examples of the industrial schoolwork on display. If you want to get an idea of how radically things have changed on the island, just flip through the photographs of Edith Dabbs' *Face of an Island.*

In the early 1950s, Penn School became Penn Community Service Center, with a focus on promoting community development. Martin Luther King, Jr., came here on retreat during the early 1960s (the cottage he stayed in is still here). Peace Corps volunteers also have trained here. Today's Penn Center operates as a resource center and museum for the Sea Islands' rich but vanishing Gullah culture.

79.2 0.0   *From Penn Center parking lot, turn right onto S-7-45.*
80.0 0.8   *On left is Chapel of Ease to St. Helena's Church
(the White Church) ruins.*

㊴ CHAPEL OF EASE to ST. HELENA'S CHURCH
(The White Church) RUINS, c. 1730.
Open to public.
This Chapel of Ease for the Beaufort church features tabby and brick construction. The Methodists held it after the Civil War. It burned in an 1886 forest fire.

A Walk in the Park

Near the lighthouse in Hunting Island State Park, a mile-long path carries you through the maritime forest out to a dune edge thick with sea oats. You can return by way of the beach. There's swimming and beachcombing here, but the gradual slope means gradual waves, so few shells find their way ashore. Turtle nests are monitored and protected, and there are one or two supervised night walks during the summer. As with other parts of the island, bird watchers are advised to come in October or later; the crowds are much smaller and the birds more plentiful. The second nature walk leads to the middle of the island and follows an old roadbed down to a tidal lagoon.

80.0	**0.0**	*From Chapel of Ease parking lot, turn right onto S-7-45 and retrace to U.S. 21.*
81.3	**1.3**	*At stop sign, turn right onto U.S. 21 South.*
90.3	**9.0**	*Arrive at Hunting Island State Park.*
91.5	**1.2**	*Turn left into park entrance gate / S-7-762.*
91.8	**0.3**	*Pass through entrance gate and turn right into Visitors' Center parking lot; pick up map.*

Hunting Island Lighthouse.

⓴ HUNTING ISLAND STATE PARK

Hunting Island State Park handles a million visitors a year. Stop at the Visitors' Center just inside the entry to enjoy exhibits about the island's lighthouse, the changing coastline, early photographs of the island, and more. Pick up a map to this largest of the beach parks as well.

The narrow, one-way roads twist and turn through old dunes grown thick with palmetto and slash pine. To the north rises the Hunting Island Lighthouse. Erectors built it with cast iron so it could be moved back as the beach eroded. A wise decision: Raised in 1875, it was moved here only 14 years later. At the base of the light, an interesting display interprets generally the history of lighthouses and specifically those in South Carolina. On a climb to the top, the winding cast-iron steps seem to get steeper until you reach a rewarding bird's-eye view of the island, ocean, shoals, back bays, and distant St. Helena.

91.8	**0.0**	*After touring park, return to park entrance.*
94.8	**3.0**	*At the entrance gate, turn left onto U.S. 21 South.*
96.5	**1.7**	*Turn right into Marsh Boardwalk parking lot.*

Outside the park's main entrance, check out two more nice spots, Marsh Boardwalk and Paradise Fishing Pier. At Marsh Boardwalk, three wooden walkways connect low sandy islands of stunted pines and cedars. Here, fiddler crabs run everywhere at low tide. A half-mile farther on U.S. 21 South, the state-owned Paradise Fishing Pier stretches into the inlet. Rent a rod and fish for whiting here or at other sections of the beach and the lagoon set aside for fishing, or watch others do it for free. It's a nice place to end the day—probably a very long one if you got this far.

97.0	**0.0**	*From pier parking lot, turn right onto U.S. 21 North.*
114.1	**17.1**	*Continue straight onto U.S. 21 North Business.*
115.7	**1.6**	*Return to Beaufort and continue on U.S. 21 North to U.S. 17 North.*
131.0	**5.3**	*Veer right and continue on U.S. 17 North to Charleston.*
183.0	**52.0**	*South side of Ashley River Bridge.*

END TOUR

Awendaw to Georgetown

TOUR FIVE

AWENDAW to GEORGETOWN

This tour travels north along U.S. Highway 17 through **Awendaw** and on to **Georgetown**. We start with the 18th-century burial ground of **Wappetaw**. Nature lovers will find the pier at **Morris Landing** an interesting stop, where off in the distance you can see Bull Island, a hurricane-battered but still beautiful barrier island. Heading north again, we pass through **The Francis Marion National Forest**, which offers much to wilderness-oriented visitors. We tour the little "fishing village" of **McClellanville**. We'll drive several miles of dirt road to visit "**The Brick Church**," built in 1768 for the parish of St. James–Santee. Close by, **Hampton Plantation State Park** offers tours of poet Archibald Rutledge's Colonial mansion and the surrounding gardens and wilderness. A nearby nature walk, **Washo**, leads to a grand place for a picnic. We cross the Santee Delta to tour the house, grounds, and outbuildings of **Hopsewee Plantation**—the birthplace of Thomas Lynch, signer of the Declaration of Independence. Finally, we arrive in **Georgetown**, one of the state's oldest communities and still chock-full of ancient houses and churches, museums, and other points of interest. If you choose, tram, boat, and walking tours help you find your way. To fit the tour into one day, take your time and go home when the sun sets.

Wappetaw Burial Ground
  Fifteen Mile Landing Road, a few yards from the intersection
  with Highway 17
  nwpconline.org
Garris Landing
  Bull Island Road / State Road 1170
  www.scgreatoutdoors.com/park-garrislanding.html
McClellanville
  843-887-3712 | *www.townofmcclellanville-sc.net*
The Village Museum
  401 Pinckney Street | 843-887-3030
St. James Santee Episcopal Church, c. 1890
  144 Oak Street | 843-887-4386 | *www.stjamesec.org*
Hampton Plantation State Historic Site
  1950 Rutledge Road | 843-546-9361
  www.southcarolinaparks.com/park-finder/state-park/1142.aspx
  Admission charged for guided tour.
Santee Coastal Reserve—Washo Reserve
  Santee Gun Club Road | 843-546-8665 | *www.dnr.sc.gov*
Hopsewee Plantation
  494 Hopsewee Road | 843-546-7891
  www.hopsewee.com
  Admission charged.
Georgetown County Visitors' Center
  531 Front Street | 843-546-8436
  www.georgetownchamber.com
Capt. Sandy's Tours
  843-527-4106

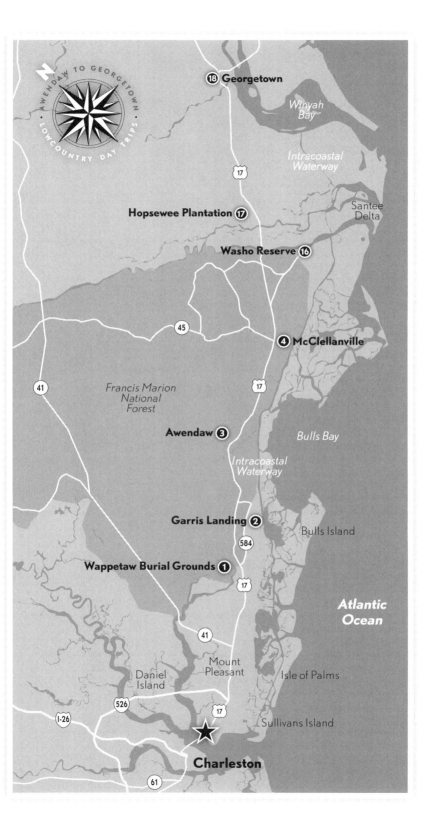

BEGIN TOUR
0.0   0.0   *Take U.S. 17 North from Charleston. Begin checking*
                  mileage at the north end of the Ravenel Bridge
                  over the Cooper River in Mount Pleasant.
14.6 14.6   *Turn left onto 15 Mile Landing Road / S-10-584.*
14.7 0.1   *On right, Wappetaw Cemetery.*

❶ WAPPETAW BURIAL GROUNDS, c. 1700
Grounds open to public.
Only a few gravestones, all dating from the 18th century, remain in this picket-fenced cemetery. In 1696, a group of New England Congregationalists shipwrecked on the outer banks of North Carolina. Befriended by the Hatteras Indians, 52 were rescued by the governor of Carolina and landed near here on Seewee Bay. Separated from Reverend Starbo's Charleston-based Presbyterian congregations, they built at least one church on this site. Badly vandalized by Union troops, it collapsed in 1897. By then, the members had moved on.

14.7 0.0   *Turn around.*
14.8 0.1   *Cross U.S. 17 and continue on Seewee Road /S-10-584.*
18.2 3.3   *Turn right onto Bull Island Road / S-10-1170.*
19.7 1.5   *Arrive at Garris Landing pier parking lot.*

❷ GARRIS LANDING
Garris Landing, formerly Moore's Landing, is the headquarters for the Cape Romain National Refuge and its 64,000 acres of saltwater marsh, tidal creeks, and bays. The original intent was to preserve migrating duck populations, but the refuge turned out to be a fortuitous home especially for the loggerhead turtle. Cape Romain is now one of the best-protected and most productive nesting areas for this endangered species. The Landing's concrete pier extends well out into Sewee Bay and is good for spotting shorebirds, especially bright-billed skimmers.

19.7 0.0   *From Garris Landing, retrace Bull Island*
                  Road / S-10-1170 to U.S. 17.
21.2 1.5   *At stop sign, turn right onto U.S. 17 North.*
31.0 9.8   *At Murrell Road, make a U-turn onto U.S. 17 South.*
31.1 0.1   *Turn right into parking lot for Palmetto Trail trailhead.*

A Brief Comment on the Surrounding Area
The Swamp Fox Hiking Trail is only one of many trails in the Francis Marion National Forest, but it's conveniently short. Take bug spray. It covers more than 250,000 acres and includes practically all the land on the left side of the highway for about 40 miles. At the center, a broad area called Hell Hole enjoyed a reputation as a haven for criminals and runaway slaves during its earliest days.

In 1935, this land and more were bought as part of the New Deal effort to save the South. Until then, the woodlands were being burned yearly to grow grass for free-roaming cattle and hogs. Locals hoped that a well-managed forest would encourage investment in nearby mills and bring jobs. Civilian Conservation Corps crews came in, constructed roads, and removed animals.

The U.S. Forest Service now promotes the natural growth of longleaf pine, a tree once prized by the naval industry because it made good masts and decking. They also used the sap for rosin, turpentine, and tar. Today, laws protect endangered species, fragile Carolina bays, and some of the forested areas.

Still, trails accommodate hikers, and broad, paved logging roads run beside wilderness areas crossed only by paddleboat. It's a delicate balancing act, to say the least.

❸ AWENDAW

When explorer-naturalist John Lawson passed this way in 1700, he mentioned only two small plantations here at Avendaugh-bough. The name was shortened to Awendaw. On crossing the Awendaw Bridge in 1926, Dr. William Johnson saw little change from Lawson's day, and reported, "There is much about these parts that makes me think of wild men of ye olden times."

Garris Landing Information
For information on recreation in the Cape Romain National Refuge, contact the Wambaw Ranger District in McClellanville or the Witherbee Ranger District in Huger.

28.7 **0.0**	*Exit parking lot to right onto U.S. 17 South.*
28.8 **0.1**	*Make U-turn at first paved crossover onto U.S. 17 North.*
38.7 **9.9**	*Pass caution lights and turn right onto Pinckney Street / S-10-9.*

❹ MCCLELLANVILLE

After the great hurricane of 1822 swept away the summer colony at the mouth of the Santee River, Archibald McClellan leased lots here to half a dozen families. In 1852, R.T. Morrison bought the adjoining land and began to divide it. The Civil War brought a sudden influx of refugees to the little "Santee seashore" village, and in the years after, impoverished planters and their descendants gradually came to live here on a year-round basis. When it was incorporated in 1926, the town had a population of about 500 and 22 stores occupied the main street. By then, farming, lumbering, and oystering provided the chief sources of income, freight came in from Charleston by boat, and on Friday and Saturday people arrived to buy their weekly provisions. City planners expected that the completion of the Cooper River Bridge and the paving of U.S. 17 would bring long-awaited "boom times"; instead, customers drove out of town to shop. Stores closed, and by 1970 the population declined to 350. It's been growing slowly ever since, and now the citizens, used to their solitude, feel threatened being further "discovered." This entry didn't take much research: I spent my summers playing in the town creek and have lived here since the early 1970s.

39.5 **0.8**	*On right is McClellanville Public School.*

❺ MCCLELLANVILLE PUBLIC SCHOOL, c. 1921
Not open to public.
This substantial piece of monumental architecture dates from the time when the village held political clout. In 1916, three of Charleston County's state legislators came from here. The building has been restored and was McClellanville's middle school until it closed at the end of the 2008-09 school year. Its future is unclear.

39.5   200 ft   *On right is New Wappetaw Presbyterian Church.*

❻ NEW WAPPETAW PRESBYTERIAN CHURCH, c. 1875
Not open to public.
Some descendants of the Congregationalists stranded on Hatteras three centuries ago ended up here. (Remember, their graveyard was our first stop.) Originally, the building had a Victorian tower and belfry. Today, you'll spy a centered steeple and a new cross. Note the smaller live oaks and great wisteria bushes beside the road. WPA workers planted this thicket. Most of the large white frame houses date from the 1890s or later. Owners intended to use a good many only as summer homes.

39.6   0.1   *On left, just beyond Oak Street, is
                         McClellanville Methodist Church.*

❼ MCCLELLANVILLE METHODIST CHURCH, c. 1903
Not open to public.
The building dates from the turn of the 20th century, but the Methodists who worshipped here probably got their start in the 1830s when the Episcopal congregation closed their church and followed their priest to a Methodist meetinghouse on the Santee River.

39.8   0.2   *On right is Dupre House.*

❽ 423 PINKNEY STREET, **The Dupre House**, c. 1790
Not open to public.
This gray-shingle, raised cottage is the oldest building in town. It was taken apart and floated down the Santee in the first year of the Civil War. The marsh in that era reached the front yard; everything beyond is dredge fill.

39.8   200 ft   *Turn right into parking lot of Municipal
                           Offices and the Village Museum.*

❾ 401 PINKNEY STREET, **The Village Museum**
The former headquarters of the Cape Romain Wildlife Refuge, this concrete block house with red tile roof was a 1935 triumph in this type of utilitarian design. The government tower beside it was built to guard the refuge from poachers, but eventually was turned over to the Forest Service. A town hall stands next door. Through a number of exhibits, the museum outlines the history of the area starting with the Seewee Indians and moving through time to the growth of the timber and seafood industries in the 20th century. The museum is also a great source for picking up brochures and other local advice.

39.8   0.0   *Turn around in Government Dock parking lot;
                         turn left onto Pinckney Street.*
40.1   0.3   *Turn left onto Oak Street / S-10-71.*
40.1   100 ft   *On left is Deer Head Oak.*

❿ DEER HEAD OAK
Children and photographers favor this site, estimated to be about 1,000 years old.

40.2   0.1   *On left is St. James Santee Episcopal Church, Chapel of Ease.*

⓫ ST. JAMES SANTEE EPISCOPAL CHURCH, **Chapel of Ease**, c. 1890
Open to public.
In 1890, the Episcopal congregation moved their services from the old "Brick Church" on the Santee to this shingle-sided, Gothic Chapel of Ease. Planter Alex

Lucas designed it, and four black craftsmen did the work, hand-cutting the chancel screen's scrollwork.

40.2 0.0 *On right, across the street, is the R.V. Morrison House.*

⑫ **142 OAK STREET, The R.V. Morrison House**, c. 1860
Not open to public.
R.V. Morrison and his wife Aletha raised 11 children in this little two-story house. Aletha later spent her mornings in the garden, kissing passing youngsters and inquiring, "And whose child are you?"

The Rest of Oak Street
This was once Water Street, and the "dock"—the large ditch on your left—was deep enough to float small freight boats. Since then, dredge fill has drastically altered the shape of things all over town. The white board-and-batten cottage facing the water was hastily built in 1861, but not finished until the late 1900s. Several houses on your right doubled as inns. In those days, locals enjoyed a sandy beach that has since fallen victim to modern times. R.T. Morrison's wharf once stood at the end of Oak Street. A turpentine works was here, and laborers loaded pulpwood onto barges at this spot when I was a boy. They had the "fish houses" by then, too, and that's what you'll find now.

St. James Santee Episcopal Church and The Dupre House, McClellanville.

40.3 0.1 *On left are the shrimp docks.*

⑬ **SHRIMP DOCKS**
Many shrimp boats, clam dredges, and smaller oyster boats dock here. Seafood is "packed out" and sold. The public piers buzz with forklifts and moving boats, plus other waterfront dangers, so be careful.

Visitors often describe McClellanville as "An Old-Time Fishing Village." While McClellanville was the nation's largest exporter of terrapins in 1900, practically no commercial fishing happened here before World War II. These days, you're almost certain to see several shrimp trawlers.

More profitable, but less conspicuous, the small clam dredges use a long conveyor that clammers lower to the bottom of the creek bed. The boat drives forward its sled-like head as a large pump washes clams and oysters up onto the moving belt. A topside crew picks these off as they pass. Assembly-line work, freezing weather, and daylight til dark, but the pay is good when the water's clean. Pollution lowers the margin considerably. A good day's work used to be 100 bushels, but, like everything else these days, there are fewer oysters to go around.

Shrimp and Oysters

Before entering the ocean, shrimpers lower the large outriggers, and the large wooden doors in the racks pull the nets to the bottom and spread them wide. A "tow" lasts two hours. A shrimper's day lasts 12 to 16 hours, and trips of a week or longer are common. Visit the docks during winter and sometimes you can buy oysters fresh from the arriving clammers.

The docks themselves have changed. In the late '50s and early '60s, the workers spoke a faster, thicker form of Gullah, and the women still sang when they headed shrimp. When the Wells Brothers' fleet of Yellow Riggers (named for their rustproof paint) packed out on September nights, Captain Happy's deaf-and-dumb "striker," or assistant, would juggle five empty Pepsi bottles and laugh silently. Legendary Doonie Watts told us unprintable stories about foreign ports. It's still exotic, but not that exotic: too much stainless steel and fluorescent light.

40.3	**0.0**	*Turn around and retrace Oak Street to Pinckney Street.*
40.5	**0.2**	*At stop sign, turn left onto Pinckney Street / S-10-9.*
41.5	**1.0**	*At stop sign, turn right onto U.S. 17 North.*
47.3	**5.8**	*Turn left onto Rutledge Road / S-10-857.*
47.3	**1.4**	*Just over a small bridge, turn left onto Old Georgetown–Charleston Road / S-10-1335 (dirt road—sometimes impassable when wet).*
49.0	**0.3**	*On right, small black-water pond, Carolina bay.*

French Santee

The French Huguenots probably arrived here shortly after 1685 and laid out James Town 15 miles to the north. Paddling up the Santee River in 1700, explorer John Lawson reported them well-situated and doing a brisk business with the Indians. "The French being a temperate industrious People...have out-stript our English," he writes. "Tis admirable to see what Time and Industry will (with God's Blessing) effect." In 1706, when these settlers asked to be included as an Anglican parish, 100 French and 60 English families were living here on the south bank of the Santee. They would soon earn fortunes from rice planting.

Carolina Bays
On your right, you'll see a small black-water pond—probably the deeper portion of a Carolina bay. These mysterious elliptical depressions punctuate much of the Southeastern seaboard, but are most prevalent in the Carolinas. The name "bay" may refer to the sink, but more likely it refers to the evergreen bays that early naturalists found growing in these depressions. Because of the uniform alignment of the "craters," some folks suggested that a meteorite shower formed them, a reasonable but controversial argument now eclipsed by a more urgent concern for the bays themselves. Sadly, landowners have drained many and planted pine, rendering most unrecognizable.

50.8 1.8   *For those who have persevered, pull off on the right when you reach the brick wall surrounding the grounds of The Brick Church, St. James–Santee.*

⑭ THE BRICK CHURCH, aka WAMBAW CHURCH, c. 1768
Open to public.
This is the fourth church to serve what was originally a predominantly French Huguenot congregation. The classical porticoes attached to the north and south represent a surprising departure from the rural church design of the day. Long noted for their architectural distinction, these entries probably had a utilitarian and political function. Even at this late date, the French congregation arrived from the north along a road now almost vanished, while the English, coming along the King's Highway, entered through the south doors.

A Bible and prayer book Rebecca Motte gave to the church disappeared during the Revolution. Evidently the holy pair sailed to England, where they were found in a bookstore and returned. The silver altar service that Thomas Lynch gifted never was.

By 1847, the worshippers abandoned such distinctions; the church bricked the French port to make a vestry, and the altar occupied this portion of the aisle. The high-backed pews are probably original, though. The entry door bears what might be a hastily scratched Masonic seal, but it didn't keep Union soldiers from destroying the pulpit and chancel. A modern-day priest rendered the finely crafted pulpit that stands before the restored Palladian window you see today. Although the church members migrated to McClellanville, they return to worship here once a year the Sunday after Easter.

50.8 0.0   *Turn around and retrace S-10-1335.*
52.9 2.1   *At stop sign, turn left onto Rutledge Road / S-10-857.*
53.3 0.4   *Turn right into entrance gate of Hampton Plantation State Park.*

⑮ HAMPTON PLANTATION STATE HISTORIC SITE, c. 1730-50
Open to public.
When workers caringly restored the Hampton Plantation house, they purposely left portions of the walls exposed so visitors could "read" the story of the house for themselves. The story is a lengthy one. It begins when Huguenot Elias Horry acquired the land between 1700 and 1730. Some historians believe that he had built a small house by 1736 when he died, others claim his son Daniel may have built it as late as 1750. No matter who gets the credit, we see the original today— a saltbox dwelling with an entrance on the water. The stairs originally faced the opposite direction, but the unusual feathered paneling probably dates from the home's earliest years.

Rice cultivation increased the family's fortune, enabling Daniel and his wife

| Hampton Plantation.

to add the massive portico and two large wings (one containing a great blue-ceilinged ballroom) before the Revolution. After the death of Horry, his wife Harriet continued to operate the plantation successfully. She and her mother, Eliza Lucas Pinckney, wearing sashes painted with the president's likeness, stood on these steps to greet George Washington, and preserved the large oak on the lawn because he recommended it.

Despite these early and colorful residents, however, Hampton is best known as the home, Archibald Rutledge, the state's poet laureate. He grew up here during the difficult years following Reconstruction. In the 1930s, he added an avenue of 154 hollies and 800 dogwoods to the existing camellia garden and path that leads to the creek. The family home, and especially the woods around it, inspired him and became material for the naturalist, hunter, poet, essayist, and short story writer. He returned whenever possible; in 1937, he retired here for good and, with the help of the loyal black residents, began rescuing the house and grounds. Two collections of essays followed, *Home by the River* and *The World Around Hampton*. Some of his best writings, they give a good account of the struggle to reclaim the plantation and his delight in nature; they also mark the end of the romantic plantation era.

We'll let Dr. Archie have the last word here: "Though the civilization that it cradled and nourished has passed away, the charm survives. The home remains lovely after the guests are gone."

53.3	**0.0**	*Return to main gate, turn left onto Rutledge Road / S-10-857.*
55.1	**1.8**	*At stop sign, cross over U.S. 17 and continue straight on South Santee Road / S-10-857.*
56.6	**1.5**	*Turn left onto Santee Gun Club Road (dirt road).*
59.2	**2.6**	*On right, Washo Reserve bulletin board with tour guide folders.*

⑯ SANTEE COASTAL RESERVE–WASHO RESERVE

Two severe hurricanes during the 1890s ended rice planting here. But the land proved fertile to a group of wealthy Northern sportsmen who bought Washo and a half-dozen other places to form the Santee Gun Club. Grover Cleveland hunted here in times when a 100-duck day was common. Those days passed, and in 1974, the gun club donated the entire 24,000 acres to the Nature Conservancy, which turned over all but the 1,000 acres surrounding the Washo Reserve to the state's wildlife department.

One of the prettiest spots on God's green earth, the reserve is open to the public. Beware the summer months, though, when the mosquitoes and deerflies can defy description. A three-mile course, the Washo Trail, starts along a slave-built dike. The impoundment to the right is thick with cypress and tupelo gum; at times, brilliant green aquatic vegetation coats the black water. A boardwalk extends into this area, famous for its wading bird rookery. Look for ospreys and alligators as you walk. They may be hard to spot through the picture-book forests of cypress, hollies, and live oaks—but the mosquitoes and deerflies won't be.

59.2	**0.0**	*Retrace Santee Gun Club Road to paved South Santee Road.*
61.8	**2.6**	*Turn right onto South Santee Road / S-10-857.*
63.3	**1.5**	*At stop sign, turn right onto U.S. 17 North.*
64.2	**0.9**	*On both sides of U.S. 17 is Santee Delta.*

The Santee Delta

As you're about to cross the first bridge over the Santee River, the ruins of burned Peachtree Plantation are on your left. Here, inventor Johnathan Lucas built the rice mill "that would do for rice production, what Eli Whitney's gin did for cotton." On your right is Fairfield (not open to the public), the home of statesman Thomas Pinckney. Although the affluent built their mansions on the riverbank, their wealth came from the delta we're crossing.

In 1700, naturalist Lawson reported this area to be a great swamp forest "affording vast Ciprus-trees, of which the French make canoes, that will carry fifty or sixty Barrels." It remained a cypress swamp until after the Revolution. Then clearing, ditching, and diking converted forest to field, and by 1830, farmers grew rice all the way to the ocean's edge. The spots where the rush appears particularly thick are old canals, and the dikes are sometimes marked by low growths of cedars. On the small islands and in the marsh itself, slaves established communities complete with barns, mills, and meetinghouses, and, in some places, large brick hurricane towers that provided storm refuge. Though not connected to the mainland, most of these parcels were referred to as separate "plantations." We're looking at Tranquility, Blackwood, Indianfield, and dozens more.

| **66.5** | **2.3** | *Turn left across U.S. 17 South into Hopsewee Plantation.* |
| **66.7** | **0.2** | *Arrive at Hopsewee Plantation parking lot.* |

⑰ HOPSEWEE PLANTATION, c. 1740
Open to public.

Hopsewee Plantation is best known as the birthplace of the youngest signer of the Declaration of Independence, Thomas Lynch, but actually it was the builder, Thomas Lynch, Sr., who intended to sign. Thomas, Jr., was born at Hopsewee in 1749. He and his father were involved in events leading to the Revolution, and both attended the Second Continental Congress. Thomas, Sr., apparently suffered a stroke just before the signing and died on the way home.

"He is a solid, firm judicious man," wrote John Adams of the older Lynch, who, sometime around 1740, crossed the Santee from Fairfield and built the main portion of this house. In 1762, Robert Hume bought it. His son John supposedly turned down a Scottish earldom just to remain "Earl of Marshmud" here at Hopsewee. Grandson John Hume Lucas (also grandson of the inventor Johnathan) rebuilt the neglected house in 1846, adding the double piazzas across the front. He's probably also responsible for the distinctive slave cabins, noted for the kitchens' wide overhang and graceful fascia, suggesting a Caribbean influence. Duck inside to see a typical Lowcountry cooking arrangement of great open fireplaces

| **H**opsewee Plantation.

*Caribbean style slave cabin at **H**opsewee Plantation.*

as well as displays of cooking utensils and early agricultural implements—hoes, scythes, tillers, and mortar.

Tours of the main house operate five days a week. The carefully restored interior maintains its original candlelight molding and especially wide pine flooring. The Georgian layout may also be original, but the central hall probably came later and the stairs are in the house's new "front" entry. Expanded and embellished by consecutive owners, this house, like Hampton, is a far more authentic mansion house than some of its better-advertised rivals.

66.7	**0.0**	*From Hopsewee Plantation parking lot, retrace drive to U.S. 17.*
66.9	**0.2**	*At end of drive, cross U.S. 17 South, turn left onto U.S. 17 North.*
79.2	**12.3**	*Cross Sampit River Bridge. Historic Georgetown is visible on your right.*

A Short History of Georgetown
Discounting an ill-fated 1526 settlement by the Spanish, the history of this area begins in 1705 when the English Proprietors granted the land. Within 15 years, enough settlers had arrived to warrant an Anglican parish called Prince George–Winyah: "George" for the king and "Winyah" for the soon-to-disappear Indians. Ship stores—tar and lumber—were produced here, but they had to be shipped through the Port of Charles Town. From the Santee north came discontent over this trade monopoly, and in 1732, Georgetown became an official port. It was already a "city" by then, the colony's third oldest. Elisha Screven had laid out a town grid with lots for churches, markets, jail, and school. His original streets constitute the historical district today, but his plan was disrupted when others claimed the 100-acre common. As a consequence, churches weren't built on Church Street.

Located at the junction of six rivers, Georgetown prospered as a trading center. Ship stores and shipbuilding, and the planting of indigo and rice, made early fortunes. When the Revolution came, many of the town's merchants and planters remained loyal to the king. The community survived this indiscretion amazingly well, and soon after the war enjoyed an unimaginable wealth. Rice cultivation made this one of the richest sections in the nation.

⑱ GEORGETOWN

Crossing the river named for the Sampit Indians, you see ships docked to your right and a great dome that stores imported salt. On the left is the paper mill— an International Paper pulp-processing plant started in 1936. Georgetown has depended on mills since the turn of the 20th century, when the Atlantic Coast Lumber Company began what would become the East Coast's largest lumber mill. It folded during the Depression, so the paper mill provided welcome revenue. Georgetown Steel Mill, now closed, lies on your right. In the late 1960s it brought jobs, but also a smokestack discharge that added a "Rust Belt" look. A few blocks to the right, the centuries-old village enjoys a long-overdue comeback.

80.1 0.3   *Just beyond the steel plant, turn right onto Front Street.*
80.6 0.5   *Go eight blocks and park your car to visit the*
             Georgetown County Visitors' Center.

⑲ 531 FRONT STREET, Harper Building, c. 1850
Georgetown County Visitors' Center
Brochures and information on local tours and spots of interest are available in this historic building, which was moved from its original location on Screven Street. First, enjoy a drive thorugh this historic area. Later, you'll have an opportunity to park and visit some of these sites.

80.6 0.0   *From Georgetown County Visitors Center, turn right*
             on U.S. 17 South.
80.8 1 blk   *Turn left onto St. James Street / S-22-80*
81.2 4 blks   *Turn right onto Front Street.*
81.2 20 ft   *First house on the left is 405 Front Street.*

⑳ 405 FRONT STREET, The Withers-Daley House, c. 1737
Not open to public.
The town's oldest house, it originally was only one room deep with porches front and back.

TOUR 5 **GEORGETOWN**

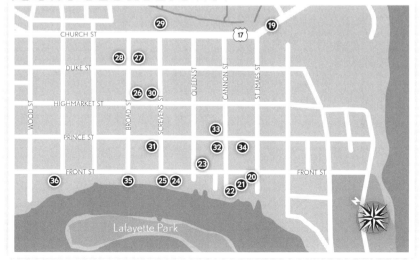

81.2 **1** blk   *Turn left onto Cannon Street.*
81.3 ½ blk   *The building on the left is 16 Cannon Street.*

㉑ 16 CANNON STREET, The Red Store Warehouse, pre-Revolution
Not open to public.
This Colonial warehouse stored silk, indigo, and fine wines. The town's finest inn once adjoined the building. U.S. Vice President Aaron Burr's daughter Theodosia Burr Alston sailed from here on the *Patriot* and was never seen again.

81.3 **0.0**   *Across street on right is 15 Cannon Street.*

㉒ 15 CANNON STREET, The Heriot-Tarbox House, c. 1765
Harbor House Bed and Breakfast
Indigo built this fine house. Sections of the vault-like foundation served as summer cool storage. Candles lit in the dormer "candle windows" announced that the woman of the house was alone and should be protected. Builder Heriot was loyal to the king, one of whose soldiers was shot on this porch by Marion's raiders.

81.3 ½ blk   *At dead end, make U-turn and retrace Cannon Street.*
81.3 **1** blk   *At stop sign, turn left onto Front Street.*
81.4 **1** blk   *Sixth house on the right is 528 Front Street.*

㉓ 528 FRONT STREET, The Man-Doyle House, c. 1775
Not open to public.
This "grand old mansion house of the village" is a typical Georgian double house with the double-tiered front portico. Built by Miss Mary Man of nearby Mansfield Plantation in about 1775, the building once enjoyed a prestigious water view and no doubt was the mansion against which others were measured. Note the wood of the pediment simulating stone, the ornate cornice molding, and beaded siding. Prominent in Georgetown's history, the house is a fine example of pre-Revolutionary construction.

81.5 **1** blk   *Continue on Front Street. On left is 633 Front Street.*

㉔ 633 FRONT STREET, Kaminski Building, c. 1842
Open to public.
Now an annex to the Rice Museum, this building began as a hardware store in 1842. The cast-iron front went on in 1859, and Heiman Kaminski added the distinctive three-story light well after the Civil War. An art gallery fills the rear of the store. The Maritime Museum Gallery in the annex provides a special treat for maritime history buffs: the Brown's Ferry Vessel. These remains represent the oldest example of American shipbuilding ever found. The 50-foot freighter dates from 1730. This fascinating example of early American craftsmanship was rescued from the bottom of the nearby Black River near Brown's Ferry.

81.5 **25** ft   *Next building on the left is the Rice Museum.*

㉕ CORNER OF FRONT and SCREVEN STREETS,
The Rice Museum, c. 1842
Open to public. Admission charged.
Since the Revolution, this site has been the town market, but the present Greek Revival building wasn't constructed until a fire swept the waterfront in 1841. Three years later, builders added the distinctive clock tower. The second floor, once the town hall, now holds the Rice Museum. Here we learn that in the flood plain of a half-dozen rivers, plantation owners (or rather their slaves) planted 40,000 acres of rice in 1850. The amount of work required to lay out these fields has

been compared to the building of the pyramids. Much of the museum bears witness to their reluctant labor, performed mostly without animals. In paintings and glass-cased models or dioramas, we see the land being cleared, ditched, and diked. At times, it was necessary to flood and drain the land, so they installed a series of water-control structures, or trunks. Visitors see demonstrations of harvesting, winnowing, and milling the grain, along with the tools used: hoes, mortars, wooden shovels, and fanner baskets. An intricate gear-filled model of a rice mill represents the full-sized machines that once stood beside the Black River. There's also a display on indigo production.

|**T**he Rice Museum, Georgetown.

81.6 **1** blk   *Turn right onto Broad Street / S-22-379.*
81.8 **3** blks   *On right, in third block, is Prince George, Winyah*
                          Episcopal Church.

㉖ CORNER OF HIGHMARKET and BROAD STREETS
Prince George Winyah Episcopal Church, c. 1747
Open to public.
The British burned this building after using it as a stable. The church then added a new roof and pews. The tower was added in 1824. The windows of the chancel addition were taken from a slave chapel built by Ploden Weston. Over the years, a small army of inattentive boys scratched a great fleet of rice schooners and other graffiti into the sides of the box pews. See if you can find "Yes, mama" among the scribbles. The churchyard contains stones dating to 1767. Governor Robert Alston is buried here, as well as the founder of Porter Military Academy, Anthony Toomer Porter.

81.9 **1** blk   *On right is Hebrew Cemetery.*

㉗ 400 BROAD STREET, **Beth Elohim Cemetery**, c. 1772
Open to public.
Georgetown's Jewish community is the state's second oldest and probably predates the earliest graves here, dated 1762. Look closely to see Hebrew inscriptions and Stars of David.

81.9 **0.0**   *Across street on left is 417 Broad Street.*

㉘ 417 BROAD STREET, **Bethel African Methodist Episcopal Church**, c. 1882
Open to public for tram tour.
Organized as a congregation in 1865, freed slaves built this AME Church in 1882, and in 1908 it was remodeled and bricked over. The hand-painted windows can be appreciated from the outside, but Swamp Fox Tram is the only guide service that tours the interior, including the crimped tin ceiling.

82.0 **1** blk   *Turn right onto Church Street.*
82.1 **1** blk   *Turn right onto Screven Street,*
                          noting Baptist Cemetery on left.

㉙ CORNER OF CHURCH and SCREVEN STREETS Baptist Cemetery, c. 1800
Open to public.
Elisha Screven set this lot aside for construction of a Baptist church that wasn't built until 1804. Among early graves sits a monument to William Screven, founder of the Baptist Church in South Carolina. The statue to the Confederate War dead once stood at the corner of Broad and Highmarket, but moved here when traffic patterns shifted.

82.2 2 blks   *On right at corner of Screven and Highmarket streets is Prince George Parish Hall.*

㉚ CORNER OF SCREVEN and HIGHMARKET STREETS
Prince George Winyah Parish Hall, c. 1845
Open to public.
This was the three-story county jail until 1950. Now, with a top story removed, the structure with 2-foot-thick walls shelters the parish hall.

82.2 0.0   *Continue on Screven Street.*
82.3 1 blk   *Turn left onto Prince Street, noting on right the yellow Georgetown County Courthouse.*

㉛ CORNER OF SCREVEN and PRINCE STREETS
Georgetown County Courthouse, c. 1824
Open to public.
Robert Mills designed this yellow Greek Revival structure, complete with a massive pediment and columns that we associate with South Carolina's best-known architect. The annex on the left is a 1948 addition.

82.5 2 blks   *On right is 501 Prince Street.*

㉜ 509 PRINCE STREET, Winyah Indigo Society Hall, c. 1857
Not open to public.
Indigo planters meeting socially paid for their drinks in indigo, and the surplus went to finance a school for the poor. Leading Charleston architect Edward Bickell White designed this red brick hall with stucco trim and stately portico.

82.5 0.0   *Across the street is 502 Prince Street.*

㉝ 502 PRINCE STREET, The Morgan-Ray House, c. 1825
Not open to public.
To all appearances, it's just a conventional town house, but this one is haunted. It was a Union army hospital: Blood still stains the dining room floor, and the bumps at night are said to be the sound of "the devil herding the bluecoats back."

82.6 ½ blk   *On right is 417 Prince Street.*

㉞ 417 PRINCE STREET, The Cuttino-Turner House, c. 1790
Not open to public.
Just as in Charleston, Georgetown had her single houses. William Cuttino built this one and the one next door for his two daughters. Both houses have had additions, but the original structures, with their narrow sides to the street, are easy to identify.

82.6 ½ blk   *At stop sign, turn right onto St. James Street.*
82.7 1 blk   *At stop sign, turn right onto Front Street.*
82.9 3-4 blks *In the next few blocks, park and visit Rice Museum and River Walk behind buildings on left as well as houses open to the public.*

㉟ RIVER SIDE of FRONT STREET, The Harbor Walk
Restaurants and shops face the water, and several small city parks occupy the high ground. Shrimp boats dock nearby. Part of the town's revitalization project, this once-derelict waterfront has been successfully refurbished.

82.9 2blks   *On left is 1003 Front Street.*

㊱ 1003 FRONT STREET, The Kaminski House, c. 1769
Open to public.
Heiman Kaminski, returning from four years of Confederate service with only two silver dollars, made a fortune with his hardware store in the lean post-war years. His son Harold, a retired naval officer, and his wife, Julia Pyatt, enlarged and furnished this house. In 1972, the family willed it to the City of Georgetown. Due to drastic alterations over the years, it's difficult to say what is original, but inside you'll find a remarkable collection of antiques. Custodians describe them as "eclectic," but these furnishings are mostly American. A 300-year-old Spanish trousseau chest huddles just inside the door; then English clocks, Persian prayer rugs, and Charleston Chippendale, portraits, and petit point scatter about. Master furniture designers Duncan Phyfe and Thomas Elfe are represented. Upstairs is a 1760 Chippendale-style commode, and in the next room, Art Deco beds. It all blends together in a curious and elegant whole that's worth experiencing.

Additional Georgetown Tours (Organized or Otherwise)
Walking is a great way to appreciate Georgetown's history, and "Miss Nell's Tours" delivers more than just exercise. Miss Nell Cribb promises real Southern hospitality, history, legends, and ghost stories, and maybe even lemonade on a front porch. Ask the Chamber of Commerce about where her tours start.
　　Feet tired? Guides aboard Swamp Fox Tram, a Jeep-pulled carriage, narrate the town's history and highlights. They're also the only ones who can get you inside the AME Church.
　　A few boats cruise the surrounding waters, and their skippers give lectures on everything under the sun. Ask at the Visitors' Center for details or call Capt. Sandy, who has been giving boat tours for more than 20 years. Plantation tours up toward the Waccamaw River provide more history but also offer a good look at the remnants of rice culture and the native wildlife. On their journeys, the boats slip through a world of crowding, thick vegetation that gradually gives way to the open Waccamaw, the distant stacks of the steel mill, and the rest of the 21st century.

80.1 **0.0**   *Return to your car and start the journey back to Charleston.*
80.6 **8** blks   *Turn left onto U.S. 17 South.*

Lafayette Memorial Highway
This highway from Georgetown to Charleston honors the Marquis de Lafayette, who landed on North Island near Georgetown in 1777. Several volunteers, including Baron de Kalb, a native of Germany, accompanied him. They promptly went to Charleston, then Philadelphia, and offered their services to the nation. Lafayette and de Kalb served as major generals in the American Revolution. De Kalb gave his life at the Battle of Camden, South Carolina, in 1780. In 1824 Lafayette returned to the United States, hailed during his tour as a hero of the nation. While in South Carolina he laid the cornerstone for the monument to de Kalb in Camden. The marker on U.S. 17 South of Georgetown reads, "*South Carolina is proud to honor the memory of Lafayette and his Gallant Comrade in Arms. June 13, 1977.*"

135.6   **56.0**   *North side of the Ravenel Bridge, entering Charleston.*
END TOUR

TOUR SIX

THE WACCAMAW NECK

This tour begins just beyond **Georgetown** and continues north along U.S. 17 to **Murrells Inlet**. We start at the **Hobcaw Barony Discovery Center**, a part of the Belle W. Baruch Foundation, before visiting the decidedly uncommercial seashore retreat of **Pawleys Island**. Just inland, we observe three very different Anglican church buildings at **All Saints Parish Waccamaw Church**. Up Waccamaw Neck to **Brookgreen Gardens**, we encounter one of the finest exhibitions of American figurative sculpture in the country, a botanical museum, and a wildlife park. Directly across the road, **Huntington Beach State Park** attracts bird watchers and ocean bathers. A couple of miles up the highway, we visit **Murrells Inlet**, a community famous for its seafood restaurants. To fit this itinerary into a single day, start early. If not, take your time and come back another day.

Hobcaw Barony Discovery Center
   22 Hobcaw Road | 843-546-4623
   Admission free.
Pawleys Island
   www.townofpawleysisland.com
All Saints Parish Waccamaw Church
   3560 Kings River Road | 843-237-4223 | *www.allsaintspawleys.org*
Brookgreen Gardens
   1931 Brookgreen Drive | 843-235-6000 or 800-849-1931 | *www.brookgreen.org*
   Admission charged.
Huntington Beach State Park
   16148 Ocean Highway | 843-235-8755
   www.southcarolinaparks.com/park-finder/state-park/1020.aspx
   Admission charged.
Atalaya (Inside Huntington Beach State Park)
   16148 Ocean Highway | 843-237-2162
   www.southcarolinaparks.com/product.aspx?productID=26375
   Admission charged.
Murrells Inlet
   843-357-2007 | *www.murrellsinletsc.com*

BEGIN TOUR

0.0	0.0	*From Charleston, take U.S. 17 North; begin clocking mileage at north side (Mount Pleasant) of Ravenel Bridge.*
16.5	16.5	*On both sides of the highway, you see the Francis Marion National Forest (see Tour 5).*
33.5	17.0	*On right, McClellanville (see Tour 5).*
40.8	7.3	*Santee River Delta (see Tour 5).*
42.8	2.0	*Look on left for Hopsewee Plantation.*
54.5	11.7	*Cross Sampit River; look to right for downtown Georgetown (see Tour 5).*
57.1	2.6	*Cross Pee Dee River and Black River bridges.*
57.7	0.6	*South side of Waccamaw River.*

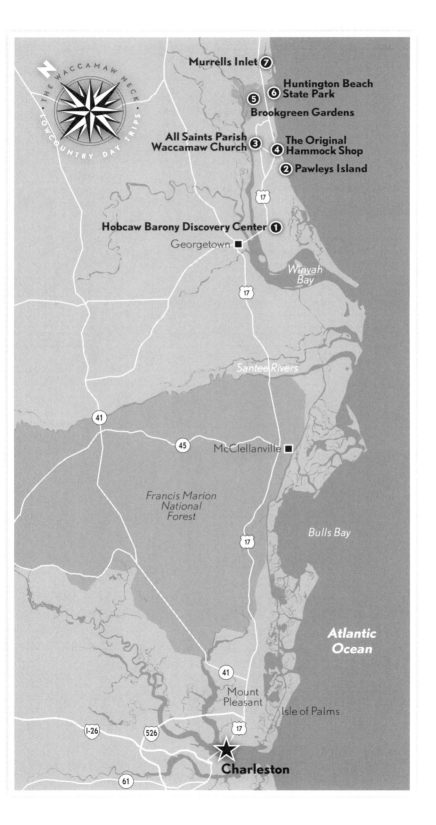

THE WACCAMAW NECK · LOWCOUNTRY DAY TRIPS

Murrells Inlet ⑦

Huntington Beach
State Park ⑥

⑤ Brookgreen Gardens

All Saints Parish
Waccamaw Church ③

The Original
Hammock Shop ④

② Pawleys Island

17

Hobcaw Barony Discovery Center ①

Georgetown ■

Winyah
Bay

17

Santee Rivers

41

45   McClellanville ■

Francis Marion
National
Forest

Bulls Bay

17

Atlantic
Ocean

41

Mount
Pleasant   Isle of Palms

I-26   526   17

★

Charleston

61

Travel and Tourism

The two bridges we crossed north of Georgetown replaced the ferry in 1935 and allowed the car to succeed the boat as the main means of transportation to and from the Waccamaw Neck. When visitors began to pass through, it was the beginning of a "recreation explosion" that continues to boom. Now, many who once only vacationed here stay year-round. This southernmost tip of the Waccamaw Neck, called Hobcaw Barony, was actually settled long before.

A History of Hobcaw Barony

Some historians contend that the Spanish, under the direction of Lucas Vásquez de Ayllón, started a colony here in 1526, but starvation and fevers plagued his 500 settlers. Ayllón died, mutiny followed, and the slaves revolted. Building a ship, 150 of the original party escaped back to Cuba. In 1718, the site was granted to one of the Lords Proprietor, John Carteret, and the 14,000-acre Hobcaw Barony remained in one block until it was divided into rice plantations just before the Revolution. In 1905, entrepreneur and statesman Bernard Baruch began purchasing the individual plots, reuniting the property, and using it as a place to relax and entertain friends, among them Sir Winston Churchill and Franklin Roosevelt. His daughter Belle inherited the land and willed the barony to the state for use as a teaching and research center.

59.3 1.6   *Turn right into Hobcaw Barony: The Belle W. Baruch Foundation Institute—home of The Belle W. Baruch Forest Service Institute of Clemson University, Belle W. Baruch Institute for Marine Biology and Coastal Research of the University of South Carolina, and Hobcaw Barony Discovery Center.*

❶ HOBCAW BARONY DISCOVERY CENTER

Formerly known as the Bellefield Nature Center, the Hobcaw Barony Discovery Center underwent an expansion and renovation in 2009. The center now features a 1,200-gallon fish tank with seasonally rotating inhabitants, a replica of a marsh midden, exhibits about the pine and cypress ecosystem, and the history of the 17,500-acre property. Just inside, a "touch table" reveals small skulls, bones, and birds nests like the ones Belle may have collected while wandering the property as a young girl. A "touch tank" in a classroom off the main gallery features creatures from a saltwater creek, but access is permitted only under the supervision of a guide. Check out the archaeological artifacts—from Indian projectile points dating to 11,000 B.C. to the rice hoes and dispensary bottles of comparatively modern times. An interactive exhibit lets you listen to the forest's sounds, while another places you inside a replicated slave cabin, complete with its newspaper insulation.

59.3 0.0   *From Hobcaw Barony Discovery Center parking lot, turn right onto U.S. 17 North.*
66.1 6.8   *Turn right onto Causeway Road / S-22-266.*
67.3 1.2   *At Pawleys Island stop sign, turn right onto S-22-10.*
68.2 0.9   *At stop sign, turn left onto S-22-265.*
68.2 1blk   *At stop sign, turn right and follow S-22-265.*
68.9 0.7   *Dead-end at south end of Pawleys Island.*

❷ PAWLEYS ISLAND

The Historical Society has done an excellent job installing markers that point out many historical beach cottages that contribute to Pawleys' tagline, "Arrogantly Shabby." Four miles long and no more than a quarter-mile wide, Pawleys Island

| **T**he Chapel" on Pawleys Island.

enjoys an almost mystical reputation as a genteelly weathered vacation spot. Three Pawley brothers took out a grant for this land in 1711, but probably didn't occupy it even as a summer retreat until after the Revolution. In 1845, future state governor Robert F.W. Allston built a causeway and moved his family onto the island for the malaria season. "The vehicles, horses, cows, furniture, bedding, trunks, provisions" were brought from nearby plantations on great flats. Servants attended summer residents, who caught up on visiting and enjoyed the seashore. Reports soon recorded nine houses and a school to accommodate 40 white residents; a church, a rectory, and more homes followed. About a dozen of these old structures remain; you can occasionally glimpse them through the thick growth of stunted oaks and cedars.

68.9	**0.0**	Retrace S-22-265 to S-22-10; continue straight through intersection of S-22-266.
70.6	**1.7**	Continue straight north on S-22-10.
71.3	**0.7**	Turn left onto S-22-46.
71.7	**0.4**	At stoplight, cross U.S.17 and continue on Waverly Road / S-22-46.
73.5	**1.8**	At stop sign, turn right onto S-22-255.
73.7	**0.2**	On left, All Saints Parish Waccamaw Church, turn into the parking lot on the right side of the road.

❸ ALL SAINTS PARISH WACCAMAW CHURCH, c. 1917
Grounds open to public.
Separated from Georgetown's Prince George Parish in 1767, this new parish, like most after the Revolution, struggled simply to maintain services. In 1832, however, Reverend Alexander Glennie revived interest and expanded the church's ministry into the slave community. In 1844, a new "building of colonial design, with massive columns on the front porch," replaced the old church. Sadly, the Civil War ended Reverend Glennie's ministry, and in 1915 the church burned. Similar in style to "the old church" but on a slightly smaller scale, the current one is the fourth to occupy the site. The church cemetery contains the remains of Westons, Wards, Allstons, Alstons, and numerous others that live on in local history and legend. Notice the graves of the great 1893 storm's victims, and that of Plowden Weston. Reverend Glennie had been brought here from England to be Weston's tutor.

Across the street sits the newest All Saints Church, a tremendous temple that the congregation refers to as "The Big Church." It is unusual compared to the earlier buildings, as in true Greek or Roman architecture, its columns actually support (or appear to support) the portico and sides. The parish house to the left was built in 1975 to match the existing 1917 church. Lightning struck the house and burned it before it could be used. When it was rebuilt the following year, workers added lightning rods to its roof and to all the buildings on the church grounds. The low buildings to the rear are the kindergarten.

73.7	**0.0**	*From church parking lot, turn left onto S-22-225 and retrace.*
73.9	**0.2**	*At stop sign, turn left onto Waverly Road / S-22-46.*
75.7	**1.8**	*At stoplight, turn left onto U.S. 17 North.*
76.0	**0.3**	*Turn right into parking lot of The Original Hammock Shop.*

❹ THE ORIGINAL HAMMOCK SHOP

Joshua Ward of nearby Brookgreen Plantation invented the Pawley's Island Hammock, a relaxing rope hammock. Ward successfully duplicated and marketed his creation with his brother-in-law, A.H. Lachiocotte. Cool and comfortable, it's truly a sinister device, for once hung and occupied, it causes even the most strong-willed person to "lose a crop." Similar styles can be found nearby, but the Original Hammock Shop has been selling the real deal since 1889.

76.0	**0.0**	*From the Hammock Shop's parking lot, turn right onto U.S. 17 North.*
81.2	**5.2**	*Turn right onto U.S. 17 North. Turn left into Brookgreen Gardens.*

❺ BROOKGREEN GARDENS, c. 1931

Waccamaw Neck was the land of the rice princes, a place rich in history and myth, and Brookgreen Gardens is particularly noteworthy. Brookgreen and three other former plantations—Springfield, The Oaks, and Laurel Hill—make up the land on which the garden sprawls. It changed hands several times before the Huntingtons bought it in 1930.

The Huntingtons

Born illegitimately to Collis Huntington and his mistress (who later married), Archer Milton Huntington received a uniquely free-form, globe-trotting education. He read much and traveled widely; Spain and its literature became his greatest love. At 33, he translated the El Cid epic that's still the standard text today. Though successful, rich, and witty, he wasn't particularly happy. His first wife ran off with a theatrical producer, leaving the door open for sculptor Anna Hyatt to rescue him from suicidal thoughts.

Brought up in Cambridge, Massachusetts, Anna had an early interest in animals, encouraged by her father, an MIT professor and noted paleontologist. Her older sister, already a sculptor, introduced her to what would be the avocation and vocation of a very long life. After training at the Art Students League in New York, she made the domestic animals of a Maryland farm and the wild animals of the Bronx Zoo her textbooks. Animal sculptures remained a specialty. In 1923, she married Archer Huntington.

They were happy; they shared an intense interest in the arts, and their seemingly dissimilar personalities complemented each other. A prolific period for the sculptor followed their union; then she contracted tuberculosis and spent a year in a Swiss sanitarium. In 1929, after returning from Europe, they purchased Brookgreen. Deciding it would be a good place for Anna to regain her health, they began planning a sculpture garden on the site of the 1901 house.

Anna designed a garden in the shape of a butterfly, and Georgetown

Fighting Stallions by Anna Huntington.

A History of Brookgreen and Its Inhabitants

Each of the original plantations near Brookgreen ran from the ocean to the Waccamaw River. Local travel in that day was by boat on the Waccamaw River. The first owner of Brookgreen Plantation, William Allston, served as a captain under Francis Marion, the American patriot who consistently rankled, eluded, and defeated the British during the Revolutionary War. Allston's son, Washington, studied art abroad. A friend of Samuel Coleridge, Washington Irving, and Samuel Morse, he became a leading artist of the day, and was known as "the American Titian" for his similar use of color.

Joseph Alston and his wife, Theodosia Burr (the daughter of Aaron Burr), occupied nearby Oaks Plantation. After Burr ended his political career by killing Alexander Hamilton in a duel, Alston helped finance his father-in-law's attempted empire in Mexico, which prompted charges of treason against Burr. Joseph was elected governor in 1812, but tragedy soon followed. His only son died of malaria, and Theodosia, journeying to see her father, disappeared at sea, leaving behind two heartbroken men and a romantic legend.

Francis Marion Weston and Plowden C.J. Weston, the student and supporter of Reverend Alexander Glennie, lived at adjoining Laurel Hill.

In 1800, the Ward family bought Brookgreen, and Joshua John Ward discovered and propagated world-famous "Carolina Golden Big Grain Rice." At Brookgreen and seven other plantations, he grew almost four million pounds of rice in 1850, and by some estimates was the country's wealthiest planter.

The Civil War ended the golden age of rice, but planting continued at Brookgreen under the Hasell family. They and the related Willetts and two Dr. Flaggs maintained a school, church, and infirmary for both blacks and whites. In 1920, Dr. Julius Mood bought the collection of plantations and ran it as a hunting club. His daughter, Julia Peterkin, featured the locale in her novels, including the Pulitzer Prize-winning **Scarlet Sister Mary**. *Waccamaw Neck grew poorer still during the Depression. Eventually, the Huntongtons purchased Brookgreen and the other three plantations.*

horticulturist Frank Tarbox, Jr., planted it. Archer managed the building of brick walls and fountains. His wife sculpted, the couple generously supported other artists, and Brookgreen became America's first sculpture garden as well as a botanical museum of Southeastern flora and fauna. Verses from appropriate poets added to the cultural appeal. The couple visited in 1946 and 1947, and then retired to the North for good. Archer died in 1955, but Anna maintained an active interest in Brookgreen for many more years. She sculpted almost up to her death in 1973 at the age of 97. Brookgreen's trustees and staff continue the couple's work to this day.

Guide to Statues Along Entrance Road
Fighting Stallions
Done by Anna Huntington when she was 75, this tremendous aluminum casting was placed here at the entrance in 1951 to catch the eye of passing motorists. It proved so successful that it became the symbol of the gardens.
Plaque and Entry
Just beyond, a plaque announces the formation of the gardens by the Huntingtons in 1931 "for the appreciation of American sculpture and the preservation of Southeastern Flora and Fauna." Longleaf pines, oaks, and hollies shade the road.

I *Live oak limbs at Brookgreen Gardens.*

Spirit of American Youth
Located in what's known as the "flagpole circle," this sculpture depicts a "young man reaching for the heavens." Donald DeLue sculpted the original to keep watch over 10,000 Allied soldiers buried in Normandy.

81.8 0.6   *Admissions plaza.*

After paying admission, continue straight and then turn right onto Allston Circle Drive. You'll pass the limestone Youth Taming the Wild.

Youth Taming the Wild
Done by Anna Huntington in 1927, this was one of the earliest pieces placed at Brookgreen. The struggle depicted may represent intellect against animal strength or a youthful country taming its frontier; the viewer is invited to interpret whatever meaning he or she likes. This piece was shipped from New Jersey, and when Brookgreen's laborers coaxed it off the barge, they sang, "Come on, Horse, come on, Horse, we got a stable all fixed for you." And here it is.

82.9 1.1   *Follow Allston Circle Drive and turn left into the parking lot for the Tarbox Welcome Center, Keepsakes Gift Shop, Rainey Sculpture Pavilion, and the Sculpture Garden. Park and begin walking here.*

The Tarbox Welcome Center
Pick up a complimentary visitors guide with a description of the daily programs, tours, excursions and current exhibitions. Then watch the interesting 10-minute film, *Gray Oaks of Mystery*, which recounts the Brookgreen Gardens' history. Here, too, you'll find another appropriate introduction, The Huntington Busts.

The Huntington Busts
Though the Garden doesn't otherwise include portrait busts of individuals or commemoratives to them, an exception was made for the founders. Anna's sister sculpted her portrait, and Anna did her husband's bust. "We are classicists," he declared at one point, but it's obvious from the eclectic range of the works presented in the gardens that he did not mean this in the narrowest sense. Craft was important, and the end product of this craft should be something recognizably human or animal.

Keepsakes Gift Shop
The gift shop sells several good books on the garden and its sculptors, including *Brookgreen Gardens Sculpture* by Beatrice Proske and *Brookgreen Gardens Sculpture, Volume 2* by Robin Salmon. You're welcome to abandon this text now, for the following is purely subjective rambling that leaves out most of the 600-plus statues on display.

Walk to the Rainey Sculpture Pavilion.

The Rainey Sculpture Pavilion
Located at the entrance to the Huntington Sculpture Garden, the Sculpture Pavilion contains two indoor exhibition spaces that feature rotating exhibits: the Carl Paul Jennewein Gallery and the Joseph Veach Noble Gallery.

Exit the Sculpture Pavilion and walk straight ahead into the Huntington Sculpture Garden. Look for a pair of lions.

Lions
These bronzes by Anna Huntington done in 1930 frame the entrance to The Diana Pool.

The Diana Pool
The pool serves several purposes, probably the most important being to reflect light upward. It's a meditative spot with tropical fish and the occasional great blue heron or egret. Years ago, I asked the gardens' former director, Gurdon Tarbox, why people threw pennies into the pool. He laughingly admitted that he had no idea, but said the bank hated to see him coming with those bags of "dirty money." In the center of the pool stands *Diana of the Chase*.

Diana of the Chase
One of Anna Huntington's best known works, this 1922 piece was cast several times. Diana, goddess of the woods, huntress queen, is often depicted in mid-chase, but here she pursues her quarry up, a shot at waterfowl rising from the surrounding water.

Walk around The Diana Pool and continue through gates on the far side of the pool. Live Oak Allée runs straight in front of you.

Live Oak Allée
Brookgreen actually encompasses several gardens. Its spaces are laid out much like a house, with each room or section given a distinctive planting and thus a different setting for the sculpture. The Huntingtons incorporated these live oaks, originally the entry to the plantation, into their plan from the beginning. The serpentine, pierced brick walls allow light through but at the same time provide a neutral backdrop for the works.

Just through the gates, which Anna Huntington designed, turn left; first sculpture on right is Narcissus.

Narcissus
A young faun made of Tennessee marble takes delight in its own reflection. German-born Adolph Weinman crafted several other pieces with similar classical themes, including the mammoth *Riders of the Dawn*. This garden brims with fauns, fawns, and sylvan situations.

Continue on walk; turning the corner to the right on left against the wall is Reaching Jaguar.

Reaching Jaguar
Anna Huntington modeled this work on "Senor Lopez," a particularly large and ferocious resident of the Bronx Zoo that she studied in 1907. She went each morning to watch the animal step down for its morning meal and worked from memory of these brief moments. This natural, sketch-like treatment of the poised cat is a tough act to follow for any of the other "animaliers," including Huntington.

Continue on walk. Next on left is My Niece.

My Niece
Jo Davidson was the most famous of American portrait sculptors, but he still had time to do a few figures like this one.

Continue on walk to Zeus.

Zeus
The raised thunderbolts add meaning once we know that this work was meant for the top of the AT&T Building in New York. Best known for his architectural work, Robert Aitken also did the reliefs in the pediment of the United States Supreme Court building. Here in South Carolina, he rendered *The Marine on Parris Island*.

At walk intersection, turn back and walk into the Palmetto Garden.

Palmetto Garden
Alleyways of palmettos and ceramic jars give this bright open "room" a Moorish feel that Archer Huntington enjoyed. The pool holds another of the Gardens' anchor pieces, *Samson and the Lion.*

Samson and the Lion
Sculptor Gleb Derujinsky shows Samson rending the young lion, but it seems neither unrestrained nor natural. Derujinsky also sculpted the effusive *Ecstasy* in the far corner—a little lively for my staid taste. As

Jaguar by Anna Huntington.

you continue to walk in the Palmetto Garden, note *Can-Can* by Jane DeDecker and *Grandmother Rita* by Richard Blake. Also note the unusual planting of this Mediterranean "room."

Go out the side gate through which you entered.

You are now in the lower left-hand corner of the giant butterfly designed by Anna Huntington. Great oaks and magnolias circle much of this enclosure, but the center where the house stood, though thick with shrubbery, opens to the sky.

Turn left; at end of walk turn right to see The Afternoon of the Fawn.

The Afternoon of the Fawn
Bryant Baker did this delicate carving himself. Ordinarily, a piece of these proportions would be done in bronze, but Anna Huntington requested marble. It broke during delivery.

To your right, seek refreshment at the Old Kitchen.

The Old Kitchen
Plantation kitchens were placed away from the main house to prevent fires, but this one survived instead of the house. It's now a refreshment area, where you can stop for something warm or cool to drink, depending on the season. It also serves soups, wraps, and sweets.

From here, enter the Offner Sculpture Center next door.

The Elliot and Rosemary Offner Sculpture Learning and Research Center
The Offner Center began with a single gift. Sculptor Richard McDermott Miller left more than 400 of his works in bronze, plaster, wax, and terra cotta to Brookgreen Gardens. His collection and sculptures from many other artists found a permanent home when the center opened in 2007. Here's just a sample of the more than 600 pieces stored here.

King Penguin and Owl
Two of the 10 playful birds Paul Manship did for the Bronx Zoo gates in 1932. Minnesotan Manship's early discovery of archaic Greek sculpture influenced him greatly, and he in turn influenced many of those working in the 1920s and

I **P**egasus *by Laura Fraser.*

'30s. His distinctive sculpture is well represented here at Brookgreen.

The Puritan
Surrounded by a billowing cloak, this hard-faced Calvinist is executed in relatively low relief. Nineteenth-century sculptor Augustus Saint-Gaudens is often called "the father of American sculpture" for his break from the Neoclassical tradition in favor of realistic treatments like this.

Benediction
The cloaked angel steps forward in a manner similar to *The Puritan*, but its face is indistinct and shadowed—an abstraction. Daniel French designed it for a war memorial. Incidentally, French was capable of rendering the realistic as well as the symbolic—he sculpted the Lincoln in the Lincoln Memorial.

Jaguar Eating
That's Senor Lopez again. This companion piece to the first Anna Huntington cat portrays breakfast time at the Bronx Zoo.

El Cid Campeador and Joan of Arc
Two different pieces—small models of the two great equestrian statues for which Anna Huntington is most well known—liberators of Spain and France.

The Driller and River Driver
The art of the '20s and '30s often celebrated the working man, but works like these by Mahonri Young and Charles Tefft don't usually lend themselves to garden settings.

Bronco Buster
This was the first attempt at sculpting for illustrator Frederic Remington. Needless to say, the 1895 work proved to be a tremendous success.

Iris
All the sculptors at Brookgreen are American by birth or naturalized. Paul Jennewein came here from Germany as a young man. His *Iris* is the goddess of the rainbow and descends to bring the messages of gods to men.

Debbie II
This isn't a goddess, just a very realistic naked woman. Debbie wore clothes in an earlier work—a sweater so finely ribbed that sculptor Isidore Margulies was accused of literally casting her from life. Margulies says such realism is really an illusion. "I want the viewer's eye to fill in those details that I left out."

From the front of the Offner Center, look straight in front of you across the winding walk to Man Carving His Own Destiny.

Man Carving His Own Destiny—"Struggling to hack out his own character, carving his own future by the effort of his will" is how Czech-born Albin Polasek described his work.

Look left and walk to Shark Diver.

Shark Diver
"Only within the suspension of water can the human form be released to its ultimate flow of grace and action," wrote sculptor Frank Eliscu. To suspend a figure like this required a masterful refinement of the lost wax process.

Just after Shark Diver, follow the straight path then turn left to find Pegasus.

Pegasus
When the blood from the severed head of Medusa fell into the sea, it produced the winged horse Pegasus, who, once caught and tamed, was given to the Muses. Laura Fraser presents this "symbol of inspiration" carrying its artist-rider above the clouds. The sculptor worked on the model for five years and then the stonecutters took over. This began as about 40 tons of granite in the quarry at Mount Airy, North Carolina. The stonecutters brought it here in three pieces and whittled half of that away. Still, little chance of it getting airborne.

To left at end of green is Fountain of the Muses.

Fountain of the Muses
There were nine Muses, the daughters of Jupiter and Mnemosyne, goddess of memory, but these aren't they. The figures dancing across the pool are five artists who have been inspired, and a faun, centaur, and goddess keeping them company. Those strange little things spurting water are fish. Swedish-born Carl Milles is an undisputed giant of 20th-century sculpture, and this display came here by way of the Metropolitan Museum of Art.
Like winged *Pegasus*, the pleasure and purpose of this one evades me.

Return to Pegasus, and look straight ahead to the marsh. In front of us are old rice fields. Return through gates and turn to left. At dead end turn right. We're once more in the upper left-hand corner of the butterfly. On left is Diana.

Diana
The most hunter-like of the gardens' Dianas, Manship's version is set off by the wilderness of abandoned rice fields beyond. The companion, *Actaeon*, is at the far end of this walk. Silhouette-like and angular, the enameled eyes and stylized hair show the influence of archaic Greek sculpture.

As you face Diana, do an about-face. Almost opposite is Mares of Diomedes.

Mares of Diomedes
Hercules tamed these man-eating mares, but this wasn't the title chosen by sculptor Gutzon Borglum, who had Old West horse-stealing in mind. He is best remembered for carving the four presidents on Mount Rushmore.

With your back to the horses, veer right to pool.

The Alligator Pool
Archer Huntington designed this pool to act as a reservoir for several surrounding fountains. Note how the overflow spills into a surrounding trough that leads to other lower fountains. His wife sculpted the sunning alligators.

In center of pool is The Alligator Bender.

The Alligator Bender
Nathaniel Choate carved the original statue out of mahogany. Then in Italy (he liked to be where the marble was), Choate created this Seminole Indian version.

Walk to far side of the pool to examine gold Dionysus.

Dionysus

Inspired by 18th-century French sculpture, Edward McCartan crafted this piece. "The forms are purified and the lucid composition polished to a glowing brilliancy of line," wrote Proske in her book about Brookgreen. This one gets special care for its gold leaf over bronze. Dionysus was the god of wine, but also a promoter of civilization, lawgiver, and lover of peace. Bright and elevated, he occupies a commanding position in the gardens' main axis—a landmark for wandering visitors.

Continue counterclockwise around the pool, then take the path to St. Francis.

St. Francis

Architect and sculptor Julian Harris writes, "He was not a powerful man; he was an ethereal man. Everything was simplified in his life, so in doing this work I tried to express what I saw in reading and studying St. Francis." A short verse accompanies the saint who seems a worthy enough companion of gods and alligator wrestlers.

Look behind you toward the rice field. In plantation days, these steps led down to the boat landing. You can still follow them down the creek edge and along the Trail Beyond the Garden Wall. Or, pass the stairs and continue following the path to Persephone.

Persephone

This may be the only human figure here by Fredericks. Queen of the realm of the dead, this goddess was allowed to wake each spring and let life begin once more.

Continue on walk, then look to opposite walkway to Sea Horse.

Sea Horse

Across the hedge and opposite walk is a strange creature by Joseph Kiselewski, who specializes in religious sculpture but has done several pieces for the young and young at heart. This unlikely sea horse appears to be at least half porpoise.

Actaeon *commands the end of the walkway.*

Actaeon

Here is the soon-to-be-deceased companion of Manship's *Diana*. Actaeon spied on the goddess while she bathed in her secret pool. In revenge, she turned him into a stag, and his own dogs tore him apart.

Right in the corner beyond Actaeon *stands* Primitive Man and Serpent.

Primitive Man and Serpent

Roland Perry traveled through Germany and Norway. "Unrestrained naturalness and liveliness of expression," says Proske of his work. The original title was *Thor and the Midgard Serpent.*

Continue to right and follow path around corner. Enter the Dogwood Garden to left. You can't miss Riders of the Dawn *in the center of the pool.*

Riders of the Dawn

You'll be happy to see that Weinman's 40-ton stampede has been placed here where it can balance the equally monumental *Pegasus.*

Walk to the right of the pool and exit to Brown Sculpture Court.

Brown Sculpture Court
Formerly the Museum of Small Sculpture, this roofless gallery contains a permanent collection of smaller works and many of the white marble pieces in the collection. It also displays photographs of artists in their studios as well as the small models for larger works. I'll mention just a few of the pieces found within.

The Peace Garden Room for Children.

Rain
Avard Fairbanks created this crouching figure with the headdress of rain in the popular Art Deco style of the day.

Maidenhood
Marble has a much finer texture than limestone because the gases have escaped before it solidifies. Sculptor George Barnard said of this study in serenity, "I finished the marble in a way I finished no other flesh." In later years, the model who posed for this piece was the cause of a scandalous murder.

End of the Trail
One of the most popular of all American sculptures is this 1915 piece by James Earle Fraser. Though working out of a European classical tradition, American sculptors looked to their native land for subject matter—a vanquished and vanishing subject, in this case. This probably looks familiar to you, but Fraser did one even more popular; he put the Indian on the buffalo nickel.

Toro Bravo
Charlotte Dunwiddie left Germany just before World War II and lived for some years in South America. Here she presents the bull at the moment just before it enters the bullring. It has stood in darkness until now and, suddenly blinded by the light, pauses a moment before charging.

The Wounded Comrade
This work by Carl Akeley, a wounded bull elephant supported and protected by two female elephants, is one of the most popular pieces in Brookgreen.

Walk out the front of The Brown Sculpture Court and turn left to enter The Peace Garden Room for Children.

The Peace Garden Room for Children
Children delight in the kid-friendly plants and whimsical statues in this outdoor sculpture garden/learning space. Youngsters explore wooded nooks, while parents sit and watch from an elevated vantage. Check out these favorites.

The Thinker
We've seen a lot of animals, but most are treated in a more realistic fashion than this chunky little ape. Fredericks' style is distinctively his own. Children love his lighthearted and deceptively simple works.

Voratio
This strange caterpillar by Jane Armstrong is the closest thing to abstraction we'll come across. Presumably, the title is a godlike reference to the animal's appetite.

Mother and Baby Bear

Back to back, these two squat like giant children's toys. It's not surprising, then that youngsters appreciate this work. Sculptor Fredericks says, "I love animals of all kinds and I did this group basically for children because I'm very fond of children. I love a child's reaction to a sculpture because it's such an honest reaction."

The Baboons

Fredericks' fame began with his *Baboon Fountain* at the 1939 World's Fair, and here are two cast from the half-size originals and presented to Brookgreen in 1985.

From the Children's Garden, exit through a gate to the left; in front of you will be a large pond. Bear left and follow the path around to Time and the Fates of Man.

Time and the Fates of Man

We're in wide-open space now, and Manship makes good use of the sunshine. Three women—young, middle-aged, and old—spin out the passage of time while the sun marks the hour in the brick plaza.

Next stop on the same path, another interpretation of The Thinker.

The Thinker

Brace yourself for Henry Clews' *The Thinker*. I used to laugh at this; now I don't. The old man is attempting to come up with a new thought, a vanity indicated by the peacock feathers. From top to bottom, it's packed with symbolism, a searing indictment of a materialistic society, the same spiritually barren society that fed the sculptor. Clews finally got so disgusted he went to France and fixed up an abandoned chateau on the Riviera.

Continue to next pool and Gazelle Fountain.

Gazelle Fountain

A wheeling gazelle crowns the top of this final pool. Another work by Fredericks, this one is as graceful and full of motion as the mother bear is stolid, but they share lightheartedness.

Look left to Don Quixote *and* Sancho.

Don Quixote

This is rocky ground for the Spanish knight-errant, tilter at windmills. For Anna Huntington, he's a sad figure, depressed. His horse Rocinante was modeled here at the Atalaya studio from an animal so poorly it had to be hung from a sling, but with a little attention the model gained a new lease on life. Rocinante seems to have been a particular favorite of Archer Huntington; he named his yacht for him and found in the poor horse's "stumbling up to God" a triumph as grand as Napoleon's.

Sancho

Anna Huntington gave the honor of doing this knight's companion to Jennewein, who created this well-fed, content retainer. No rocks beneath his feet.

Continue straight through the breezeway to the other side of the Rainey Sculpture Pavilion. See Flying Wild Geese.

Flying Wild Geese

In this piece, Marshall Fredericks uses almost flat surfaces, rendering them broad, rounded, and silhouetted against the sky.

Len Ganeway
This old farmer reading his paper on the park bench is popular with visitors, and you may have to wait your turn to sit beside him. There's no danger that he's been "cast from life," but note the detail in the rubber boots, overalls, and worn face with ample mustache. We assume this is a portrait of a real person, probably the artist's neighbor, but actually, Len Ganeway is the pen name of the newspaper editor who commissioned the work. Sculptor Derek Wernher explained, "He's just a little guy reading a newspaper. Once I got the head, I got the person, and the rest of it fell into place."

Wild Turkey, *The Lowcountry Zoo.*

We're through: the three-hour Brookgreen. Actually, that's not much better than the famous "three-minute Louvre," but there's no law that says we have to see it all.

So now we are left to sit beside Len Ganeway and mutter to ourselves that last retort of all Philistines, "We know what we like."

But do we? We can't respond as children do by climbing into the lap of the mother bear. Did you find a dozen works that brought you genuine pleasure? If so, return and you're sure to find a dozen more. Artist Derek Wernher gets the last word. Of people who write tours of sculpture gardens: "They want all this verbiage. They want to know what you feel is the essence. Well for Christ's sake, there it is. You can go through stylistic interpretations and blah, blah. But an art work is a helluva lot more than that."

82.9 0.0   *From parking lot, turn left onto Allston Circle Drive.*
You'll pass In Memory of the Workhorse *on the right.*

In Memory of the Workhorse
This 1964 piece gives you some idea of the length and breadth of Anna Huntington's career; it was inspired by a small piece, *The Storm,* which she had modeled in France 57 years earlier. She loved all animals, but horses were a favorite subject.

Enroute to the zoo portion of Brookgreen Gardens, you'll pass the Wall Lowcountry Center, the embarkation point for creek cruises and overland excursions to historical sites. Near the entrance flies Diving Eagle.

Diving Eagle
Notice the wreath that the eagle is delivering to the waves. Added in 1980, this 6-foot bronze by Albino Manca was cast from the first enlargement. An earlier 18-foot version is located at Battery Park in New York and dedicated to those lost at sea during World War II.

83.5 0.5   *Turn left into the Lowcountry Zoo parking lot.*

The Lowcountry Zoo
In this accredited AZA zoo, you'll find only local native animals and plants. A guided tour gives a complete introduction to them both. On the trail that wends past the animal exhibits, we pass live oaks and Spanish moss, then enter less familiar terrain. Beauty berry, black cherry, bladder pod, and fiddlehead, the first of the dozen ferns, are here. First stop: the Floyd

fiddlehead, the first of the dozen ferns, are here. First stop: the Floyd Domestic Animals of the Plantation. In a barnyard pasture bounded by natural wood fencing and dotted with live oaks graze rare historic breeds of domestic animals used by settlers.

It may take you off the path a bit, but Whispering Wings Butterfly Exhibit is open spring through fall. Step inside the mesh structure to feel the gentle touch of a Southeastern species butterfly land on your hand, or to watch them emerge from their cocoons. A separate admission fee applies.

Past the plantation, animals, and butterflies rises the 90-foot-high Cypress Swamp Aviary. The freshwater tide moves in and out of this swamp bottom, where ibis and herons are the most obvious of the enclosed species. Many people don't like to see animals in captivity, but most of the birds and animals here were born in captivity or were rehabilitated but cannot be released back into the wild. We see cypress trees and knees up close and then head for the otters.

What was once one exhibit has become two. River Basin Retreat includes underwater viewing that allows us to see the otter's graceful movements in the water. Then we see them in their natural habitat, where they wrestle and play. A display board here gives general otter information. The cold-blooded alligators are decidedly more sinister, whether wallowing in muddy holes or sunning themselves for all to see.

Around the bend, gray and red foxes laze. It's thought that the red fox was brought over from England for fox hunting when the native gray fox kept climbing trees to escape the hounds.

Five raptor aviaries follow. These smaller exhibits give zookeepers easy access to this group of rehabilitated but sometimes gimpy native raptors, such as bald eagles, owls, and hawks.

Turkey Edge holds several wild turkeys and a large pond popular with resident Canada geese and mute swans.

Bring your binoculars to the next aviary. Unlike their rehab neighbors a few habitats away, these birds of prey can fly. Spy them in the treetrops.

Finally, a 23-acre enclosure surrounded by a dry moat and high fence holds a large herd of savannah deer. Like all the animals, they seem tame and content enough with their surroundings. We follow the edge of the fence for several hundred feet and a sign directs us to the parking lot.

The Lowcountry Zoo's master plan calls for more native species in the future. Stay tuned for new exhibits of black bear, red wolf, puma, skunks, armadillos, bobcats, and bats.

83.4 0.0   *From Nature Wildlife Park parking lot, turn left onto Allston Circle Drive and continue to U.S. 17.*
84.8 1.4   *At stop sign, cross U.S. 17 and turn left.*
85.2 0.4   *Turn right at entrance to Huntington Beach State Park.*

⑥ HUNTINGTON BEACH STATE PARK

The tour of this 2,500-acre park starts at the entrance. Take the small brochure handed out at the gate and begin your loop through the mainland forest, after which the park road crosses a causeway dike—a dramatic introduction to the environs. Stop by the Education Center, added in 2002, where you'll find live animal exhibits, including a touch tank with a stingray, horseshoe crab, and other sea creatures.

85.8 0.6   *On right is the Mullet Pond.*

Don't feed the alligators! One of the old-timers.

The Mullet Pond
Alligators star in this freshwater to brackish lagoon—about 100 of them. Unless it's deep winter, you'll see their eyes and noses sticking above the water. Most are about five feet long, with a few babies mixed in. The real old-timers retired to the far end after public feeding was stopped. Don't feed the alligators! They can be dangerous. Banana waterlily and cattail grow most noticeably, but storm tides sometimes cross over and kill them back. The duckweeds, widgeon grass, and other rushes provide more tolerant food for waterfowl. Year-round you'll see gallinules, coots, and grebes, and during the winter, a great variety of migrating ducks. Herons and egrets work both sides of the causeway.

85.8 0.0   *On left is Tidal Salt Marsh.*

Tidal Salt Marsh
Low tide exposes an extensive mud flat with broad oyster beds. At high tide, only the top of the marsh shows—a fertile cycle we can examine up close from the Marsh Boardwalk.

86.8 1.0   *At stop sign, turn left.*
87.0 0.2   *Turn left into Marsh Boardwalk parking lot.*

Marsh Boardwalk

On this day seagulls feed in Oak Creek where the Marsh Boardwalk pier ends; on the far shore a variety of wading birds roost.

87.0	**0.0**	*From parking lot, turn left.*
87.8	**0.8**	*On right is Hot and Hot Fish Club historical marker.*

Hot and Hot Fish Club, Drunken Jack Island, and the Flagg Storm

A historical marker on the northern end of the island commemorates the Hot and Hot Fish Club. This famous fish fry was originally held on Drunken Jack Island, just inland from where we stand. Fishermen brought the day's catch ashore and cooked during the afternoon, so there were at least two courses— hot and hot. The honorary president provided a ham or roast, and the vice president, the wine.

87.8	**0.0**	*Continue straight to parking area.*
87.8	**200** ft	*Park in this North End parking lot.*

North End and Jetty

Walking onto the beach, you get a good cross-section view of the dunes. The "back dunes" are usually the highest and thick with sea oats. Ahead lie the secondary and primary dune rows. Note the beach amaranthus growing here. Coming up almost on the surf's edge, it's a remarkable plant. Far tougher than the better-known marsh grass and sea oats, it's the unsung hero of the dune fields. Wind-driven sand piles against it, it grows higher, and more sand piles up until sea oats can take root.

Watch for sanderlings, the most common of the numerous sandpipers here, some ringbilled gulls, and the occasional willet. The farther north we walk, the farther off the beaten path we go. There's a turtle program here, too, but we're getting toward the northern limits of the loggerheads' nesting range. Still, an appreciable number of nests are guarded and hatched out every year. Sand crabs are the big danger (elsewhere it's raccoons). In the far distance, the black rock of the jetty was completed in 1980 to aid in party boat and commercial fishing. Look at the debris at our feet. If you pass this way, especially after a storm, you'll find a variety of beachcomber's delights—corals, spider crabs, cockles, razor clams, coralline, sea cucumbers, sponges, penshells, purse crabs, devil's pocketbooks, gooseneck barnacles—all within a few paces.

On our right, a variety of terns and dowitchers fill a large, shallow lagoon known as Sandpiper Pond, while a nearby sand flat harbors least terns and Wilson plovers. We keep our distance since the birds chose this place to escape predators like us. The jetty is paved, but be very careful climbing onto it; sand shelves form above the stone. Legs have been broken here. You can walk out to the end, a favorite place for fishermen, or turn left and follow the road back to the beach and the car.

87.8	**0.0**	*From parking lot, retrace south and continue south to Atalaya parking lot.*
89.1	**1.3**	*Turn left into parking lot.*

Kerrigan Nature Trail.

On this trail, we turn inland and follow the old causeway that once led to Brookgreen. We're past the northern limits of Sea Island cotton, but it's possible that provision crops were grown here during plantation days. The pines, once survivors of 90 years of salt spray, have lost out at last, but other plants have survived. Wax myrtles are common undergrowth; note the waxy leaves. The sheen on their leaves, and on the leaves of the live oaks and the smilax and pennywort at

The surf rolls in at Hntington Beach State Park.

our feet, protects against the salt air.

The vines here are particularly thick. Grape, yellow jessamine, Virginia creeper, and peppervine twist about with verileafed smilaxes, but most exceptional of all is the poison ivy—watch for it. Notice the pennywort, too. It grows all over the park. The little dark-green umbrellas grow smaller and smaller the closer they are to the ocean. Though particularly noticeable with this plant, you'll see that all the inland vegetation becomes more stunted close to the dunes.

Stop, listen for calls, and take a good look. There are still ample birding opportunities here. Birders have recorded more than 80 bird species on the island. A much-traveled path carries us out to the beach once more.

Atalaya, c. 1938
We enter the rear of Atalaya through the front sunroom, where we pick up a map of the interior. Or, stop by the Interpretive Center, opened in 2007. Guided tours are available, as are interpretive signs throughout. Once inside the National Historic Landmark, note how the inner garden grows thick with palms, for they and the solid old building have survived storms remarkably well. This was meant to be the original entry and is certainly the nicest part of the plan. The tower in its center once held a cypress-tank water supply for the complex. The brochure explains most of the house, so I'll just comment on the most obvious omission. While a flat-roofed house of solid, fireproof masonry with small, narrow windows and tiny rooms connected by lengthy corridors suits the Spanish Moors of the late 1300s, it's a curious choice for a South Carolina beach house, especially one to be occupied in the winter by someone

Five Facts About Atalya

1. *Atalaya means "watchtower."*

2. *There are no blueprints: Archer Huntington kept the ideas in his head and conveyed his intentions to his contractor, William Thomson, bit by bit.*

3. *The "dripping" mortar style was called "the Huntington squeeze."*

4. *The building measured 200 by 200 feet and was built around an existing beach house that was moved just before being enclosed.*

5. *It's said that a Moorish castle from his beloved Spain inspired Archer Huntington.*

recuperating from tuberculosis. Servants kept the fires going continually in the many fireplaces, but it's hard to imagine life beyond the edge of the hearth. Actually, it's hard to imagine a comfortable life here, period.

Local guide Genevieve Peterkin remembers it that way. When occupied, Atalaya was all painted, the cream-white flaking from the brick. Indian blankets, hung from the walls, and furniture that was austere but stylish decorated the rooms. No doubt a happy couple, guests, and servants gave a far less forlorn presence to the place. Anna Huntington sculpted the aging horse for *Don Quixote* in this studio. There was an oyster-shucking room, and close by, two bear pens. What more could you ask of a Moorish castle?

In the end Atalaya is an architectural folly, but only in the kindest sense of those words—a building so outrageously romantic that it defies all logical complaint.

89.1	**0.0**	*Turn right out of Atalaya parking lot, retrace to park entrance gate.*
89.2	**0.1**	*Turn left.*
90.2	**1.0**	*At park's entrance gate (if you want to continue to Murrells Inlet), turn right onto U.S. 17 North.*
91.6	**1.4**	*Veer right onto U.S. 17 North Business.*
94.6	**3.0**	*For the next three miles the road is lined with dozens of good seafood restaurants.*

❼ Murrells Inlet

Over lunch, our guide Genevieve Peterkin declares with a broad smile that, contrary to rumors, the founder of this inlet was neither a pirate nor a member of the Morrall family. He was just a planter named Murrell who settled here in about 1740. The community of both summer and permanent residents was long noted for its seafood, and today its restaurants carry on that tradition. Plan to stay for dinner.

Several old houses remain, but they're on semi-private lanes, and you're asked to stay clear. In the center of the community and facing the marsh, the old Belin Methodist Church was originally on Pawleys Island. My host's grandfathers and others dismantled it, put it in ox carts, and brought it here. Builders doubled the church in length and added new columns: The old ones were filled with bees and honey. In 1992, a new church, built in the same style as the older one, was erected.

97.6	**3.0**	*Return on U.S. 17 South Business to U.S. 17 South.*
97.6	**0.0**	*Cross U.S. 17 North, turn left onto U.S. 17 South and return to Charleston on U.S. 17.*

We head back to Charleston on U.S. 17.

172.8	**75.2**	*North side of Ravenel Bridge entering Charleston.*

END TOUR

TOUR SEVEN

THE SAVANNAH RIVER

This is a naturalist tour that begins on U.S. 17 approximately 53 miles south of Charleston and takes a roundabout path to the **Savannah River**. In the little pineland village of Grahamville, we visit **two small but handsome churches**. Then we drive 20 miles toward the coast to see **Rose Hill**, a great Gothic Revival plantation house. At the **Victoria Bluff** Game Management Area, a trail circles through a distinctive "Florida flatwoods." A short drive brings us to marsh-surrounded **Pinckney Island** —great for birding, hiking, or just getting away. We head inland once more, but not far, to the summer retreat of **Bluffton**. Much of it survived the Civil War and even the 20th century—a true village. Eight miles beyond is the small antebellum **Bull Hill Methodist Church**, and then we reach the **Savannah River Wildlife Refuge**. Here the unusual four-mile Laurel Hill Wildlife Drive circles slave-built rice fields and shows off the state's best duck marshes. You drive about an hour and a half south of Charleston before this day trip begins, so if you want to fit it all in, leave early and take a picnic lunch.

Church of the Holy Trinity
2718 Bees Creek Road | 843-726-3743 | *www.holytrinityofgrahamville.org*

Euhaw Baptist Church
2576 Bees Creek Road | 843-726-3343 | *www.euhawbaptist.org*

Rose Hill Plantation
843-757-6046 | *www.rosehillmansion.com*

Victoria Bluff Heritage Preserve
Sawmill Creek Road and Highway 278 | 843-546-3226, ext. 13
www.dnr.sc.gov/managed/heritage/victoriablf/description.html

Pinckney Island National Wildlife Refuge
Off Highway 278 on the north side of the bridge to Hilton Head Island
843-784-2468 | *www.fws.gov/pinckneyisland*

Hilton Head Island–Bluffton Chamber of Commerce
843-757-1624 | *www.hiltonheadisland.org*

Bull Hill (St. Luke's) Methodist Church
3080 Okatie Highway | 843-705-3022

Savannah National Wildlife Refuge
694 Beech Hill Lane | 843-784-2468 | *www.fws.gov/savannah*

BEGIN TOUR

0.0	**0.0**	*Begin on U.S. 17 South at the south side of the Ashley River bridge.*
53.0	**53.0**	*On right is Sheldon Church Road S-7-21 (see Tour 4). Continue on U.S. 17 South.*

❶ SHELDON CHURCH and **SHERMAN'S MARCH**

Sherman marched through this area, thoroughly destroying it. Just off to our right, he burned Sheldon Church. Between here and the Savannah River, only a handful of buildings were left standing. The army was large, so he broke it into

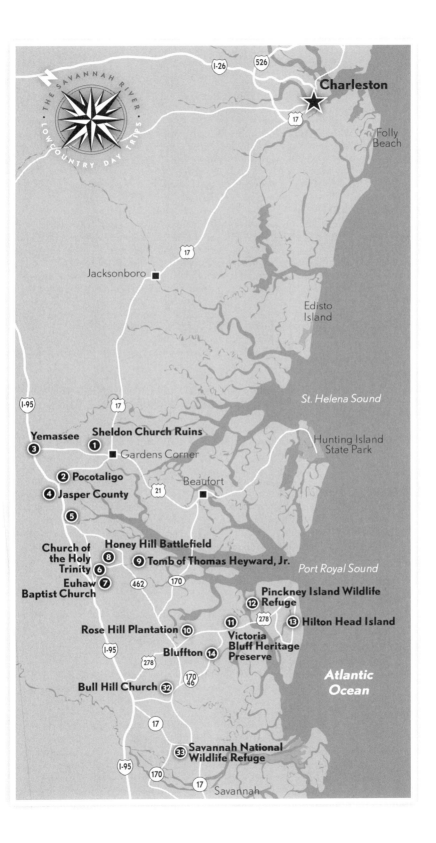

four advancing forces that could supply themselves by following parallel but slightly meandering routes between Savannah and Columbia. Small parties of "bummers" who came and went rode out from these divisions, bringing in food and spreading the path of destruction far wider than the actual march's route. It appears that Sherman knew exactly what he was doing. He bypassed Charleston because there were too many rivers and marshlands to cross.

58.9 5.9   *Arrive at Pocotaligo Community.*

❷ POCOTALIGO

This small rural community was once the chief town of the Yemassee Indians. The Yemassee War began here in 1715, when the Indians surprised and killed one of the most ambitious Indian traders, Thomas Nairne, and about 90 other settlers. During the Revolution the British built Fort Balfour on the opposite side of the Pocotaligo River and surrendered it to Colonel William Harden. Three hundred citizens welcomed George Washington when he toured. The Civil War brought destruction and decline.

59.2 0.3   *At intersection with U.S. 21, continue straight on U.S. 17 South.*

❸ YEMASSEE

Off to our right on U.S. 21, Yemassee began as a railroad stop. NBC newscaster Frank Blair is from this unlikely spot, and even more unlikely, Frank Lloyd Wright built his only Southern plantation house nearby.

59.4 0.2   *Cross Pocotaligo River and enter Jasper County.*

❹ JASPER COUNTY

Formed in 1912, when it separated from Hampton to the north (the vote was 283 to 24), Jasper is our youngest county. In 1877, Yankee railroad directors started the first of the state's shooting preserves here. There were hard feelings at the time, but the outsiders brought "understanding and money." By 1912, these hunting clubs owned much of the land.

60.9 1.5   *U.S. 17 South and I-95 combine; continue south.*
64.8 3.9   *Cross Coosawhatchie River.*

❺ COOSAWHATCHIE

This small rural community also began as an Indian village. A colonial settlement grew up around a bridge, and in 1788 it became the county seat of Beaufort. Unionist James Petigru practiced law here until 1819 and was still alive when the Civil War came. "Everybody in South Carolina has seceded except Petigru," was the popular saying. "South Carolina is too small to be a nation and too large to be an insane asylum," is one version of his reply. This village of a dozen shops and houses never grew appreciably. Prisoners confined to the jail here died of malaria before they could be brought to trial, and those citizens free to walk the streets were often no better off. In 1840, the county seat was moved to the nearby but healthier Gillisonville. Robert E. Lee chose Coosawhatchie for his headquarters during the first months of the war and directed his coastal defenses from this strategic position beside the newly constructed railroad from Savannah to Charleston. As we head toward Ridgeland and Grahamville, we travel in a straight line, following the tracks of a rail line, a constant source of fighting during the Civil War. Coosawhatchie was in Sherman's path, and little survived.

Church of the Holy Trinity.

72.7	7.9	*Veer right at Exit 21 off of I-95.*
73.0	0.3	*At stop sign, turn left onto S.C. 336 East.*
73.5	0.5	*At stop sign, turn right onto S-27-13. Continue straight where S.C. 336 turns left.*
73.8	0.3	*Go straight at this stop sign. You're now in Grahamville. Immediately turn left into parking area of the Church of the Holy Trinity.*

Grahamville
Nearby Ridgeland has nearly swallowed this little village, a situation unthinkable to its earlier inhabitants. At the time of the Revolution, Ridgeland could only boast a tavern—George Allison's Punch House—but it grew as a railroad depot at the expense of the older summer retreat. In turn, Grahamville had grown at the expense of the earlier but unhealthy Euhaw community, which is just down the road. The population peaked when Union troops forced residents away from the Sea Islands. They settled in Grahamville. One little antebellum church survives.

❻ CHURCH OF THE HOLY TRINITY, c. 1855
Open to public.
In 1829, William Heyward donated this crossroad site for the construction of an Episcopal chapel. Twenty-six years later another wealthy planter, James Bolan, funded the construction of this Gothic Revival building. It's unusual for the substantial buttressed bell tower to be off to one side and for the windows and doors to have rounded arches instead of the familiar Gothic points. Union troops carried off the Bible, but it was returned in 1928 and is on display in the vestibule. The chaste white plaster walls and simple altar are surprising and pleasing changes from the dark and ornate interiors of most Gothic construction.

73.8	0.0	*From church parking area, turn left and continue on S-27-13.*
73.9	0.1	*Turn left into Euhaw Baptist Church parking lot.*

❼ EUHAW BAPTIST CHURCH, C. 1907
Not open to public.
Though the building dates only from the last century, this Baptist congregation is far older. It is the second-oldest Baptist organization in the South, dating back to a church of the same name established on Edisto Island in 1686. Euhaw was

one of four churches that formed the Charles Town Baptist Association and was the mother church of the tiny Beaufort congregation. The church moved to this location in the 1740s. During the Civil War, Union troops burned the already abandoned Euhaw building. It was not replaced until half a century later, when the present structure was built. With its towers flanking the entry, the taller one containing the open belfry, it is a pleasing Victorian complement to its Gothic Episcopal neighbor.

73.9	**0.0**	*Turn right from Euhaw Baptist Church parking lot onto S-27-13.*
74.0	**0.1**	*At stop sign, turn right on Old House Road.*
74.3	**0.3**	*At junction of S.C. 336 East, continue straight.*
75.8	**1.5**	*On left, historical marker for Battle of Honey Hill.*

⑧ HONEY HILL BATTLEFIELD, c. 1864
Not open to public.
On November 30, 1864, 5,000 Union troops under General J.G. Foster attempted to sever the railroad connection to Savannah, and thus cause its evacuation. Colonel Charles Colcock stopped them here by setting fire to a field and hastily gathering 1,000 defenders. The Confederates lost about 50 men, the Union about 1,000. It was the last such Rebel victory.

75.8	**0.0**	*Continue on Old House Road.*
78.4	**2.6**	*At stop sign, turn right on S.C. 462 / S.C. 336 East.*
78.5	**0.1**	*On left, historical marker for Thomas Heyward, Jr.*

⑨ TOMB OF THOMAS HEYWARD, JR., c. 1809
Beaufort claims this patriot as her native son, but he's buried on private property at the end of the oak avenue. Thomas Heyward started practicing law in 1771, served on several Revolutionary War councils, and was a delegate to the Continental Congress. He signed the Declaration of Independence when he was only 30. In the years following, he served as a judge and was a founder of the Agricultural Society of South Carolina.

78.5	**0.0**	*Continue on S.C. 462/S.C. 336 East.*
86.1	**7.6**	*At intersection with S.C. 170, turn right.*
90.3	**4.2**	*Turn right onto cloverleaf and merge with U.S. 278 East in the direction of Hilton Head Island.*
94.0	**3.7**	*On left is entrance to Rosehill Plantation.*

⑩ ROSE HILL PLANTATION, c. 1858
Open to public, but call ahead to gain entrance to gated community.
Though there's no definite proof, it seems likely that well-known Charleston architect E.B. White designed this great Gothic Revival house. The owner, Dr. John Kirk, had studied medicine at the University of Pennsylvania and then returned here to practice and grow wealthy as a planter. Begun in 1860, the mansion was never completed and was referred to after the war as "Kirk's Folly." It sat unfinished, slowly deteriorating, until purchased in 1946 and lavishly restored. Steep-roofed and asymmetrical, the building represents a radical departure from the more conventional Greek Revival plantation homes of that area.

I**T**he cabbage palmetto, *Victoria Bluff Heritage Preserve.*

94.0 **0.0**   *Continue on U.S. 278 East.*
97.9 **3.9**   *Turn left on Sawmill Creek Road / S-7-744.*
99.1 **1.2**   *On right, parking area and entrance to*
             Victoria Bluff Heritage Preserve.

⑪ VICTORIA BLUFF HERITAGE PRESERVE

This 1,200-acre property was at first destined to be the site of an industrial development. Strong objections from environmentalists, however, led to the eventual ownership by the South Carolina Marine Resources Department. Two hundred acres went for the Waddell Center, and the remainder was turned over to the Carolina Heritage Trust to administer. It's open for archery hunting for a split two-week season during November and December, so you'll want to avoid that time, but the trail is open the rest of the year. Use a good bug spray and watch out for snakes if they're in season. The property has been cut by fire lines, and it's these that form a number of paths. A main trail rambles along the outer perimeter of the preserve, while several others criss-cross through its center, past pine and saw palmetto flatwoods rarely found this far north. A kiosk at the parking lot contains a laminated map of the area as well as copies you can take with you.

Note the cabbage palmetto at the start. The stems are smooth and the strands ragged, but it is often mistaken for the little saw palmetto (with saw-like stems) that's predominant here.

We start to our right. These are evergreen woods; only the wildflowers, fungus, and mushrooms like the pink russela add a little color. The opening on our left is a depression left by a lime sink. We'll walk through one later. Don't be confused by the ribbons on the trees; deer hunters leave them.

Bear to your left and cross over an Indian midden that's been pushed up in an effort to keep three-wheel vehicles off the trail. There are many such shell piles scattered through the woods. We follow the fire line, veering left past a large live oak. There are more shells and the paths dip into a depression thick with royal and cinnamon ferns. Loblolly pines stand to the left and red maple and tupelo to the right. Black root, native indigo, and blueberry grow here along with pond pine. Look for rusty lyonia—rust-colored on the underside of the leaf—in this typical Florida landscape: This is the only place in the state where it grows. We cross an open, flat area, take the left fork of the trail, and enter a wet area. There's a big live oak on our left and an old fence. We turn left once more and pass a large metal water-monitoring device. A hard left turn carries us into a low bay. The rare pond spice grows here with panic grass, bracken fern, and St. Andrew's cross. You're almost home; turn left on the road and it takes you back to the car.

100.3	**0.0**	*Return to U.S. 278 East, turn left.*
103.1	**2.8**	*Cross first bridge and turn left into Pinckney Island Wildlife Refuge.*
103.2	**0.1**	*On right, historical marker.*
103.6	**0.4**	*Parking lot.*

⑫ PINCKNEY ISLAND WILDLIFE REFUGE

This is one of the best sites for water birds along the coast. Park your car on the first large island and check out the information kiosk in the parking area. Pick up a trail guide and navigate your way on foot or bicycle across 14 miles of nature trails. Interpretive signs dot the first few miles.

The refuge, established in 1975, is actually made up of five small islands surrounded by several thousand acres of marsh. We have access to the largest of these, Pinckney Island. Approximately four miles long, but sometimes no wider than the road, it was the Sea Island cotton plantation of Charles Cotesworth Pinckney.

The original inhabitants preceded Pinckney by as much as 12,000 years and left behind numerous shell middens, some fairly large. The marsh crowds in on every side, but your eye surely will catch the dramatic concentrations of snowy egrets and white ibis. The island, cultivated for 150 years, now grows with wax myrtle and pine. Stuck away inside this growth, five small ponds harbor a variety of wildlife. Don't be confused by the pond names—snowy and cattle egrets, and Louisiana, night, and little blue herons nest in ponds named Osprey and Ibis.

104.1	**0.5**	*Retrace to U.S. 278. (If you would like to see Hilton Head Island, cross U.S. 278 West and turn left on U.S. 278 East. Return to this spot to continue tour.)*

⑬ HILTON HEAD ISLAND

There are several places of interest on Hilton Head Island, among them an old fort on the north end and a small Indian shell ring on the south. However, the traffic is heavy, and there are guarded gates to pass. In the mid-1950s, I crossed here on the ferry *Pocahontas*; I remember only one car on the island and dozens of the now fabled little marsh tacky ponies. But that's another ferry that's come and gone.

104.1	**0.0**	*At stop sign, turn right onto U.S. 278 West.*

118.6	**4.5**	*Turn left at light onto S.C. 46.*
109.4	**0.8**	*At traffic circle, take second right and continue on S.C. 46.*
110.2	**0.8**	*At stop sign, turn right onto May River Road / S.C. 46.*
110.2	**1**blk	*Turn left onto Calhoun Street.*

⑭ BLUFFTON

Other than naming the May River, the French made no other contribution to civilizing the area that would become a summer retreat. The Spanish, however, plotted to keep it in the hands of their Indian allies. After the Yemassee revolt in 1715, the Lords Proprietor divided these "Indian Lands," and Sir John Colleton drew the surrounding Devil's Elbow Barony. His grandson, also Sir John, built plantations at Victoria Bluff and Foot Point. By the time the British destroyed these places in 1779, Colleton already had divided his barony into six tracts, sold them, and died. Benjamin Walls received Bluffton.

Since Sherman's troops destroyed all the Beaufort County records, it's difficult to say exactly who came when. It appears, though, that the Pope and Kirk families sought refuge from malaria here as early as 1800. Other cotton and rice planters

TOUR7 **BLUFFTON**

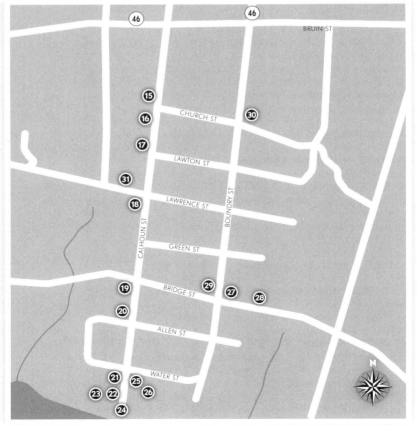

| The People's Store, Bluffton.

from Hilton Head and elsewhere followed, and in the 1830s the streets took shape. The town grew and soon boasted both Episcopal and Methodist churches, a private school, a Masonic lodge, and several stores.

Politics was serious business in the otherwise relaxed community, and in 1844 the "Bluffton Movement" for secession began beneath one of the giant oaks. Robert Barnwell Rhett, the enfant terrible who would grow up to be "the Father of Secession," was its promoter, but the rhetoric faded when secession actually arrived.

During the Civil War, residents evacuated, leaving their homes with furnishing, still in place. Confederate pickets offered token resistance, and in June 1863, 1,000 Union troops in three vessels burned two-thirds of the community. Only 13 homes, eight of which remain, and the two churches were left standing.

In the years following the war, Bluffton grew back as a commercial center with at least seven large general stores on Calhoun Street. The riverboat linked it to the outside world until the completion of the Savannah River Bridge in 1926. Businesses then declined, for customers now drove away for their supplies, but popularity as a summer village increased: Savannah residents could commute. Real prosperity didn't return, however, until the development of Hilton Head and other resort communities.

Bluffton remains a true village; let's take a tour. But first, let me say before going a step farther that I lived here between the ages of 6 and 11 (1950-55), and to make things worse, I've talked over old times with my "Aunt" Anne Bridges, who was also living here then. Trust us; Bluffton is a magical place.

110.2   1st blk   *Look for 20 Calhoun Street, Planter's Mercantile.*

⑮ 20 CALHOUN STREET, Planter's Mercantile, c. 1890
Not open to public.
The Patz brothers, Abram and Moses, built this building. Dry goods, groceries, furniture, buggies, coffins, fixtures, and much, much more could be bought here and at a half-dozen similar stores on this street. When I was a boy, we still slid pennies across the counter here at Planter's in exchange for licorice and hard candies.

110.2   Same blk   *Next door on right is Patz House.*

⑯ 26 CALHOUN STREET, Patz Brothers' House, c. 1892
Not open to public.
The Patz brothers built the Victorian house next to the Mercantile as their residence. Notice the two doors; it's a duplex. A now out-of-print book published by the Bluffton Historical Society, *No. II, A Longer History of Bluffton, S.C., and Its Environs* (referred to here as *The Longer History*), says that the wives of the two brothers feuded and didn't speak to each other for years. Abram accidentally drank carbolic acid when he went to the Mercantile one night looking for an antacid medicine. After that, his brother sold out. The residence is a good example of Folk Victorian architecture.

110.3   Same blk   *Next door on right is Carson House.*

⑰ 38 CALHOUN STREET, Carson Cottage, c. 1868
Open to public.
J.J. Carson built the next house on the right, now a restaurant, low to the ground with a veranda. At the battle of Chancellorsville, Carson rescued the mortally wounded "Stonewall" Jackson and rushed him through enemy lines. Carson also organized the first Baptist church here in 1902.

110.3   **1** blk   *Continue on Calhoun Street. On right at corner of
                            Lawrence and Calhoun streets is The Peoples Store.*

⑱ 56 CALHOUN STREET, The Peoples Store, c. 1904
Open to public.
Next on your right is "The Store" that Jesse Peoples started. He had five children by his first wife and 10 by his second. I think that at least six sons were named after the 12 disciples, and Matthew and Luke ran the store until the early 1950s. The story goes that the hardware stock had been sold down to one of everything, and then the doors locked for good. An itinerant barber came around once a week to scalp us in the shed room on the left. The Store is a gift shop today.

110.3   **1** blk   *On far right corner of the intersection of Calhoun Street
                            and Bridge Street is the Fripp-Lowden House.*

⑲ 80 CALHOUN STREET, The Fripp-Lowden House, c. 1909
Not open to public.
Schoolteacher Sallie Fripp occupied this little house. In the garden she bred the camellia that bears her name. When I was here, her son-in-law, who played the violin beautifully and worked as the town plumber, still occasionally opened the Fripp family store that once stood across the street.

110.3   Same blk   *On right next door is Seven Oaks at
                          corner of Calhoun and Allen streets.*

⑳ 82 CALHOUN STREET, Seven Oaks, c. 1860
Not open to public.
Colonel Middleton Stuart was the first known owner of Seven Oaks, but the family didn't return after the Civil War. In the 1920s, the old summerhouse was operated very successfully as a boardinghouse.

110.4   Nxt blk   *Second house on right of Calhoun Street
                         is Allen-Lockwood House.*

㉑ 94 CALHOUN STREET, Allen-Lockwood House, c. 1850
Not open to public.
This simple summer cottage facing the churchyard was built for William Allen. Colonel Allen had a net worth of $100,000 in 1860 but was bankrupt in 1866. His daughter bought the house at a forced sale for $10.

110.4   Nxt blk   *Next right of Calhoun Street is the Church of the Cross.*

㉒ 110 CALHOUN STREET, Church of the Cross, c. 1857
Grounds open to public.
Charleston architect E.B. White designed the church, but the tower and vestibule of his plan were omitted with pleasing results. Carpenter Gothic is the style, one favored for Episcopal construction for the rest of the century. This one, however, is

unusually large, cruciform, and noted for its rose-colored lancet windows.

Armed with her great ear trumpet, "Miss Susie" defended the front pew against all comers, new and old, and we children were expected to memorize a Bible verse every week. "God is love" and "Jesus wept" were passable and well-worn responses. Our betters told us that the Union fired on the church and it was saved by the Rebels, but the Yankee report says it was intentionally spared. No tombstones or memorials are in sight—just an ancient marble-based sundial that promises, "I count only sunny hours."

110.4   ½ blk   *Walk into the parking area just behind the church and go to the corner. Stop and look to your left.*

㉓ 9 WATER STREET, Huger-Gordon House, c. 1795
Not open to public.
From the corner of the parking lot, you can see the Huger-Gordon House, which faces the May River. Judged by the brickwork, some portions have been dated back to 1795. That makes it the oldest house in town, as well as the only waterfront home to survive the Union invasion. Minié balls lodged in the doorframe give evidence of its narrow escape.

110.4   50 ft   *At end of Calhoun Street is Steamboat Landing.*

㉔ STEAMBOAT LANDING
The steamboat docked here at the end of Calhoun Street, an occasion of great celebration in its day. In *Bluffton Boy*, Andrew Peoples describes how the whistle of the Beaufort boat brought out the excited multitudes, and he, forgetting that he was in charge of his little sister Mildred, rushed to join them. The unattended baby carriage went careening down this bluff, to be stopped at the last moment.

110.4   Same blk   *Across street from church is Squire Pope House.*

㉕ 111 CALHOUN STREET, Squire Pope's Summer House, c. 1850
Not open to public.
Actually, this is only the carriage house and another small building combined to make a home for the impoverished widow of one of Hilton Head's wealthiest planters. All we have to judge the original Pope summerhouse by are these outbuildings and the garden, which still survive.

110.4   0.0   *Behind Squire Pope House is Dr. Jakey's office site.*

㉖ DR. JAKEY'S OFFICE SITE
My Aunt Anne tells of a young man going to have his tooth pulled and finding Dr. Jakey stirring a pot of grits over an open fire. The good dentist would pull on the tooth awhile, and stir awhile, and pull, and stir, until the grits were done and the tooth came out at the same time. That was a half-century before my time, but I keep thinking of the long-abandoned dentist's office being here just beyond the Squire Pope House. (Aunt Anne says that it was a half-mile upstream.) Anyway, I'm certain of this: There was a four-hole outhouse for the patients—four holes cut in the shape of a club, a diamond, a heart, and a spade. And when the office collapsed, it left a grandly mechanical dentist's chair exposed to the weather and encircled by vines.

110.4   0.0   *Continue on Calhoun Street.*
110.5   2 blks   *Turn right onto Bridge Street / S-7-13.*
110.5   1 blk   *At 4-way stop, cross Boundary Street / S-7-66. On your left is the Fripp House.*

㉗ 48 BRIDGE STREET, The Fripp House, c. 1835
Not open to public.
A Pope, not a Fripp, built this distinctive two-story frame house. An unusual combination of raised cottage faced with Federalist portico, the great rambling house sits on particularly high brick pillars, which perhaps helped it catch the breeze. The Sams family bought it from the Popes and sold it to the Fripps, who held onto it for 34 years.

110.5   Same blk   *Next door on left is The Card House.*

㉘ 34 BRIDGE STREET, The Card House, c. 1825
Not open to public.
Next on your left is an equally rambling structure of unknown origin. Legend calls it the oldest house in town, but it doesn't show up in the records until 1847. The name "Card House" supposedly comes from a high-stakes poker game played here in which William Eddings Baynard won a 1,000-acre Hilton Head plantation from John Stoney. Miss Hattie Colquitt, a later owner, suggested instead that it got its name because it looked like a house children would build with a pack of playing cards. It does.

110.5   1 blk   *Cross bridge, turn around, retrace*
Bridge Street one block. Turn right
onto Boundary Street / S-7-66.
On left is the Heyward House.

㉙ 70 BOUNDARY STREET, The Heyward House, c. 1840
Not open to public.
Wealthy May River planter John Cole built this home in the Carolina or Summer Cottage style. Now the welcome center for the Bluffton Historic District, it remains mostly unchanged. In the back you can spot a small, clay-floored kitchen and a one-room slave house.

110.6   4 blks   *Cross Church Street/S-7-299.*
On right is the Campbell Chapel AME Church.

㉚ 23 BOUNDARY STREET, Campbell Chapel AME Church, c. 1853
Not open to public.
The Longer History says it was built by the Methodists, which is probably so, but my Aunt Anne says Miss Heyward (the resident of the last house) told her it was a Camolite church at one time, and the name seems to bear that out. Probably Methodist and Camolite both, this little building was empty by 1874 and was given to the African Methodist Episcopalians (AME), who held services there for another century. The simple Greek Revival design was a popular one of the day, but here the siding is board and batten rather than the traditional horizontal type.

Campbell Chapel AME Church, Bluffton.

110.6	**0.0**	*Continue on Boundary Street.*
110.6	**1** blk	*At stop sign, turn left onto May River Road / S.C. 46.*
110.7	**1** blk	*Turn left onto Calhoun Street.*
117.0	**3** blks	*Turn right onto Lawrence Street / S-7-377.*
117.0	**½** blk	*On right is The John Seabrook House.*

㉛ 47 LAWRENCE STREET, The John A. Seabrook House, c. 1850s
Not open to public.
Probably built by Edisto planter John Seabrook in the 1850s, this house fell into Yankee hands in 1876, when the postmaster bought it. A typical raised cottage, it is well preserved and unchanged—something that could be said for this whole unchanging little village. Except that, in 1953, a two-wagon medicine show came this way and set up on the far side of Calhoun Street. It was run out of town on the fourth night. Soon after, a family living a block over on Boundary Street got a television set. We were all invited in to look at the set—which wasn't actually turned on—and to see the collapsible TV tables that they ate on. The rest is history, or at least what passes for it.

110.7	**0.0**	*Turn around.*
110.8	**½** blk	*At stop sign, turn left onto Calhoun Street.*
110.8	**3** blks	*At stop sign, turn left onto May River Road / S.C. 46.*
116.9	**6.1**	*Turn right onto Gibbet Road / S-7-34.*
118.1	**1.2**	*At stop sign, turn right onto*
		Okatie Highway / S.C. 170.
119.6	**1.5**	*Turn left into St. Luke's parking area.*

㉜ BULL HILL METHODIST CHURCH (ST. LUKE'S), c. 1821
Grounds open to public.
John Bull gave a four-acre site for the construction of an Episcopal church in 1786. The first Bull Hill church was gone by 1821, though, and workers erected the present one nearby. The Civil War ended services, and in 1875, the Methodists bought the church and still worship here. A neat little Greek Revival-style meetinghouse, it's surrounded by some interesting graves, among them that of Dr. J.H. Mellinchamp.

119.6	**0.0**	*Return to road and turn right on Okatie Highway / S.C. 170.*
122.3	**2.7**	*At traffic circle, turn right onto S.C. 170 West / S.C. 46.*
124.1	**1.8**	*Cross New River Bridge.*
124.6	**0.5**	*Turn right on S.C. 170 West.*
127.7	**3.1**	*At stop sign, turn left onto S.C. 170 West.*
128.4	**0.7**	*At stop sign, cross near land and*
		turn left onto U.S. 17 South.
129.6	**1.2**	*Bear right onto U.S. 17 South.*
		(Do not take U.S. 17 South A.)
132.1	**2.5**	*Turn left into Savannah National Wildlife Refuge Drive.*

㉝ SAVANNAH NATIONAL WILDLIFE REFUGE
Stop first at the visitor center, opened in March 2009, to use the facilities, gather information about the refuge, and watch a video introduction to the more than 29,000 acres that compose the refuge. About half of it is freshwater marshlands, 3,000 acres of which is diked and accessible to hikers during daylight hours. Four miles are set aside for automobile touring.

A Note About the Wildlife

Opportunities for sighting wildlife in the refuge abound, especially water birds and alligators. Be very wary of the latter, as they lie motionless in the sun. Appearances to the contrary, they can move like a flash if they see prey or if they're frightened.

Birding is good here year-round. Migration happens in October and April, but full winter ponds provide ducks with good habitat during the colder months. It's considered one of the best spots for watching canvasbacks, ringnecks, widgeon, brant, and shore birds.

|Vast expanses at the Savannah National Wildlife Reserve once were rice fields.

The Laurel Hill Wildlife Drive

This one-way, 4-mile drive meanders about the impoundments of four early rice plantations and offers a simultaneous look at the wetlands. I made this trip in early September with my father, who worked out of the Savannah Refuge as a wildlife biologist between 1948 and 1955. As on all our trips together, he's the naturalist, but on this one he adds bits of refuge lore as well.

Developed by expanding South Carolina planters, rice cultivation came relatively late to the Savannah River region. By the time of the Civil War, though, it rivaled even the incredible output of the Georgetown fields. Still, it was a frontier of sorts, and the homes were usually modest, like the one that stood on this knoll at Laurel Hill. Although Sherman's troops burned other nearby houses, they mysteriously left this little neighborhood intact. Nevertheless, the dwellings of the owners and slaves, and the mills and barns, are all gone today.

After passing ruins from a former mill, now covered by vegetation and not marked because of vandalism, we spy evidence of modern industry on the far bank of the river. Water and air are constantly monitored for the protection of wildlife, and people. As you drive, look at both sides of the dike. That's tidal on your right, usually brackish with a low salt content, but the water's fresh on left. Wild rice, no relation to the domestic variety, shows its yellow-green seeds above a sea of cattail and cut-grass. Each pond is managed differently. Good duck foods grow here— smartweed and giant foxtail (easy to spot, for it looks like a fox's tail).

Look for the old wooden structure on your right. Though it served as a bridge, it was actually a water-control structure built in the early days of the Refuge. Flash boards were placed in or taken out of the slots so that large amounts of water could be moved. It was not just a spillway: If a hurricane or a freshet threatened to cover the dikes, water was allowed in so that the pressure on both sides of the embankments would equalize.

Grape, mulberry, chinaberry, and morning glory crowd the roadway here along with the prettiest of marsh plants, the cardinal flower.

Note the tropical cattail to your right. The spike is taller and lighter than the common cattail we've seen up until now. On the left, another good duck food, giant cut-grass, is going to seed. And on the dike itself, ragweed and pokeberry. No trees grow here. Now, as in antebellum days, trees were discouraged because their roots would cut through the earth and cause leaks. Only cypress roots and stumps remain.

Beyond these, workers established an old bulkhead, a fix for a soft spot in the land when it couldn't be diked. From here, we enter a small island thick with yaupon and canopied with live oaks. A short handicapped-accessible trail extends into these areas.

We've entered Recess Plantation. The brick cistern to our left is thought to have provided drinking water for the slaves quartered on this knoll. Usually, they dug wells, but in this case, it must have been necessary to connect guttering to the roof edges of the cabins. Please don't touch the bricks. A short nature walk starts here if you want to hike a bit.

Once off the island, impoundments line both sides. Ahead is a broad freshwater canal that the Army Corps of Engineers built in an attempt to deepen the main Savannah River channel and prevent saltwater from coming in.

After spying a few birds and alligators, including an eight-footer that was lurking around the bend, we start back toward the highway. When you return to U.S. 17, a long day is coming to a close, and Charleston beckons.

132.1	**0.0**	*At exit gate from Refuge, turn right onto U.S. 17 North.*
136.1	**4.0**	*Continue on U.S. 17 North.*
139.6	**3.5**	*Turn right onto I-95 North cloverleaf.*
167.5	**27.9**	*Veer right at Exit 33 onto U.S. 17 North and continue on this route to Charleston.*
228.7	**61.2**	*Arrive at south side of Ashley River Bridge.*

END TOUR

Four Hole Swamp to Jacksonboro

TOUR EIGHT

FOUR HOLE SWAMP to JACKSONBORO

This is a five-star trip for naturalists, with a wonderful blend for historians as well. First, we travel about 45 minutes north of Charleston to the **Audubon Center at Beidler Forest**. Then we pass along **historic railroad tracks** and through the little station town of **St. George** to reach **Indian Field**, the earliest Methodist campground and tabernacle in the country. Next, there's **Colleton State Park**, where we can picnic beside the Edisto River. Then, it's on to **Walterboro**, an antebellum pineland village grown larger, but still rich in lovely homes and public buildings. Heading back to Charleston, we pass the **Pon Pon Chapel** ruins, the ancient **Bethel Presbyterian Church Burial Ground**, and the **tomb of a Revolutionary War martyr, Isaac Hayne**. We end the day at the **Edisto Nature Trail**.

Audubon Center at Francis Beidler Forest
    336 Sanctuary Road | 843-462-2150
    www.sc.audubon.org/Centers_FBF.html
    Admission charged.

St. George
    843-563-9091 | *www.visitstgeorgesc.com*

Indian Field Campground
    Off Highway 15 at Indian Field Circle

Colleton State Park
    147 Wayside Lane | (843) 538-8206
    www.southcarolinaparks.com/park-finder/state-park/1876.aspx

Walterboro
    843-549-9595 | *www.walterboro.org*

Parker's Ferry Battle Site
    Off S.C. 64 at Parker's Ferry Road

Pon Pon Chapel of Ease Ruins
    Parker's Ferry Road

Tomb of Colonel Isaac Hayne
    Off Highway 64 on Parkers Ferry Road | 843-538-8206
    www.southcarolinaparks.com/product.aspx?productId=3567

Edisto Nature Trail
    Off U.S 17 North, near Old Jacksonboro marker

BEGIN TOUR

0.0	**0.0**	*Leave Charleston on I-26 West and start mileage at intersection of U.S. 17.*
33.0	**3.0**	*Exit right at Exit 187, Ridgeville—St. George Exit.*
33.3	**0.3**	*At exit stop sign, turn left onto S.C. 27 / Ridgeville Road.*
34.4	**1.1**	*At first stop sign, turn right onto U.S. 78 West.*
36.9	**1.7**	*First bridge crosses a section of Four Hole Swamp which, downstream, becomes Francis Beidler Forest.*

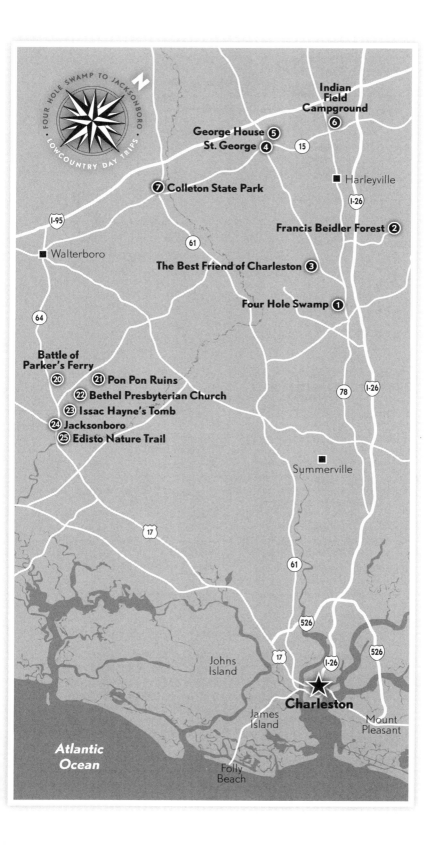

❶ FOUR HOLE SWAMP

Technically, Four Hole is a swamp-stream, an arm of the Edisto River just off to our left, and black water flows through it at a perceptible rate. Some scientists think wind and the tide of the receding Atlantic Ocean carved out the swamp's basin, usually no wider than a mile and a half, but a ridge of limestone close by the Edisto River keeps the drainage partly blocked. At times, the water here rises as high as 3½ feet.

On our way there, we travel through one of the few Lowcountry areas that was never divided into plantations. Farmers worked the land, or it simply remained wilderness. In fact, a small tribe of Edisto Indians still lives nearby. As you can imagine, parties on both sides of the Revolution fought over this bridge site on U.S. 78 several times. To early travelers, the bridge was a necessity, because the 60-mile-wide swamp proved a considerable barrier.

37.0	0.1	*Fork right onto U.S. 178 West/East Main Street.*
37.7	0.7	*Turn right onto Beidler Forest Road / S-18-28.*
41.8	4.1	*Bear straight onto Mims Road when S-18-28 curves sharply to left.*
42.8	1.0	*Turn right through Francis Beidler Forest entrance gates onto Sanctuary Road.*
43.7	0.9	*Arrive at Francis Beidler Forest parking lot.*

❷ FRANCIS BEIDLER FOREST

The entrance to the forest begins between two fields and then runs through a second-growth forest, all of which seems typical of much of the state, but just ahead a unique experience awaits. Francis Beidler Forest is the largest remaining virgin stand of bald cypress and tupelo gum trees in the world—a treasure owned by the National Audubon Society.

We begin our visit inside the Audubon Center, where staff members and displays interpret the swamp habitat and inhabitants. I highly recommend that you sit down at one of the interactive, touch-screen computers and preview what you might see before taking your walk.

Before embarking on the 1.75 miles of boardwalk trail that circles through the uncut cypress and tupelo stand, we borrow a helpful handbook to guide us through only a small portion of the 1,700 acres. Numbers on the handrail correspond to the numbers in the printed guide. Educational spurs lead off the main boardwalk to interpretive sites that discuss the swamp's aquatic insects and fish, or the features of an old-growth forest.

Together, my father, an Audubon Society staffer, and I start on high ground, but looking ahead we see a descent and a rapid shift in vegetation. The amount of time water stands in a particular place determines what will grow there, a fact that becomes more evident as we stroll first among loblolly pines, named for the loblollies or low spots where the first settlers found them growing. Pond pines grow here as well. More susceptible to fire, they can't thrive as the loblollies do on the often-burnt uplands. We pass quickly downhill into the hardwood flats, and note the lichens and fungus that appear as colorful spots among the decaying browns of the forest stumps and branches. On this hot July morning, the swamp is dry in most places. There's scat on the walk and a variety of tracks in the mud. We come upon wrens, cardinals, and even a deer. Alligators, turtles, and an anhinga crowd Goodson Lake, but we don't spot the impressive pileated woodpeckers, prothonotary warblers, or any of the more retiring residents.

As we drop down a three-foot incline that brings us to the swamp bottom, the vegetation thins until finally three tree species remain, and these for the most part are above our heads. That's water ash on the bottom (understory), tupelo next (midstory), and cypress above (overstory). On the coast, salt dictates what survives,

Francis Beidler Forest
These great swamp forests once ran throughout the coastal plain, but early settlers clear-cut and burned them to make inland rice fields. After the Civil War, loggers heavily lumbered the unburned areas. Francis Beidler was one of these early lumbermen. He bought this section in the 1890s and, being one of the few conservationists of his day, simply held onto the land without cutting the trees. His family continued to preserve the forest, and when the estate was liquidated, their cooperation and gifts made possible the construction of the visitors' facilities, now the Audubon Center.

Bald Cypress

Towering as high as 120 feet, each bald cypress is supported at the bottom by a swelling butt (21 feet for one of these) and a root system that spreads out 100 feet wide. These tangling roots pop up as strange knees. Most of the knees are small, knobby wooden stalagmites that rise the water level and then stop, but in places, they grow monstrous. One knee is as big as a human and because of its distinctly human shape is named "the Madonna." These growths may help the trees breathe, but there's no proof of this, and the tree will continue to live even if the knees are cut off (they are at Cypress Gardens). They do, however, stabilize the tree. The deeper the water, the more knees and the thicker the butt, and even in the softest spots, these giants don't blow over.

but here it's simply water. As long as man doesn't interfere, the best-adapted plant life is obviously the great bald cypress. Lightning and old age are the main enemies now that man is no longer a threat. Indeed, the principal feeling of the swamp is one of ancient growth and gradual decay.

In the driest of times, fire may rage, but for the most part the fungus and molds are left to work away at the fallen, slowly rotting trees. In these spots we see red maples or sweetgum sprouting well beyond their upland bounds. It's not all cypress after all: The tupelos are almost as grand. A tiny green fly orchid may not be quite so majestic, but it has found a foothold, and we're in luck for it only blooms during the summer.

We pass along the creek's edge and then visit the lake, where an observation tower enables viewers to spot turtles, fish, and possibly the lake's resident alligator. Gradually, we circle up toward higher ground. Our guide, a basket maker in his spare time, points out the vine supplejack weavers use. The conversation turns to what cypress is worth: We all happen to be fans of good wood. Cypress was and continues to be prized for interior paneling and exterior siding. Now, real knot-free "black" cypress can't be bought. It takes 300 to 500 years to grow trees like the ones we've just passed, and some here date to 1,000 years. Unfortunately, none of us can wait around quite that long. We spot a doe that's come searching for a drink of water, and then it's up the hill and out.

43.7	0.0	*From parking area, retrace to entrance gates of Francis Beidler Forest.*
44.6	0.9	*Turn left onto Mims Road.*
45.6	1.0	*At stop sign, go straight onto Beidler Forest Road / S-18-28.*
49.7	4.1	*At stop sign, turn left onto U.S. 178 East.*
50.4	0.7	*At stop sign, turn right onto U.S. 78 West.*
54.0	3.6	*Look to left at railroad tracks that run parallel to U.S. 78.*

❸ THE BEST FRIEND OF CHARLESTON

Once we've passed through the crossroads of Dorchester, the Norfolk Southern Railroad tracks parallel the highway on the left. They originally served the South Carolina Railroad Company as the Charleston to Hamburg line. Completed in 1833, its 136-mile course made it the longest railroad in the world. The purpose was to rescue Charleston from the competition of Savannah by siphoning off cotton being grown inland of Augusta. Needless to say, Georgia wasn't interested in sharing her newfound wealth. The railroad didn't show much profit, but it was a great convenience to the inland planters of Carolina, who for the most part welcomed its coming.

The Best Friend of Charleston was the first American-made locomotive for public service. It was probably the first to blow up, too, which it did when the fireman sat on the annoying steam-release valve soon after service began. Passenger service was not all that could be desired, but it was soon putting towns like Summerville, St. George, and Branchville on the map.

63.9	9.9	*In downtown St. George, turn right at stoplight onto Parler Avenue / U.S. 15 North.*

❹ ST. GEORGE

St. George was named for its first settler, James George. Though the town was first called George's Turnout and then George's Station, the "Saint" was added because it originally had been part of St. George's Dorchester Parish. In those early days, it prospered as a depot and water stop, but incorporation didn't come until 1874. By then cotton farming had revived, and a large lumber mill made good use of the railroad. The great Victorian houses date from this period, and there's a courthouse built when Dorchester was separated from Colleton County in the 1890s. The main street, U.S. 15 or Parler Avenue, wasn't paved until 1930, so until then they raced horses here on the Fourth of July.

64.2 0.3   *Four blocks on left is 609 Parler Avenue, at corner of Minus Street.*

❺ 609 PARLER AVENUE, The George House, c. 1851
Not open to public.
This is the only antebellum house remaining here. In 1847, Bishop William Capers founded a Methodist church in St. George, a log building close to the railroad. James George donated the land for the church and went to Charleston and bought a Bible for it. There was a time when you couldn't go five miles here without hitting a Methodist church or finding a child who was named after a Methodist preacher. Well, that may be an exaggeration, but there's no denying that the state's first bishop, Francis Asbury, and his circuit riders found a willing audience here, which brings us to our next stop.

64.2 0.0   *Continue on U.S. 15 North.*
66.8 2.6   *Turn left onto Indian Field Circle / S-18-73.*
67.3 0.5   *Turn right on Asbury Drive to circle Indian Field campground.*

❻ INDIAN FIELD CAMPGROUND, c. 1848
Open to public.
Early Methodist circuit riders preached beneath crude brush "arbors" and then in "pole churches." Indian Field, however, contains a tabernacle, the oldest such structure in the United States. Here the place of worship expanded to become a tremendous open-sided shelter for those gathered at week-long "camp meetings."

The idea must have spread quickly, for Bishop Asbury himself preached at Indian Fields in 1801. The spot may have shifted a few hundred yards since then, but by 1848, the meeting place had taken on its present form. The tabernacle is basically unchanged. Modern shingles have replaced wooden ones, however.

Indian Field Campground.

The floor has always been dirt. The benches are a modern luxury. At one time the worshippers brought their own seats or stood—men to one side of the aisle, women to the other, and slaves to the rear.

Ninety-nine equally rustic cabins' or "tents" form a circle about the tabernacle. (The good shepherd had saved the 99 sheep but still searched for the 100th that was lost.) With dirt floors, and ventilation strips in place of windows, the narrow buildings are similar, barnlike constructions. Studs and clapboard siding show on the interior—guests sleep in a second-story loft. It is doubtful they are as old as the tabernacle, but some still contain axe-hewn beams and poles, and the design is repeated even if the building is torn down completely and replaced.

The increase of creature comforts is something of a joke with the old-time campers. Wooden pallets and old springs have supplanted piles of straw on the floor. Cooking is now done on "cook furnaces" —homemade barbecue grills with chimneys—instead of open fires or Dutch ovens. There are outhouses across the road from each cabin. Light bulbs are a luxury—some cabins have as many as four—as are refrigerators.

The empty campground, of course, can't do justice to a full one. In 1878, "meeting week" was set the week of the first Sunday in October, and this practice continues. Visitors of any denomination are invited to worship, sing, and enjoy the fellowship.

67.7	0.4	*Complete circle of Indian Field campground, return to cabin 9; go straight onto S-18-73.*
68.2	0.5	*At stop sign, turn right onto U.S. 15 South, return to St. George.*
71.2	3.0	*At intersection of U.S. 15 and U.S. 78 in St. George, continue straight on U.S. 15 South.*
79.5	8.3	*Right of U.S. 15 South, sand pits and Canady Stream Plant towers. As we reach the river basin of the Edisto, there are sand mining operations. Ahead is a small state park that's just down the road—and river—from the nearby Canady Stream Generator.*
80.0	0.5	*Cross Edisto River.*
80.3	0.3	*Turn right into entrance of Colleton State Park.*

❼ COLLETON STATE PARK
The park has a nature trail running through a thick grove of loblollies and dogwood. Picnickers, swimmers, kayakers, and campers are accommodated, and the park is midway along the Edisto Canoe Trail—an organized project of the state parks system. It's also a great place to drop a line for bass, catfish, crappie, and beautiful redbreasts.

80.3	0.0	*After visiting state park, return to U.S. 15, turn right onto U.S. 15 South.*
84.6	4.3	*On right, Island Creek Meeting House historic marker.*
90.4	5.8	*Arrive at Walterboro city limits. U.S. 15 becomes North Jefferies Blvd.*
91.7	1.3	*Turn right onto Benson Street. Park on street.*

Walterboro's History
Up until 1783, Paul and Jacob Walter had spent their summers in nearby Jackson-borough, but gradually malaria had reduced Paul's family to a single child, and now his wife appeared to be dying as well. Traveling inland for 18 miles, the two brothers found a high, sandy hill beside a deep, hickory-filled valley. They built two-room log cabins and moved their families here. The place proved safe and others followed.

Local historian Beulah Glover found this 1800 source that gives a rare glimpse of "democratic" frontier summer camping.

In order to guarantee social union luxury was discouraged. The houses were of logs, merely barked and lined with clap board ... no frame house, no iron in the building, wooden hinges, shingle roofs ... chimeneys [sic] were made of logs well covered with clay, tables of pine yet how comfortable

*did we make these houses; a little taste and a contented heart made them
as neat and pleasant as a splendid mansion.*

The same writer goes on to describe roads and paths cut between the homes,
with nightly fires burning on the tops of tree stumps serving as street lamps.
Supplies were brought the 16 miles from the Pon Pon or Jacksonborough area,
and a beef was killed and shared each week. In addition, a single store's second
story served as a meetinghouse for traveling preachers, and as a community
center and ballroom the rest of the week. It was an idyllic situation, the writer said,
and added an unusual architectural note on the cabins.

*This little community lived in great unanimity. The refreshing scent of the
pine ... so thick a wood preserved a constant shade and a healthy fragrance.
Having no glazed windows a wide bush shed surrounded the house, kept us
cool and rendered it unnecessary to close the wooden shutters during rain.*

After the first frost, this community dissolved, and its members returned to their
plantation homes, but in 1817 the county seat was placed here, and by 1830,
changes had occurred. The town still centered about the valley, which was considered
its true heart, but the summer population had swelled to 900. There was a
courthouse, a jail, three churches, a market, and a male and female academy. Greek
Revival mansions, or at least substantial raised cottages, replaced log cabins, but
then the turmoil of the nationwide nullification debate disturbed the tranquil village.
Let's take a walk and see what remains.

91.7   0.0   *To left of 109 Benson Street facing Jefferies
Boulevard is Old Colleton County Jail.*

⑧ CORNER OF JEFFERIES BOULEVARD and BENSON STREET
The Old Colleton County Jail, c. 1856
Colleton Museum & Gift Shop.
Charleston's leading architects, Lee and Jones, designed this miniature castle
with parapet—a Gothic Revival façade no doubt considered appropriate for a jail.
A modern renovation changed the interior, but you can appreciate it just as well
from the street. Now it houses the Colleton Museum & Gift Shop and Walterboro-
Colleton Chamber of Commerce.

TOUR 8 **WALTERBORO**

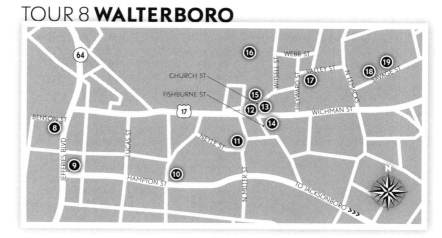

91.7	**0.0**	*Turn around and return to Jefferies Boulevard. At stop sign, turn right.*
91.8	**2** blks	*Turn left onto Hampton Street; on left is Colleton County Court House.*

Colleton County Court House, Walterboro.

❾ CORNER OF JEFFERIES BOULEVARD and HAMPTON STREET
Colleton County Court House, c. 1822
Public offices.

Approach the courthouse from Hampton Street to appreciate the portico designed by South Carolina's first and best-known architect, Robert Mills. The original building is only the center part, which bears a strong resemblance to Mills's Fireproof Building in Charleston. In 1822, this was the extreme eastern edge of a town centered on Old Hickory Valley. Appropriately placed by the steps is the Confederate Monument, found in all older county seats.

Antebellum Homes
Traveling along Hampton Street, we pass a variety of distinctive antebellum and Victorian homes. By the mid-1890s, the town had the biggest railroad depot on the Savannah to Charleston line. Sawmills and farming brought a renewed prosperity. The business district shifted to its present location a block over to our left. We cross Memorial Avenue, earlier known as Railroad Avenue, where some of the finer and fashionable homes still stand.

91.8	**0.0**	*Continue on Hampton Street.*
92.1	**3** blks	*As you cross Memorial Avenue, look to left to see Walterboro Water Tower.*

❿ WALTERBORO WATER TOWER, c. 1915
Not open to public.
This 133-foot landmark is constructed of concrete and holds 100,000 gallons of water. The small slits are windows.

92.2	**1** blk	*Turn left onto North Miller Street.*
92.3	**1** blk	*On left at corner of North Miller and Neyle streets is the Methodist Church.*

⓫ CORNER OF MILLER and NEYLE STREETS
Fishers of Men Total Deliverance Ministry
Not open to public.
During its lifetime, this once simple meetinghouse structure has been an Independent Methodist church and a Baptist church. In fact, it is sometimes referred to as the "Old" First Baptist Church.

Hickory Valley
We've reached the original Hickory Valley settlement area. Early residents measured out from the Little Library here three-quarters of a mile in every direction to design the town, so this was both literally and symbolically the center

Library Society and Bedon-Lucas House.

of the community. In 1879, a tornado destroyed the church and many early houses, and uprooted the trees that had shaded the citizens for almost a century.

92.4	1 blk	*At stop sign, turn right onto Wichman Street / U.S. 17A.*
92.5	1 blk	*Turn left onto Fishburne Street and park. On left is Walterboro Library.*

⑫ 803 WICHMAN STREET, Walterboro Library Society, c. 1820
Open to public.
The Little Library survived a tornado, but actually it has been moved since then from the spot on our right now occupied by St. Jude's Church.

92.5	0.0	*To right facing Fishburne Street is St. Jude's Episcopal Church.*

⑬ 907 WICHMAN STREET, St. Jude's Episcopal Church, c. 1882.
Open to public.
The Episcopalians built this Carpenter Gothic church to replace the one destroyed by the cyclone.

92.5	0.0	*Look to right across Wichman Street to St. Peter's AME Church, which faces Fishburne Street.*

⑭ 902 WICHMAN STREET, St. Peter's AME Church, c. 1900
Not open to public.
This striking Gothic Revival building was constructed only a few years after its Episcopal neighbor.

92.5	0.0	*Look behind Library Society Building to 205 Church Street.*

⑮ 205 CHURCH STREET, The Bedon-Lucas House, c. 1820
Open to public.
The large columned home built by Richard Bedon, now home to the Colleton County Historical and Preservation Society, was one of the few in the immediate neighborhood to survive the cyclone. Bedon donated the land for the library.

92.5	0.0	*Continue on Fishburne Street.*
92.5	1 blk	*At stop sign, turn right onto Church Street.*
92.6	1 blk	*Turn left onto Witsell Street / S-15-240.*
92.6	½ blk	*On left is Hickory Valley.*

⑯ THE REAL HICKORY VALLEY

Walters and the others first settled around this deep, tree-filled ravine to the left, Hickory Valley.

92.6	½ blk	*Turn right onto Webb Street / S-15-291.*
92.7	**1** blk	*Turn right onto Heyward Street / S-15-290.*
92.8	**1** blk	*Turn left onto Valley Street / S-15-289.*
		On right is The Klein-Patterson House.

⑰ 104 VALLEY STREET, **The Klein-Patterson House**, c. 1824

Not open to public.
This Greek Revival house originally had double piazzas, now replaced with great columns. Either version is a far cry from the "democratic" log structures that served for the first summer camping. The commercial district shifted as well, for the town's first drugstore was on this lot.

92.8	**0.0**	*Continue on Valley Street / S-15-289.*
92.9	**1** blk	*At stop sign, turn right onto North Lemacks Street / 15-152.*
92.9	**1** blk	*Turn left onto Savage Street / S-15-79.*
		On left is The Glover-McLeod House.

⑱ 109 SAVAGE STREET, **The Glover-McCleod House**, c. 1824

Not open to public.
Locals dubbed this great house surrounded by a camellia garden "Mounds" because the owner buried two white horses on either side of the entry.

93.0	½ blk	*Next door on left is Perry-Smoak-Lubs House.*

⑲ 125 SAVAGE STREET, THE PERRY-SMOAK-LUBS HOUSE, c. 1814

Not open to public.
The next house, also garden-surrounded, is a raised cottage. Architecturally, this was the transition between cabin and mansion. Building high off the ground put the residents above the mosquitoes.

93.2	**1** blk	*At stop sign, turn right onto U.S. 17A / South Wichman Street. As we travel U.S. 17A / South Wichman Street, we'll pass several more antebellum raised cottages and some larger Victorian homes.*
94.0	**13** blks	*Turn left onto Lucas Street.*
94.2	**2** blks	*At second stop sign, turn left onto Hampton Street.*

The Road to Jacksonboro

Locals tell a story of a famed prankster who dragged a dead fox through a church on Saturday night, then loosed his dogs to run wild through the congregation the following morning. A far more serious "joke" got him run out of town soon after, but we're leaving of our own free will. The road we're on leads to Jacksonboro. Several historical markers dot the roadside, but sometimes you have to look closely for them.

95.1	**0.9**	*Arrive at junction with S.C. 64 and take S.C. 64 East.*
106.5	**11.4**	*Turn left onto Parker's Ferry Road at historic marker for Battle of Parker's Ferry.*

⑳ BATTLE OF PARKER'S FERRY

The battle wasn't actually fought here, and there's nothing to see, but shortly after the death of Colonel Hayne (next marker), Francis Marion arrived to aid Colonel Harden. The British had confiscated the area's rice and were landing at the nearby ferry. With 400 men, Marion waited at the causeway and ambushed a force of 540 Hessians, British, and Tories. Beaten badly, the enemy withdrew to Dorchester and then to Charleston. There had been at least a half dozen other skirmishes and battles in the area, but this one, coming shortly after Colonel Hayne's execution and just before the Yorktown surrender, is noted as an important psychological victory for the Americans.

107.3	**0.8**	*At stop sign, cross S-15-40 and continue on Parker's Ferry Road briefly.*
107.4	**0.1**	*Turn right into churchyard at ruins of Pon Pon Chapel of Ease.*

㉑ PON PON CHAPEL OF EASE RUINS, c. 1754
Open to public.

In 1725, this parish received an Angelican chapel of ease, but the present ruins dates from 1753. It burned sometime between 1796 and 1806, and is still known as "the Burnt Church." Worshippers must have considered the building, with its distinctly marked water table, arched windows, and unusual Jacobean gables, grand for a mere chapel, but not much remains. A dozen old gravestones, some dating from the late 18th century, offer the briefest of records for the passing years. An antebellum marker describes "A tender and Affectionate Mother, Endowed with the ornament of meek and quiet spirit."

107.4	**0.0**	*Turn left onto Parker's Ferry Road from churchyard.*
108.3	**0.9**	*At second stop sign, turn left onto S.C. 64 East.*
109.0	**0.7**	*On left is historical marker for Bethel Presbyterian Church site.*

What remains of the Pon Pon Chapel of Ease, nestled among the trees.

㉒ BETHEL PRESBYTERIAN CHURCH

This was one of the early Presbyterian churches founded by Reverend Archibald Stobo. Founded in 1728, the church was here until the congregation moved to Walterboro. The building was already abandoned when it burned in 1886. The current brick building dates to 1969. Several dozen gravestones from the 18th and 19th centuries survive. Captain Dent, who commanded "Old Ironsides," gets special mention, but there are others of interest. A Mr. Bowman was well remembered: "Firm and generous friend, A keen sportsman and true Patriot lies here. His friends morn their lost. These woods that so often Echoed, The Crack of his Rifle, (still) Hear his cheerful cry."

109.0	**0.0**	*Continue on S.C. 64 East.*
109.8	**0.0**	*Turn left onto dirt road beside Isaac Hayne's historical marker.*
110.8	**1.0**	*Arrive at Colonel Isaac Hayne's gravesite.*

㉓ COLONEL ISAAC HAYNE'S TOMB

During the Revolutionary War, the British took Colonel Hayne prisoner at the fall of Charleston. After he promised not to fight the English, they paroled him. When ordered to fight against his comrades, however, he refused, broke parole, and rejoined the Americans. Captured, he was hanged by the British. His inscription reads in part: "In life a soldier of his Country, In death a martyr to her sacred cause. His memory an undying inspiration to his fellow countrymen, His monument the freedom of his Native Land." Crepe myrtle, holly, and live oaks cover the knoll, which is also the homesite of the Hayne and Parks families.

110.8	**0.0**	*Retrace on dirt road to S.C. 64.*
111.8	**1.0**	*At stop sign, turn left onto S.C. 64 East.*
113.2	**1.4**	*At stop sign, turn left onto U.S. 17 North.*
113.5	**0.3**	*On left is the location of Old Jacksonboro, merely a field now.*

㉔ Old Jacksonboro's History

Originally, the Pon Pon (translated as "black water") Indian village occupied this site. Then the spot was granted to John Jackson, and by 1735 a settlement had started. A town plan of 1780 shows 113 lots, and the community boasted a free school, race track, tavern, Masonic lodge, and Episcopal and Presbyterian churches close by. Two years after Charleston fell to the British, Jacksonboro became South Carolina's capital for a season. Then it served as county seat until 1822. The particularly deadly malaria that invaded the Lowcountry following the Revolution finally put an end to the original town. In 1783, the Walters had moved inland to Walterboro, and eventually everyone else followed. The newer Jacksonboro we drive through on Highway 17 started when the railroad came through in 1859 and was further aided by the phosphate mining of the 1890s.

113.6	**0.1**	*Turn left into parking lot of Edisto Nature Trail.*

Westvaco

MeadWestvaco Corporation sponsors the trail; it's probably the best example of community corporate responsibility we'll encounter. Westvaco began in 1888 when it pioneered a process for producing wood pulp. Today, it operates 50 plants in 30 countries with 20,000 employees and has expanded beyond paper making

| E*disto Nature Trail.*

into a variety of industries. The company holds more than 70,000 acres near Edisto, most of it loblolly pine. The path winds through some of this land, a quarter of which will be developed as part of the company's East Edisto Master Plan. According to the plan, which will take upwards of 50 years to fully realize, the remaining three quarters will remain rural.

㉕ EDISTO NATURE TRAIL

This excellent self-guided nature trail shows the many uses to which the land has been put over the past three centuries. Choose between two trails at Edisto, a half-mile or a mile. Take the longer if you have time. It leads quickly out of the familiar loblolly forest and travels not only through a river swamp bottom but also through time. Trees and plants are identified along the way; there's a trail map available in the mailbox on the site or at a nearby gas station. For your own safety, stay on the path, use the handrails on the bridges, and obey the other safety notes. Watch out for poison ivy. Bug spray is also recommended.

Unlike Four Hole Swamp, this is not virgin but third-growth forest you are entering.

My father and I begin on a wide path that was once "Old Charleston Road." On both sides, tremendous loblolly pines fill an abandoned field. (It's sometimes called "old field pine" since it volunteers so readily in these areas.) We pass yellow jessamine, our state flower, and spy berries of the familiar wax myrtle before crossing to a second old road, The King's Highway. Crossing a canal, we drop into the river-bottom swamp of the Edisto. Another abandoned field has been planted with fast-growing slash pine. This species lost some of its early popularity with timber companies because it did not fare well in ice storms, but here the weather is still warm enough for it to grow.

Local wildlife makes great use of Edisto's abundant plants. Raccoons enjoy the fruit of muscadine grape vines. Black cherries, Southern crabapple, and American beautyberry or French mulberry are other favorites. Squirrels nibble away at loblolly cones. They cut them while still green, and the debris litters the path.

A sawmill water hole was dug to provide water for the steam engine, but liquor-still operators often dug identical wells and before that, water holes were dug for the half-wild cattle. At this point, we spy a labeled dwarf palmetto. Unlike the cabbage palmetto, it grows no bigger.

A boardwalk leads us onto an old slave-built dike. Early in the 1700s, inland swamps were cleared of cypress and gum and planted in rice. The fields were usually smaller here than in the marshland because the ground of each field had to be perfectly level so that it could be flooded properly. The canal system is not so elaborate either, but still we see numerous ditches running through what was once rice fields and is now forest.

Yaupon is marked here, but is struggling because it's so far removed from the coast. The "black drink" of the Indians, it was a local tea for white settlers, who were still drinking it in the 1920s.

These rice fields might have been abandoned even before the Civil War, but in the years after, rice cultivation would eventually end. Phosphate mining began during Reconstruction and continued into the 20th century. The topsoil was scraped away (in this case not too deeply) and the rock was mined for use as fertilizer. All that remains are the dirt mounds and pebbles in the path.

On the boardwalk here we see the bald cypress with accompanying knees. This was probably the predominant species to begin with, and the site is not unlike what we saw at Four Hole. The barge canal on the river probably dates from rice planting days. Flats carried the rice out of the Edisto River, where it could be carried to the mill. There's an old building site here, a knoll with a few bricks, and just beyond that the site of a phosphate factory. Some scraps of iron gear and bolts are visible, but nothing else reveals the work except some spots of gravel.

We cross from the dike to the bed of an old railroad tram. This one may have served the phosphate mill we just passed, but during the early part of this century, these narrow-gauge tracks crisscrossed the Lowcountry. Timber crews followed in their wake, loading the rail cars with logs that could be dumped into rivers like the Edisto and floated to distant mills, or sawed on the bank and sent away by barge or ship.

Leaving the tram road, we're once more on the edge of the loblolly hardwood forest where we began. There's a spring marked here, dry on this summer day, and then we pass through the great trees of the long-abandoned field and back into the present.

Compared to Four Hole, we've seen less wildlife and no giant cypress. Nevertheless, there's something reassuring in the fecundity of this forest. If not bulldozed and concreted into complete oblivion or poisoned by acid rain, nature has a remarkable ability to restore herself here in the Lowcountry, and with surprising speed can soften and eventually cover over man's enterprise.

113.6 **0.0** *Turn left out of Nature Trail parking lot onto U.S. 17 North.*
143.5 **29.9** *Cross south side of Ashley River Bridge.*
END TOUR

West Shore of the Cooper River

TOUR NINE

WEST SHORE OF THE COOPER RIVER

Including Goose Creek, Cypress Gardens, and Pinopolis. We start this tour just north of Charleston in the historic **Goose Creek** area, stopping first at **St. James, Goose Creek Church**. En route to our final destination, **Moncks Corner**, we cross the Back River to visit the **Indigo Vats**, and then head north through the pine forest of **Bushy Park**, a well-hidden industrial park. At **Cypress Gardens**, a spot famous for its boat trips through cypress-filled ponds, we take time to wander the azalea- and camellia-lined pathways. Traveling scenic **old Highway 52**, we reach Moncks Corner. Nearby **Pinopolis** beckons with its pretty pineland village dotted with pines, crepe myrtle, and some 1840s homes. We end our day here with visits to **Pinopolis Methodist Church** and **St. John's Baptist Church**.

St. James-Goose Creek Church
100 Vestry Lane | 843-884-4375
Naval Weapons Station
Off of Red Bank Road
Lower Berkeley Waste Water Treatment Plant
2111 Red Bank Road | 843-572-4400
Bushy Park / Indigo Vats
Near 1522 Bushy Park Road | 800-882-0337
www.berkeleysc.org/historicalsites.html
Cypress Gardens
3030 Cypress Gardens Road | 843-553-0515 | *www.cypressgardens.info*
Admission charged.
The Nesbitt House, houses the Berkeley County Chamber of Commerce
1004 Old Highway 52 | 843-761-8238
Pinopolis Methodist Church
1833 Pinopolis Road | 843-761-8477 | *www.gbgm-umc.org/pinopolis*
St. John's Baptist Church
1142 Sugarhill Drive | 843-761-8116

BEGIN TOUR

0.0	**0.0**	*Leave Charleston on I-26 West. Begin clocking mileage when you go under the bypass, I-526.*
3.4	**3.4**	*Take exit 209A—Goose Creek exit, and merge onto U.S.52 West—Rivers Avenue.*
5.4	**2.0**	*Just past the exit for U.S. 78 West, take right toward Goose Creek Road. The route is prominently marked: Army Logistics Base/Naval Weapons Station/Nad Road.*
5.7	**0.3**	*Merge left onto Goose Creek Road. Cross RR tracks and then Goose Creek bridge.*
6.2	**0.5**	*At stoplight, take a right onto Snake Road / S-8-208.*
6.5	**0.3**	*Look for historic marker on right for St. James– Goose Creek Church. Park briefly on Vestry Lane or a few yards farther near the stoplight to get out and read the marker.*

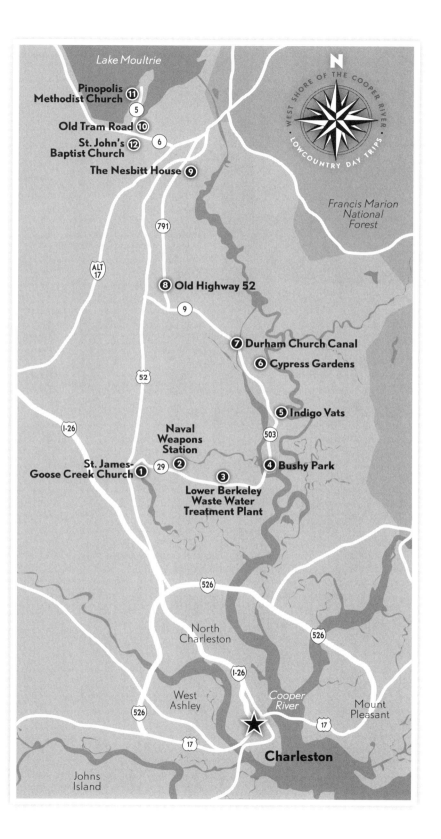

Lake Moultrie

Pinopolis Methodist Church ⑪ ⑤

Old Tram Road ⑩ ⑥

St. John's Baptist Church ⑫

The Nesbitt House ⑨

Francis Marion National Forest

791

ALT 17

⑧ **Old Highway 52**

⑨

⑦ **Durham Church Canal**

⑥ **Cypress Gardens**

52

⑤ **Indigo Vats**

I-26

Naval Weapons Station

503

St. James-Goose Creek Church ① 29 ②

③ ④ **Bushy Park**

Lower Berkeley Waste Water Treatment Plant

526

North Charleston

526

I-26

West Ashley

Cooper River

526

Mount Pleasant

17

17

★

Charleston

Johns Island

I**St. James-Goose Creek Church.**

Goose Creek's History

We start at Goose Creek, a sprawling suburb of Charleston. The original community, however, was almost as old as the colony. Governor John Yeamans of Barbados settled here; it was Yeamans' Creek then. He harassed the earlier settlers and then did the infant colony the favor of dying. They cultivated rice and indigo as well as more political turmoil—the most powerful planters of the day, the Barbadian Goose Creek men, continually fought to control the colony's government. In 1706, they established the Church of England as Carolina's official church. Politics, not faith, seems to have motivated them most. In a twist of irony, their grand mansions have fallen into ruin, while the second-oldest rural Anglican church in South Carolina still stands.

❶ ST. JAMES GOOSE CREEK CHURCH, c. 1719
Open only by appointment.

Started in 1708, this little jerkin-headed building wasn't completed until about a decade later. Many observers grouped it among the most interesting of English churches; historian and church member Sam Stoney called it the most baroque. It's certainly unique, for it may be the only one in existence containing the Royal Coat of Arms for the House of Hanover, and one of only two with a hanging hatchment. The Izard family hatchment was probably left after a funeral. Extensively restored in 1840 and again after severe damage by the great earthquake of 1886, the building has been well looked after.

If you've arranged a tour, you'll notice how on the church's exterior cherubs face the window arches and a pelican feeds her young on the pediment. The pelican is at least the third—one contractor tried in vain to model the bird from a reluctant Muscovy duck.

This was the symbol of the Society of the Propagation of the Gospel in Foreign Parts, which supplied ministers to Anglican churches. The first here, Samuel Thomas, did not find life easy. His replacement, Reverend Francis LeJau, was often exasperated by his contrary congregation and meager-to-nonexistent salary. The church was built during his tenure, but he died just before its completion; he lies buried before the altar.

Inside, elaborate dadoes flank both sides of the sounding board and finely worked pulpit. The brightly colored Lion and Unicorn preside high above, almost as if to suggest that the king's word was above God's.

7.5	**1.0**	*Continuing on Snake Road, turn right at stoplight onto Red Bank Road / S-8-29.*
8.9	**1.4**	*On left is the entrance to the (former) Polaris Missile Facility.*

❷ NAVAL WEAPONS STATION
Not open to the public.

More of a community than one site, the Naval Weapons Station occupies land on both sides of the road. More than a century ago, the citizenry here made red tiles and had Methodist camp meetings at the Red Bank Landing. But that was before Dr. Ravenel invented the first effective semisubmersible submarine, and the concept of "nuclear deterrent" was just a futuristic dream.

8.9	**0.0**	*Continue on Red Bank Road.*
11.7	**2.8**	*On left is Lower Berkeley County Waste Facility.*

❸ LOWER BERKELEY WASTE WATER TREATMENT PLANT

Part of the Berkeley County Water and Sanitation system, this treatment plant is the third largest in the tri-county area with its daily capacity of 22.5 million gallons. Its average dry-weather flow is about 10.5 million gallons daily, which are discharged after aeration, clarification, and disinfection into the Cooper River.

11.7	**0.0**	*Continue on Red Bank Road.*
12.2	**0.5**	*Turn left onto Bushy Park Road / S-8-503.*
12.7	**0.5**	*On right is Back River Reservoir.*

❹ BUSHY PARK

Once a plantation, Bushy Park now houses a number of industrial plants. The Back River, famous for its rice growing and brick making, is partly impounded to ensure a constant supply of fresh water for these manufacturing processes. Still, a tiny reminder of old times persists in the midst of it all.

12.7	**0.0**	*Continue on Bushy Park Road.*
13.8	**1.1**	*Turn right into the Bushy Park Industrial Complex visitor parking lot to visit the Indigo Vats, located just left of the Bayer Heritage Federal Credit Union.*

❺ INDIGO VATS
Open to public.

At the gate of the Miles Corporation, note a set of indigo vats built in about 1750, but moved here in 1977. One is made of brick—unusual since most were wood. A sliding door separates the two linked sections. To begin the processing, workers placed the stalk and leaves into the first vat to ferment for about 14 hours. Then they drew this liquid into the lower "battery," where they beat the solution with paddles, thickening it, then allowing it to settle. Finally, they drew off the water so the sediment lumps could dry and go to market. The "indigo maker" monitored this process day and night until completion. The end product could produce three shades—copper, blue, and purple—and brought fortunes to some early planters. It also proved valuable enough to the English that they paid an extra bounty to keep it out of the hands of the French.

13.8	**0.0**	*Turn right on leaving parking lot and continue on Bushy Park Road / S-8-503.*
19.3	**5.5**	*At stop sign, turn right onto S.C. 9 East / Cypress Garden Road.*

Circa 1750 indigo vats.

Cypress Gardens

Originally part of Dean Hall plantation, Cypress Gardens held the home of William Carson, who married the daughter of Unionist James Petigru. A Unionist widow when war came, Mrs. Carson carried her younger son off to Italy, where she supported herself as a painter. Her older son, James, fought for the Confederacy and, after a career as a mining engineer, retired here to the river.

Benjamin Kitteridge bought Dean Hall in 1909 and, inspired by the wild azaleas growing about the old rice reserve, turned it into a more formal garden. Azaleas were his pride, and he planted thousands, many of which now tower like trees. Camellias were added, too, along with wisteria, tea olives, pines, dogwoods, and magnolias, but the Gardens' hallmark remains the cypresses.

| **19.4** | **0.1** | *Turn right to enter Cypress Gardens.* |
| **19.7** | **0.3** | *Cypress Gardens Parking lot.* |

❻ CYPRESS GARDENS, c. 1927

Upon entering Cypress Gardens, pick up a map that shows several miles of paths and lists the main points of interest. Spring's dazzling azaleas bring the site the most notoriety, but paddlers also appreciate the quiet boat ride through the black water of the cypress-crowded reservoir. Wildlife abounds, from squirrels to alligators, and an education staff helps interpret the surroundings. In recent years, the gardens have added a Butterfly House, in which nectar and larvae plants nurture a bevy of birds and butterflies native to the Southeast. An outdoor alligator display guarantees visitors will see three of the prehistoric-looking reptiles even in winter. The Swamparium displays reptiles, fish, and amphibians native to the swamp. In 2010, the gardens got its first history display when a museum featuring buttons, pipes, pottery, and other artifacts from the former slave quarters of Dean Hall Plantation opened. Overall it's a fine place to refresh, as a visitor center houses a gift shop, and an educational center holds displays about the area.

| **20.0** | **0.3** | *Return to park gate and turn left at stop sign onto S.C. 9 West / Cypress Gardens Road.* |
| **20.1** | **0.1** | *Cross Durham Church Canal.* |

❼ DURHAM CHURCH CANAL

Just as you leave the Gardens, you cross the canal connecting the west branch of the Cooper with the Back River Reservoir.

| **20.1** | **0.0** | *Continue on Cypress Gardens Road.* |
| **23.9** | **3.8** | *At stop sign, turn right onto S-8-78 / Old U.S. 52 West.* |

❽ OLD HIGHWAY 52

This is the road less traveled and thus a quiet, green drive. Several well-known plantations dot the route, but they're all private. Ancient Mulberry Castle was the home of Thomas Broughton and served as a refuge and fort during the Yemassee attack. Lewisfield is typical of the fine, well-ventilated houses built even before the Revolution. Gippy, a Classical Revival house built on the eve of the war, can be seen, but it's in the middle of a residential area. Dairy cattle once roamed these pastures, and Gippy milk was sold until at least 1987.

| **23.9** | **0.0** | *Continue on old U.S. 52.* |
| **31.3** | **7.4** | *Turn right into the Berkeley County Chamber of Commerce, also known as The Nesbitt House.* |

❾ THE NESBITT HOUSE, c. 1725

Dating back to 1725, this building once housed the overseer at Dean Hall. Since then, it has been reassembled and refurbished. It now houses the Berkeley County Chamber of Commerce . Stop in; they're happy to give you information about the area.

Moncks Corner's History

Lord Proprietor Peter Colleton received the grant for Fair-lawne Barony (the land from Mulberry Castle north) in 1672. Two of Peter's grandsons, John and Peter, eventually settled in Carolina and left honorable descendants, but gradually they broke up the great 16,000-acre holding. In 1735, Thomas Monck purchased 1,000 acres of it, the corner bounded by Stony Landing, the Charles Town Road, and the rest of Fairlawn. Since Monck's corner sat on a main trade route to the nearby landing, several stores, a tavern, and racetrack were built. This community, located somewhere close to where highways 17A and 52 join, faded away after the Revolution, but the coming of the railroad and the choice of the village as county seat in the 1890s restored it. This new Moncks Corner expanded, finally encompassing the old.

Bordering on Hell Hole Swamp, a longtime hideout for outlaws, runaway slaves, and unpatriated Indians, the Moncks Corner community held a tradition of lawlessness, or at least willful independence. Prohibition only heightened this reputation, when moonshiners plied their trade even more boldly than elsewhere in the Lowcountry, if that was possible. "Not a goiter to the gallon," the 1940 WPA Guide declares of this apparently safe-to-drink distillation. Today the town is better known for recreation at nearby Lake Moultrie. Fish camps, outboard motor boats, and tasty fried catfish are what they advertise today.

31.3	**0.0**	*Return to U.S. 52 / S-8-79 and turn right.*
31.7	**0.4**	*At second stoplight, turn left onto S.C. 6 West / East Main Street.*
32.1	**0.4**	*Cross railroad tracks.*
33.6	**1.5**	*Take right fork onto Pinopolis Road / S.C.5.*

Pinopolis

Drive slowly and look carefully. We entered Pinopolis on a central paved road lined with crepe myrtles. Several dirt lanes lead off the main road, but most are dead ends and private driveways, so we'll be content with the view from here. By the time of the Civil War, the village boasted 20-30 fine houses; a few remain behind the trees.

35.3	**1.7**	*Look left sharply and quickly; at a tiny milepost at 1764 Pinopolis Road you may be able to see the bed of an old track.*

⑩ OLD TRAM ROAD

Just inside the village proper, the highway crosses the bed of an old tram road. Power lines run down it today, but you can see the cut made to secure a proper grade. Built in 1892, this 10-mile rail line connected to the main line in Moncks Corner and led off to our left to the visionary "New England City." This real-estate development went bankrupt 14 years later, and the Santee Cooper flooded its site in 1940.

35.4	**0.1**	*Pinopolis Methodist Church is on your left.*

⑪ PINOPOLIS METHODIST CHURCH, c. 1900
Grounds open to public.

On your left stands a simple Victorian with modest gingerbread trim, the Pinopolis Methodist Church, built in 1900. The Methodists, however, date back far earlier. The Wesley brothers visited Mulberry Plantation in 1735. Both Bishop Asbury and William Capers rode a circuit in this area around 1800. And just seven miles away is the Friendship Methodist Church. On the site of early camp meetings, a church

| **P**inopolis Methodist Church.

was built in 1825, and the present building incorporated one of its floor timbers at its center. The earliest church at this site, however, was a Baptist one.

35.4	**0.0**	*Continue on Pinopolis Road / Main Street / S.C. 5, touring*
		Pinopolis' side streets (approximately 1.7 miles).
37.1	**1.7**	*Return to post office on Pinopolis Road /*
		Main Street / S.C. 5.
37.1	**0.0**	*Starting at post office, retrace Pinopolis Road /*
		Main Street S.C. 5.
38.3	**1.2**	*Bear straight on Sugar Hill Drive / S-8-16.*
38.4	**0.1**	*On left is St. John's Baptist Church.*

⑫ ST. JOHN'S BAPTIST CHURCH, c. 1884
Grounds open to public.
Constituted June 15, 1851, with eight members from Goose Creek and Mount Olive churches, the first church was located at today's Methodist church site that we visited earlier. Services in this building started in 1884 and continued until 1926, when members transferred to Moncks Corner. But in 1970, worshippers renovated the building and resumed services.

38.4	**0.0**	*Continue on Sugar Hill Drive / S-8-16.*
38.8	**0.4**	*At stoplight, cross S.C. 6 and continue on S-8-16.*
42.5	**3.7**	*At stop sign, turn right onto U.S. 17A South.*
48.9	**6.4**	*At stoplight, cross U.S. 176 and continue on U.S. 17A South.*
52.9	**4.0**	*Cross over I-26 and turn left, then merge onto I-26 East.*
		Return to downtown Charleston by I-26 East.

END TOUR

East Branch of the Cooper River
TOUR TEN

EAST BRANCH OF THE COOPER RIVER

Including the Eastern Shore of the West Branch of the Cooper River,
On this tour—perfect for people who enjoy a leisurely drive through the
countryside—we steer through the heart of the **Francis Marion National Forest**,
as well as private timberland. At the northernmost part of the tour, farmland
dotted with cotton fields takes over. We stop at **Mepkin Abbey**, **Lake Moultrie
Dam**, and **Stony Landing Plantation House**. Along the way, we glimpse the
bygone rice culture with its great plantations and churches that once lined the
Cooper River. Start early, and pack a picnic.

Detyens Shipyards, Inc.
     843-308-8000 | *www.detyens.com*
Middleburg Plantation
     www.berkeleysc.org/historicalsites.html#plantations
Rice Hope Plantation
     206 Rice Hope Drive | 843-849-9000 | *www.ricehope.com*
Taveau Church
     www.berkeleysc.org/historicalsites.html
Mepkin Abbey
     1098 Mepkin Abbey Road | 843-761-8509 | *mepkinabbey.org*
Jefferies Generating Plant and Pinopolis Dam at Lake Moultrie
     463 Powerhouse Road
Dennis Wildlife Center
     305 Black Oak Road | 843-953-3387 | *www.dnr.sc.gov*
St. Stephen's Episcopal Church
     196 Brick Church Circle | 843-567-3419
     http://ststephenschurchsc.org
Old Santee Canal State Park (Stony Landing)
     900 Stony Landing Road | 843-899-5200
     www.oldsanteecanalpark.org
     Admission charged.

BEGIN TOUR

0.0	0.0	*Start mileage at north side (away from downtown Charleston) of Cooper River Bridge on U.S. 17 North.*
7.5	7.5	*Turn left onto S.C. 41.*
12.5	5.0	*On left as you cross Wando River is Detyens Shipyards.*

❶ DETYENS SHIPYARDS, INC., c. 1962
Not open to public.
This abandoned shipyard used to employ 300 employees and could accommodate
up to a 500-foot, 10,000-ton ship for repairs at one of its many dry docks.
Detyens now operates at a location on the Cooper River in North Charleston.

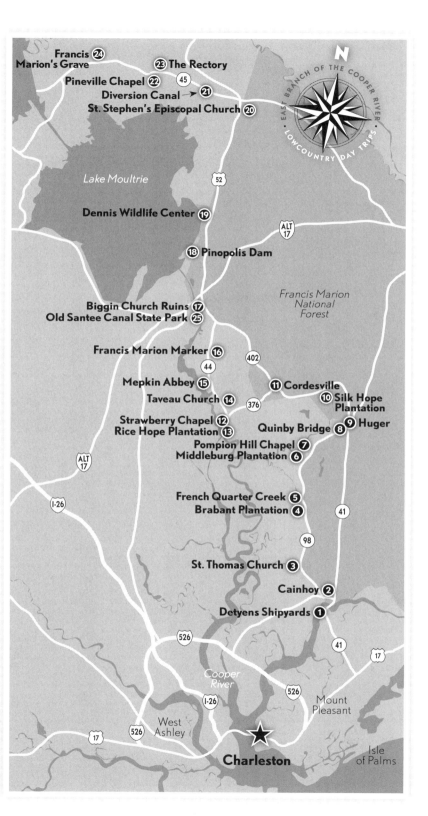

Francis Marion's Grave ㉔
The Rectory ㉓
Pineville Chapel ㉒
Diversion Canal → ㉑
St. Stephen's Episcopal Church ⑳

N

EAST BRANCH OF THE COOPER RIVER · LOWCOUNTRY DAY TRIPS

Lake Moultrie

52

Dennis Wildlife Center ⑲

ALT 17

⑱ Pinopolis Dam

Francis Marion National Forest

Biggin Church Ruins ⑰
Old Santee Canal State Park ㉕

Francis Marion Marker ⑯

402

44

Mepkin Abbey ⑮
Taveau Church ⑭

⑪ Cordesville
⑩ Silk Hope Plantation

376

Strawberry Chapel ⑫
Rice Hope Plantation ⑬
Pompion Hill Chapel ⑦
Middleburg Plantation ⑥

Quinby Bridge ⑧ ⑨ Huger

French Quarter Creek ⑤
Brabant Plantation ④

41

ALT 17

98

I-26

St. Thomas Church ③

Cainhoy ②

Detyens Shipyards ①

41

526

17

Cooper River

I-26

526

West Ashley

526

17

Mount Pleasant

Isle of Palms

★

Charleston

| **12.5** | **0.0** | *Continue north on S.C. 41.* |
| **12.9** | **0.4** | *Veer left onto S-8-33 just beyond small sign to I-526.* |

❷ CAINHOY

This small rural community had a few settlers as early as 1680, but its official existence dates from 1735. Five early buildings remain, but in this village of narrow dirt lanes and private drives, they're hard to find. The name, Cainhoy, some suggest, was from an early ferryman of that time being hailed from the far bank—"Cain hoy!" More likely, it's an Indian name. Francis Marion headquartered here for a while, and soon after, Bishop Asbury found hospitality at the Capers home. Besides a Methodist meeting ground, there was a Presbyterian church whose graveyard still exists, though it's tucked away. Bishop William Capers left this description: "Cain Hoy was the most notable place ... a high reputation for society, hospitality, and all that." The fabled Cainhoy ferry is another that's come and gone.

| **13.7** | **0.8** | *Turn right at stoplight onto S-8-98, which parallels the East Branch of the Cooper River.* |
| **16.0** | **2.3** | *Look sharp for the unobtrusive historical marker on the left that marks St. Thomas Church.* |

❸ ST. THOMAS CHURCH, c. 1819
Grounds open to public.

When town planners laid out St. Thomas parish in 1706, they discovered that the settlers of the French Quarter couldn't understand English well enough to follow the service. For this reason, they established a parish within a parish, St. Denis. The two had long since combined when the original Cainhoy church burned in an 1815 forest fire. Built soon after, this little Greek Revival building, with its high walls and full gables, is an interesting contrast to the earlier churches we've seen elsewhere.

The grounds include a cemetery, once the scene of the Cainhoy Massacre. A group of whites from Charleston attended a Negro Republican meeting in 1876. These visitors were fired upon, and at least one man was killed before they could retreat to the ferryboat nearby. Uneasy with the narrow margin of victory, the Democrats soon after gerrymandered the black and Republican voters out of Charleston and into the newly formed Berkeley County. Historian and author Maxwell Orvin says it was derisively called "the baby county or black county," a block of the political landscape that would be chipped away and rearranged for another 20 years. Affectionately referred to as "the mean one," my great-grandfather was sheriff here for much of that time.

| **16.0** | **0.0** | *Continue on S-8-98.* |
| **20.2** | **4.2** | *On left is Brabant Plantation historical marker.* |

❹ BRABANT PLANTATION
Historical marker.

Following the Revolution, South Carolina's first Episcopal bishop, Robert Smith, lived here. It also happens to be the spot where Mad Archy Campbell drew his last breath. Stories say that Mad Archy Campbell, surely the most colorful of British Revolutionary War officers, invited Charleston belle Margaret Philips to ride with him and then raced the carriage to St. James where he held a pistol to the head of the Goose Creek minister, demanding to be married to the protesting woman. The minister declared he would marry Campbell only "with the consent of the young lady and her mother." Their descendants claim the myth is just that, and that she married him gladly.

20.2	**0.0**	*Continue on S-8-98.*
20.8	**0.6**	*Cross French Quarter Creek.*

❺ FRENCH QUARTER CREEK

Following the revocation of the Edict of Nantes, Huguenots settled this region, known as the French Quarter, almost as heavily as French Santee to the north. As happened there, they were eventually absorbed into the Anglican congregation.

24.5	**3.7**	*Look left for the gates of Middleburg Plantation.*

❻ MIDDLEBURG PLANTATION, c. 1697

Not open to public.

Middleburg and French Quarter Creek.

Although it's closed to the public, you can spy the house at the end of a long avenue from the road. Simple clapboard, two stories with a narrow veranda, it was built in 1697, which makes this former home of Huguenot Benjamin Simons the oldest wooden house in South Carolina.

24.5	**0.0**	*Continue on S-8-98.*
24.8	**0.3**	*On left is the historical marker for Pompion Hill Chapel.*

❼ POMPION HILL CHAPEL, c. 1763

Not open to public.

Pronounced "Pumkin" Hill, this little Chapel of Ease was built in 1763. As at St. Stephen's, a Villeponeux and an Axson left their marks on a finely crafted little church that's gone through eight years of restoration. Though you can't see it from the road, boaters can spy it from the river. Twice a year, worshippers gather on the church grounds to feast on God's word and a picnic lunch. A cemetery that also dates back to the 1700s holds Mrs. Chicken, introduced later in this chapter.

24.8	**0.0**	*Continue on S-8-98.*
26.6	**1.8**	*Cross the new Quinby Bridge, which replaced the original from at least 1735.*

❽ QUINBY BRIDGE, c. 1735 or older
Colonel Coats, with 500 infantry and 100 cavalry, fought to a draw the combined American forces of Lee, Hampton, Marion, and Sumter. The dead were hastily buried along this roadside, and it's said that heavy rains used to wash out their bones. Locals claim the ghosts of headless British troops clatter by at night.

26.6	**0.0**	*Continue on S-8-98.*
26.8	**0.2**	*At stop sign, turn left onto S.C. 41 North.*

❾ HUGER
Present-day Huger (use the somewhat French pronunciation "Hewgee" or "Ugee") doesn't show much sign of its ancient age, but this community dates back to at least 1735.

26.9	**0.1**	*Veer left onto S.C. 402 West.*
28.0	**1.1**	*On left, Silk Hope historical marker.*

❿ SILK HOPE PLANTATION
Historical marker.
At this plantation in 1690, colonial governor Sir Nathaniel Johnson reportedly raised a multitude of silkworms and planted 24,000 mulberry trees. He's best known for repelling a Spanish and French invasion of the colony in 1706 and passing the Anglican Church Act in that year.

28.0	**0.0**	*Continue on S.C. 402 West.*
34.4	**6.4**	*At Cordesville, turn left onto Sawmill Road / S-8-376.*

⓫ CORDESVILLE
Little remains to remind us that Cordesville was one of the principal summering spots of the Cooper River planters.

38.7	**4.3**	*At stop sign, turn left onto S-8-44.*
38.8	**0.1**	*Turn right onto Strawberry Chapel Road.*
39.0	**0.2**	*On the right is Strawberry Chapel.*

⓬ STRAWBERRY CHAPEL, c. 1725
Not open to the public.
This chapel is all that remains of the would-be town of Childsbury. A victim of a nobleman's tyranny, James Child fled to the New World and hoped to regain his fortune at this ferry landing. There's no trace of Bay Street or College Square, but a school operated here until 1754, and the town had a market day and racetrack. Historians speculate that residents abandoned it by 1815 because, like so many others, it was unhealthy.

The chapel and cemetery remain. James Child left the site for the chapel in his will, and in 1725 the modest little jerkin-headed building was constructed as a Chapel of Ease. As the name implies, the chapel provided an easier traveling distance for parishioners who could be served by a shuttling priest. This chapel eventually replaced the ill-fated Biggin Church that it was meant to supplement.

In the cemetery, note the large open Harleston vault to the right of the chapel. The thin fern growing above its entry is spider brake or "Huguenot fern," so named because it was discovered growing in Charleston's Huguenot cemetery in 1868.

39.0	**0.0**	*Make a U-turn and retrace to stop sign.*
39.2	**0.2**	*At stop sign, turn right onto Rice Hope Drive / S-8-1054.*
39.5	**0.3**	*Continue on Rice Hope Drive.*
39.7	**0.2**	*Turn left and*

ǀ**S***trawberry Chapel and cemetery.*

continue on Rice Hope Drive. Gates to Rice Hope Plantation are about 50 feet ahead on the right.

⑬ RICE HOPE PLANTATION, c. 1840
Bed-and-breakfast.
Extensive gardens vie for attention as much as the historic mansion on the Cooper River. Some of them date back to the late 18th century and were redesigned in the 1930s by noted landscape designer Loutrel Briggs. The topics of interest at the plantation include early rice planting and a Revolutionary War battle, but historian Louisa Cheves Stoney says Rice Hope was best remembered for its hospitality.

39.7	**0.0**	*Return to Rice Hope Drive / S-8-1054.*
39.9	**0.2**	*Turn left and continue on Rice Hope Drive / S-8-1054.*
41.0	**1.1**	*On right is Taveau Church.*

⑭ TAVEAU CHURCH, c. 1835
Not open to public.
Coming from Edisto Island, Martha Carolina Swinton was a Presbyterian and felt strongly that her Anglican neighbors should have a chance to hear the true word. The second wife of John Ball, she bore him 11 children, outlived him, and as Miss Stoney writes, "had the temerity to marry a Taveau." This small frame church was given to the blacks soon after her death and then came under the jurisdiction of the Methodists.

41.0	**0.0**	*Continue on S-8-44.*
41.6	**0.6**	*Turn left into Mepkin Abbey gates.*

⑮ MEPKIN ABBEY, c. 1949
Guided tours available.
This Cistercian Trappist monastery at Mepkin was founded in 1949. It's still a beautiful, quiet spot, and the only Catholic place of worship mentioned in these tours. Drive by the painted brick gatehouse and follow the signs to the reception center and store, housed in a wooden building. Here, a brother will provide

Mepkin Abbey

In Italy about 1,500 years ago, St. Benedict founded the first true monastic order and gave it direction with his "Holy Rule," which stressed communal living, humility, and obedience. In 1098, the Cistercian order was founded in France. Called "White Monks" because they wear a white habit beneath a black scapular, its members felt it necessary to return to a stricter interpretation of St. Benedict's teaching. Though primarily contemplative, these men, beginning under the leadership of St. Bernard, made great advances in agricultural techniques and contributed to the development and spread of Gothic architecture throughout Europe. The Renaissance and then the Reformation took their toll on the order. The remaining monks fractured into many small independent congregations, the best known of which are "strict observance," or Trappist, like this one.

information about where you can walk on your own, whether to the terraced gardens developed by the Luce family or through the outdoor garden labyrinth or other meditative spots. Docents guide tours of the church and the monastery grounds, sharing details about the monastic life. Although mostly silent, the monks speak occasionally and can be seen carrying out their mixed duties of prayer and work—duties that begin many hours before daylight. The Clare Boothe Luce Library, also open to visitors, contains a remarkable collection of African-American religious archives as well as other significant religious materials. Accommodations are available for short retreats. Once the brothers raised chickens and sold eggs, but now they cultivate oyster mushrooms, which can be found alongside other goods in the Abbey gift shop.

Mepkin Plantation Grounds, c. 1762
On the Abbey grounds, the Mepkin Plantation is the 1762 home of South Carolina merchant, planter, and statesman Henry Laurens. In 1936, Henry and Clare Boothe Luce, best known as the publishers of *Time* and *Life* magazines, purchased the property. They gave the majority of the land to the Trappists. Mr. Luce and other family members are buried here beside the great oak avenue in the terraced garden overlooking the Cooper River.

42.4 0.8   *Proceed straight to reach the Luce graveyard parking area. Walk to the high bluff overlooking the Cooper River. Along the edge of the woods to your right, 60 feet from the Cooper River bluff, is the path leading to the Laurens burial plot.*

Grave of Henry Laurens
Remarkable for many reasons, Henry Laurens is also the first person in South Carolina to be cremated. His young daughter had been declared dead, but revived before she could be buried. Laurens dreaded the same thing happening to him, so he left strict instructions for his own disposal: That his body "be wrapped in 12 yards of tow cloth and burned until it was entirely consumed." His ashes are buried beneath this 1792 grave marker. His son, John Laurens, one of George Washington's staffers who led the decisive charge at Yorktown and helped settle the terms of surrender there, joined his father in the plot upon his return to South Carolina. The British killed him in a skirmish south of Charleston.

42.4 0.0   *Return to Mepkin Abbey gates and turn left onto S-8-44.*
46.1 3.7   *On right at intersection of Hard Pinch Road / S-8-359 is Francis Marion historical marker (difficult to see).*

⑯ FRANCIS MARION
Historical marker.
Biographer Parson Weems suggests this as the birthplace of Francis Marion, but he also claims Marion was born "no bigger than a Maine lobster, and stayed that size until he was 12," so his account is highly suspect. Family tradition says so, too, though, and an ancient black retainer of the family was certain. "Enty, he born at Cordes." (He was born at Cordes Plantation, wasn't he?) In infancy he was moved to Winyah Bay and grew up there.

46.1 0.0   *Continue on S-8-44.*
48.1 2.0   *At stop sign, turn left onto S.C. 402 West and immediately cross Wadboo Creek.*
49.5 1.4   *On left are the Biggin Church ruins.*

Biggin Church ruins.

⑰ BIGGIN CHURCH RUINS, c. 1755

Open to public.

The Church Act of 1706 established nine original parishes, including St. John's Parish. "A pleasant and healthful part of the country, where the planters were generally good, sober and teachable people." The first church, the interior of which Thomas Broughton adorned, accidentally burned in 1755. The congregation built the second the following year, strategically locating it at the intersection of three roads and Biggin Creek (now gone thanks to Tail Race Canal). As was often the case, the building also proved strategically important to military forces. In 1781, Lieutenant Colonel Coates garrisoned his troops here and burned the building when he withdrew. The congregation rebuilt it again, and Reverend Dalcho reports it prospering in 1820. Vandals damaged the interior in the next war, however, and the abandoned building burned completely in an 1890 forest fire. Today, a large portion of at least two walls remains, surrounded by an ancient, flower-crowded burial ground. The grounds also include an interesting old graveyard.

Sir John Colleton, who donated the original site, was laid to rest here, but only after he willed a watch to his unhappy wife "so that she may take notice how time passes and earnestly entreat her to make better use of the time than she has in the past." Dr. Johnson says that old "Turpentine John" Palmer and his brother, Joseph, were imprisoned in a low-arched vault (now a ruin) during the Revolution because John's son was with Marion. They attempted to cut their way out, leaving revealing slices inside the brick. Once released, they were so weak, it took them two days and nights to walk the 10 miles home. Johnson also tells of an 1812 stone that reads, "and as I am, soon will you be, Prepare for death and follow me." A St. Stephen's wag scratched under the epitaph, "To follow you I n'er consent, until I find which way you went." Not all are so strange or flippant. The Moultrie family and others rest in ordinary peace beneath these oaks and dogwoods.

49.5	**0.0**	*Continue on S. C. 402 West.*
49.7	**0.2**	*Turn left and continue on S.C. 402 West.*
49.9	**0.2**	*At stoplight, turn right onto U.S. 52 West.*
51.6	**1.7**	*Turn left at Jefferies Generating Plant sign onto Power House Road / S-8-20.*
52.9	**1.3**	*Pinopolis Dam on Cooper River that forms Lake Moultrie.*

⑱ JEFFERIES GENERATING PLANT and PINOPOLIS DAM, c. late 1930s

Not open to public beyond the gatehouse.

Constructed in just 31 months, the Pinopolis Dam didn't actually dam a river, so the 1 ½ mile-long concrete structure is set into 26 miles of flanking earthen dike. Prearranged tours are available.

From the gatehouse, the Jeffries Generating Plant powerhouse is on your left. The large Art Deco structure's soft, rounded lines say a lot about the optimistic outlook for an industrial future. (The Lowcountry was short on optimism and cash, and the only other industrial Art Deco building that's even close to our tour path is the Coca-Cola Bottling Company in distant Ridgeland.) The plant houses five turbine generators; beyond, the navigational lock still raises boats 75 feet up from the Tail Race Canal. The steel power poles on your left denote the hydroelectric switchyard, where generated power is changed into different voltages and sent on its way.

The plant that we first drove by generates electricity with steam generated by burning coal. It was built in 1953 when it was discovered that the hydroelectric plant could not keep up with increasing demand. Today only a small percentage of the Santee Cooper power comes from the original generators. Other power plants elsewhere make up the difference.

The WPA and the Lakes

By 1793, engineers knew that there was considerable drop in elevation between the Santee and Cooper rivers, but it wasn't until 1934 that the Santee Cooper Authority made the ambitious attempt to generate electrical power by diverting the water from one river to the other. The nation was in the midst of the Great Depression, and much of this section of the Lowcountry was poverty-stricken and desolate. With the sponsorship of Franklin Roosevelt and strong local political support led by Senator Richard Jefferies, 200,000 acres were eventually cleared and turned into the man-made lakes, Marion and Moultrie. They held water for two hydroelectric plants.

Nine hundred families, mostly black, had to be relocated, as well as 6,000 graves. Several large plantation houses and churches were saved, but many were lost, along with a tremendous river-bottom forest. As a result of the project, a topic still sensitive in some areas because of the forced eviction, the state's rural areas finally received electricity, and people became healthier and more comfortable. The enlarging Navy Yard had a source of power, which, with the approach of World War II, became even more important. Other industries located near the source of cheap power, and brought jobs. As an added bonus, one that eventually provided as much revenue as the generators, the lake became a paradise for fishermen and vacationers. On the minus side, the diverted water carried silt into Charleston Harbor. Now, water first diverted by the 1793 canal and again by this 1941 project has been re-rediverted whence it originally flowed—the Santee River.

52.9	**0.0**	*Retrace S-8-20 to U.S. 52.*
54.2	**1.3**	*At stop sign, turn left onto U.S. 52 West.*
58.5	**4.3**	*Turn left onto Black Oak Road / S-8-42.*
59.2	**0.7**	*Turn left into Dennis Wildlife Center.*

⑲ DENNIS WILDLIFE CENTER

This administrative building and its adjoining facilities serve as the center for wildlife research and management in the surrounding lakes and woodlands. It's not open for touring, although you should stop in the lobby of the main building to see an interesting natural history display—225 clutches of birds' eggs collected by antebellum naturalist William Elliott, wing identifications, and mounted local fish.

The main business of the center, though, is striped bass. Each river system of the East Coast has its own population of striped bass. Living part of their life in salt water, they, like salmon, lay their eggs in fresh water. It was a surprise, then, when fishermen and biologists discovered that the striped bass (often called rockfish) of the Santee and Cooper rivers had adapted themselves to the newly created Lake Moultrie and Lake Marion and were flourishing there. By the early 1950s, this fishing area had become nationally known. A fish hatchery was opened on the

Diversion Canal, and the Dennis Center helps with that work.

The hatchery is the largest producer of striped bass larvae in the world—up to 100 million a year. In addition, the center also experiments with a hybrid striped bass, catfish, and other local and exotic species. Blue catfish, introduced from Arkansas in 1964, reached a healthy size. My father and I watched a couple of 30-pounders being unloaded at a fish camp on the far side of Lake Moultrie, but the record fish came out of the Tail Race Canal in 1991—109 pounds, 4 ounces.

> *And there was mooted many a day,*
> *The question on which each gourmet*
> *Throughout the Parish had his say,*
> *Which is the best,*
> *Santee or Cooper River bream?*
> *Alas, the evening star grew dim*
> *Ere any guest agreed with him,*
> *Or he with guest.*

That's the question posed by writer Yates Snowden in "A Carolina Bourbon," and if you can't get an answer, then there probably isn't one.

59.2	**0.0**	*From Dennis Wildlife Center, turn right onto Black Oak Road / S-8-42 and retrace to U.S. 52.*
59.9	**0.7**	*At stop sign, turn left onto U.S. 52 West / Main Street.*
67.0	**7.1**	*In St. Stephen's, turn right onto S.C. 45 East / Church Street.*
67.4	**0.4**	*Just after curve turn right onto Brick Church Circle Road / S-8-122.*
67.4	**250** ft	*Turn left into St. Stephen's Churchyard.*

⑳ ST. STEPHEN'S EPISCOPAL CHURCH, c. 1769
Grounds open to public.

"The church is one of the handsomest country churches in So.Ca., and would be no mean ornament to Charleston," wrote Reverend Dalcho in 1820. That was certainly the intent of the vestry and guilders, F. Villepontoux and A. Howard, for they had wrangled hard and long to get the best materials and labor. The design emulated Charleston's St. Michael's, at least in the high-coved ceiling, which is why the exterior boasts the high gambrel roof and distinctively curved gable ends. On an arranged tour (or on Sunday morning), note the careful exterior brickwork and the signatures of contractors and masons about the doorways.

St. Stephen's Episcopal Church.

Like many other Anglican churches, this one fell on hard times immediately after the Revolution. In his reminiscence, parish resident Sam Dubose wrote, "In 1786, I was baptized by a Presbyterian minister ... who lived more than 50 miles off and whose presence among us was accidental and I never saw a minister until I was 12." Dubose put the blame on a lack of morals among some of the new Episcopal priests. In truth, the congregation moved inland after a series of freshets on the Santee wiped out crops and fevers swept through the area. They reformed in the little chapel of the Pineville community. Involved in a lawsuit, this independent group did not officially join the diocese until 1843, and then it fell on even harder times. Despite the lack of churchgoers in the area, however, St. Stephen's was restored three times in the next 150 years. Now it has opened its doors once more.

The graveyard is one of the prettiest around and crowded with stones. No matter what the status of the church, this "public burying grounds" was kept in use. It wasn't uncommon, says Dubose, to be buried on the homestead, but when the adjoining countryside flooded in 1941, many of these family plots were relocated here. Dubose adds that in those early days, a layer of boards had to be placed in the grave to keep the wolves from digging them up. This was called "English Santee" then, but you would hardly guess that from the French names inscribed. "The family of the Gaillards lie here interred," wrote Reverend Dalcho. Another comment for this resting place: "A mighty army am the Porchers." Historian Porcher wrote of the three roads that once joined at this church: "Strange that they should unite for all lead to the grave."

67.4	**0.0**	*From churchyard, turn left onto Brick Church Circle Road / S-8-122.*
67.5	**0.1**	*At stop sign, turn left onto S.C. 45 West / Church St.*
67.9	**0.4**	*Continue across U.S. 52 on S.C. 45 West.*
70.0	**2.1**	*Cross diversion canal from Lake Moultrie to Santee River.*

㉑ DIVERSION CANAL, LAKE MOULTRIE TO SANTEE RIVER

This is the diversion canal that rediverts water back to the Santee River.

74.3	**4.3**	*In Pineville, turn left onto S-8-204.*

Pineville

A designated historic district preserves what remains of this summer haven that began in 1794 and eventually blossomed to include about 75 substantial houses, public library, school, church, tavern, and racetrack. Residents placed a superstitious faith in the "good" air of Pineville; anyone who breathed it was warned to remain in the vicinity for the rest of season. Historian Porcher says the planters visited their plantations in the morning, hunted sometimes, and returned to lodge at the post office. Then came siesta and afternoon tea before visiting could begin. "Every excuse was used to have a dancing party which closed at frost with the Jockey Club Ball." Just two miles from the Santee Swamp, Pineville didn't remain safe, and in the 1830s, fatal fever epidemics scattered much of the population. Then, in the final days of the Civil War, almost all the houses were burned. (Estimates range from seven to 80.)

74.3	**400** ft	*Turn left into Pineville Chapel parking lot.*

㉒ THE PINEVILLE CHAPEL, c. 1810

Not open to public.

"More zeal and less voice" is how Porcher describes the Episcopal service. "Old Capt. Palmer, the patriarch of the village, certainly possessed no musical talents but he had zeal and fancied he had accomplished the 100th Psalm." Little the music matters, however, since a recent renovation has rendered the little church charming in its own right.

74.3	**0.0**	*From Pineville Chapel parking lot, turn right onto S-8-204.*
74.4	**400** ft	*At stop sign, turn left onto S.C. 45 West.*
74.7	**0.3**	*On right, white house with green trim is The Rectory.*

㉓ THE RECTORY, c. 1810
Not open to public.

The rectory was spared from Civil War conflagrations, as were the 1830 post office and 1826 library now tacked onto the rear. It's all part of a residence now.

74.7	**0.0**	*Continue on S.C. 45 West.*
77.9	**3.2**	*Turn right at brick gate onto dirt road to Francis Marion's grave.*
78.9	**1.0**	*Grave parking lot.*

㉔ FRANCIS MARION'S GRAVE, c. 1790s
Open to public.

Hero of the American Revolution, Marion was a master of guerrilla warfare and, with his small bank of men and boys, provided much-needed American victories. After the fall of Yorktown, he was elected to the Jacksonboro Assembly, where he urged reconciliation with Tory neighbors—even as his troops continued to fight the British. Late in life, Marion married a widow with a hot temper. It was said that he threw his hat through the window before entering the house. If it didn't come sailing out, then this veteran of shipwreck and Indian War knew it was safe to enter. At his death, however, his wife was inconsolable, so it's nice to see them lying now peacefully side by side. Their graves are maintained by State Park Service.

78.9	**0.0**	*Retrace to S.C. 45 West.*
79.9	**1.0**	*At stop sign, turn left onto S.C. 45 East.*
90.0	**10.1**	*In St. Stephen's, turn right onto U.S. 52 East.*
103.7	**13.7**	*Cross Tail Race Canal, which connects Lake Moultrie and west branch of Cooper River.*
104.1	**0.4**	*At second road after the bridge, turn left onto Rembrant Dennis Blvd. / P-0801.*
105.1	**1.0**	*Turn left onto entrance road to Old Santee Canal State Park and Stony Landing House.*
105.8	**0.7**	*Old Santee Canal State Park entrance gate.*

㉕ OLD SANTEE CANAL STATE PARK (Stony Landing)

Historic Stony Landing has been rejuvenated and incorporated into The Old Santee Canal Park. Its 250 acres are rich in natural beauty, accessible by several miles of trails and boardwalks, and by canoes. In addition, the antebellum Stony Landing house, once the Dennis family home, has been restored and is open to the public. Tours are available by request. Boat docks on the Tail Race Canal, picnic areas, natural amphitheater, submarine model, interpretive center—the park offers a variety. The centerpiece is the old section of the Santee Canal, which ends here, edged on both sides by the steep bluffs of Biggin Creek.

Stony Landing and the Santee Canal
The earliest Indian traders used Stony Landing, first called Stone Landing. They could follow the famous Cherokee Trail to this point and then carry their skins

on to Charleston by water. The trail became the Congaree Road; planters used it to bring their rice and other produce to town. Flats and even schooners replaced canoes on the Cooper River. Stores were built here, and before and after the Civil War, workers cut building stone and made cement on the site. Early planters cleared Biggin Creek, previously impassable beyond this point.

Following the Revolution, an engineer launched a far more ambitious project. Construction of the Santee Canal began in 1793 and concluded in 1800. Four feet deep, 20 feet wide, and 22 miles long, it routed backcountry produce into the

Stony Landing, Old Santee Canal State Park.

Charleston harbor. F.A. Porcher, the canal's historian, argues that the structure, the earliest such undertaking in the United States, proved a far greater struggle than it should have been. He claims that the vanity of the Swedish engineer and perhaps the personal interest of a board member caused them to ignore easier routes and pushed the canal's price up to a then-staggering $800,000. At that price it would never show a profit, but the ditching and building of locks provided much-needed revenue for planters who had lost the bounty paid on indigo and been hit by a series of bad freshets: They rented out their slaves to the corporation. Once completed, the canal also provided a very useful service to the inland settlers. Plagued by insufficient water to raise and lower the canal boats and flats through the locks, and having to compete with the South Carolina railroad, the waterway officially closed in 1850.

Even as the canal was being built, planters discovered that they could grow and gin inland cotton for a handsome profit. Thus, cotton became the major cargo during the next half century. Seven hundred and twenty boats, each paying a $22 toll, delivered 70,000 bales to Charleston in 1830. But historian Porcher reports that in 1831 he personally witnessed the strangest shipment to pass this way. "A gentleman from the upper country of high social position, but of a decidedly sportive tendency," passed by on a canal boat loaded with fighting gamecocks. "He had heard the Governor of Havana was a lover of the cockpit and with this venture he was going to try his fortune in that city." You're not likely to come upon such a sight, but the canal itself is impressive enough and is open to canoe and kayak traffic.

105.8	0.0	*To return to Charleston, from entrance gates, retrace to Rembrant Dennis Boulevard / P-0801.*
106.5	0.7	*At stoplight, turn left onto Rembrant Dennis Boulevard.*
107.4	0.9	*At second stoplight, continue straight onto U.S. 52 East.*
123.2	15.8	*Turn right onto U.S. 78 West.*
125.2	2.0	*Turn left onto I-26 East.*
140.2	15.0	*Return to downtown Charleston via I-26.*
END TOUR		

Edisto Island

TOUR ELEVEN

EDISTO ISLAND

On this day trip, we head south on U.S. 17, then turn toward the coast.
We pass through the village of **Adams Run**, whose pretty little **Willtown Church**
immigrated with the population. Then it's on to the Sea Island "principality" of
Edisto Island. Here we drive through a landscape unchanged by developers
to visit two distinctive old churches. Next, we walk the **Edisto Beach State Park
Nature Trail** that winds through a coastal forest and ends at a 4,000-year-old
Indian midden. Lastly, we beachcomb on **Edisto Beach State Park Beach**,
a spot famous for its Pleistocene fossils. You can easily fit this trip into one leisurely
day, but if you're not up to the walk, skip the lengthy nature trail in favor of
the beach.

Willtown Church (Christ St. Paul's Church)
    Route 174 in Adams Run | 843-889-2820
Edisto Island
    www.edistoisland.com
The Presbyterian Church on Edisto Island
    2164 Highway 174 | 843-869-2326 | *www.pcedisto.org*
New First Missionary Baptist Church (formerly the First Baptist Church)
1644 Highway 174 | 843-869-2432 | *www.newfmbc.org*
Trinity Episcopal Church
    1589 Highway 174 | 843-869-3568
The Old Store, Freedman's Village, With These Hands
    1444 Highway 174 | 843-869-3509
Edisto Beach State Park
    8377 State Cabin Road | 843-869-2756

BEGIN TOUR
0.0   0.0   *Take U.S. 17 South from Charleston. Start mileage
                from south side of Ashley River Bridge (far side away
                from downtown Charleston). Note: For information
                about these first 23.4 miles, see Tour 4, Beaufort
                and the Sea Islands, page 79.*
23.4 23.4   *Turn left onto S.C. 174 South.*
25.9   2.5   *Turn right, continuing on S.C. 174 South.*

❶ ADAMS RUN

This little summer retreat started in about 1839 when the Wilkinsons of nearby
Summit Plantation began to lease lots for $15 a year to planters from the Pon Pon
and Edisto River area. It was called Wilkinsonville then, but mysteriously changed
to Adamsville, then to Adams Run. (There was no Adams family on record.) At
some point, lots were sold and substantial houses built, and in 1852, a legislative
act declared the citizens of Adams Run, temporary and otherwise, "a body politic."

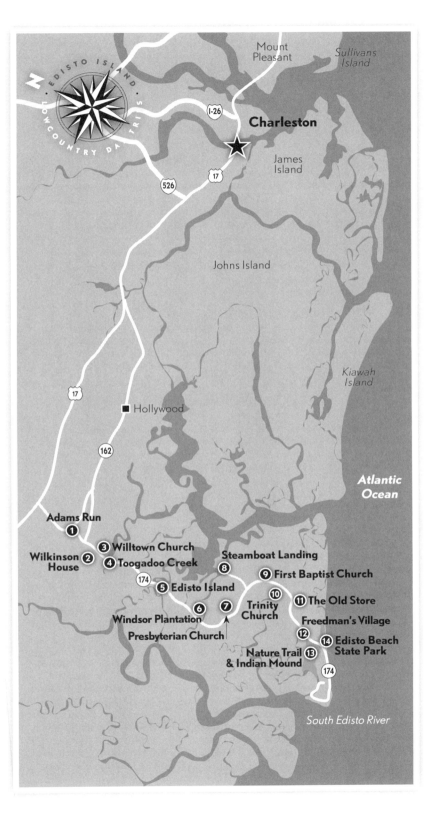

26.0 0.1   *On right, Wilkinson House.*

❷WILKINSON HOUSE, c. 1838
Not open to public.
William Wilkinson, in 1838, built the large house on the right as we come into town, but he sold it for taxes after the Civil War. During the conflict, this was a base for Confederate defenses; in the years after, a small center for agriculture-related commerce. It's the "Village" described in Ambrose Gonzolas' 1922 Gullah account *Black Border*—a distinction now grown dubious. The main coastal road came this way, but U.S. 17 bypassed the community in the late 1930s.

26.1 0.1   *Continue on S.C. 174 South. On left,*
                   Willtown Church (Christ Episcopal Church).

❸WILLTOWN CHURCH (Christ St. Paul's Church), c. 1834
You find the Willtown Church here in Adams Run because the congregation deserted nearby Willtown before the Civil War. In 1879, they disassembled the building and brought it along. It's hard to say exactly how close this comes to the brick-columned structure of Willtown. It still seems of "singular beauty and completeness," especially in this setting of oaks, dogwoods, and azaleas.
Willtown
Willtown, on the nearby South Edisto River, ranked second only to Charles Town in the colony's early days. Few records exist, but the town proved substantial enough to survive the Yemassee War, and the men of the Presbyterian congregation put down the Stono slave rebellion in 1739. By the beginning of the 19th century, however, residents began abandoning the town. A rectory that accompanied the church is all that remains, and that's on private property.

26.1 0.0   *From Christ Church, continue south on S.C. 174.*
28.4 2.3   *Cross Toogadoo Creek.*

❹TOOGADOO CREEK and THE OTHER PLACES
In discussing this little corner of the world, Dr. Johnson mentions the Clementia Springs of the Clement family. Their famous sulphur water was taken for medical purposes. He also tells of Revolutionary War patriot Mellinchamp, who received 17 saber wounds and was left for dead by the British. He crawled away and was nursed back to health by a squatter woman. When William Gilmore Simms used the incident in a novel, he just changed "squatter" to "aristocratic" so it would make for better reading.

   We soon cross the headwaters of the Toogadoo River, on the banks of which once lived Francis Wilkinson Pickens, governor of South Carolina. He was also ambassador to Russia—the apple of his eye, Lucy Holcombe, would only marry him if he became an ambassador. She had been bitterly disappointed in love, for her first fiancé had dashed off with Narciso López in 1853 to liberate Cuba, where he was quickly stood up against a wall and shot.

   On our way to Edisto we pass soybean fields and large oaks crowding against the highway. Large vistas of open marshland begin. This is the mythical community of Nelly—"You is Nelly to Edisto." So if you're going to read the history, read it quickly.

28.4 0.0   *Continue south on S.C. 174.*
31.8 3.4   *Cross Dawhoo River Bridge.*

| **D**unes, *palmettos, and pelicans on Edisto Island.*

❺ EDISTO ISLAND

In the years preceding the Civil War, this little community was so wealthy, isolated, and ready for independence that it was called "the royal principality of Edisto." By then it already had a couple of centuries of recorded history under its belt. When the Spanish first spoke of the "Orista," or Edisto, they referred to the Port Royal inhabitants, but by 1670 these Indians had been pushed to this island. The English found them there, and in 1674 the Earl of Shaftesbury (Lord Ashley Cooper) at least made an offer to buy it from the tribe. He renamed it Locke Island after his philosopher, secretary, and physician, John Locke. Shaftesbury hoped to set up a feudal estate here complete with serfs, but it's likely he never meant to come and was only trying to confuse his many enemies. Paul Grimball, secretary to the governor, was living on the island, however, so the Spanish burned his house when they returned to restate their claim in 1686. The tabby ruins remain.

Hardy Welsh and Scots immigrants came soon after. They attempted to grow rice, but switched to indigo. By 1714, the growing population requested a road and causeway. During the Revolution the islanders formed a company of patriots. According to most sources, Edisto wasn't a battleground, but in her *Historic Houses*, Harriette Leiding says that privateer Tories and Mediterranean Sea sailors in long "refuge boats" paddled up from Savannah and raided the island for cattle and whatever else they could carry off. The real scourge came after that war. David Ramsey's 1808 history reports that more than three-fourths of the inhabitants died of fever during these bad years, and some of the old family names disappeared altogether.

The days of island royalty, however, had already begun. Cotton had very successfully replaced indigo. Slaves outnumbered the tiny white population 10-to-1, and they cultivated virtually all available acres. The white boys were sent to Yale and Princeton, and even girls were educated. Within two years, William Seabrook built the mansion that would set the princely style for those to come. With little room for hunting or horseracing on the small island, fishing and fast sailboats became favored pursuits. Religion was better practiced than on the mainland, dancing parties fewer.

In 1825, Lafayette made his fabled visit, and the following year Robert Mills' *Statistics* reported that such royal treatment as he received was not just reserved for French noblemen. The hospitality of the island was indeed legendary. No tavern was ever attempted, for none was needed.

By 1862, Union soldiers and sailors had dampened such romantic notions. The inhabitants evacuated, leaving their mansions to the Union army and freed slaves. At war's end, Sherman confiscated Edisto and settled 10,000 more

freedmen there. But this emergency order was overturned, and in 1866, the white population returned to find its homes vandalized but still standing. The blacks now worked on shares, for a salary, or a combination of both. By 1900, the boll weevil had appeared, and in 1920 farmers gave up cotton for good. Truck crops replaced cotton because the completion of the Dawhoo Bridge eased getting these crops to market. Unneeded black labor migrated away. At the same time, visitors began to arrive.

A Sumter-based resort group opened up the beach, but growth was slow without electricity or other conveniences, and the island remained uninhabited enough that rumrunners ran their "cedar pencil" business on the beach's lee shore. In the late 1930s, however, the state park was started, and mainlanders discovered Edisto. In a thick stand of palmettos and high dunes, Civilian Conservation Corps workers built park buildings and the road was paved, but the hurricane of 1940 destroyed most of their work. Both private and public sectors started

Botany Bay Plantation
In 2008, the nearly 5,000-acre Botany Bay Plantation Wildlife Management Area opened to the public, providing access to two formerly private plantations. Within the boundary of the ACE Basin, the land covers a spectrum of habitats—from the beach and maritime forest and coastal scrub/shrub areas to tidal marshes and historic sites listed on the National Historic Register. Learn more about the history and culture of the island at Edisto Island Historic Museum (843-869-1954).

over. Workers moved five surviving park cabins inland to a safer spot, and refurbished the beach with sand pumped from a back lagoon. Today, as on many other Sea Islands, resorts are quickly replacing plantations.

Dawhoo Bridge, Whooping Island, and Little Edisto
You're crossing the Dawhoo River, which is also the Intracoastal Waterway. Until 1920 you crossed here by ferry. This is Whooping Island on the far side: You stood here and "whooped" for the ferryman. Beyond the next marsh expanse, Little Edisto Island begins.

35.0 3.2   *Just after crossing the second bridge (Russell Creek Bridge), pull off on the right side of the road and look back across the creek downstream toward Windsor Plantation.*

❻WINDSOR PLANTATION, c. 1857
Not open to public.
The cleared fields around Windsor Plantation were so low workers had to dike them to protect the cotton from spring tides. E. Mikell Bailey received the house as a wedding gift. Built high on piers to catch the breeze and stay above the storm tides, it's typical of many Sea Island homes, which differ from the Federalist and Greek Revival mansions on Edisto proper. Take a good look anyway, for these other homes are well off the road; this is probably the only one you'll see clearly.

35.0	**0.0**	*Continue on S.C. 174 South.*
38.3	**3.3**	*Turn left into parking area of Presbyterian Church on Edisto Island.*

| **Presbyterian Church on Edisto Island.*

❼ PRESBYTERIAN CHURCH ON EDISTO ISLAND, c. 1830
Grounds open to public.
This Presbyterian church claims the distinction of being "the oldest existing in its original location and of unbroken continuity in South Carolina." Church membership, however, did not grow appreciably until 1821, when William States Lee began a memorable pastorate that lasted half a century. In 1830, cotton wealth and renewed religious enthusiasm made the current building possible. Six years later, famed planter William Seabrook left the church $5,000. A cove ceiling was added to the interior and the large bell tower and portico replaced the original modest entry. The planters living on the inland portion of the island entered through the "burrough door" on the left. The others entered through the "seaside door" on the right.

Reverend Lee brought a large number of blacks into the church, something the Presbyterians usually could not accomplish. But during the Civil War, these freed slaves took over the building, and in 1866 Lee led a small white membership into a Sunday service and reclaimed the building "in the name of God and by authority of the U.S. Government."

Although the church is locked, we can wander around the graveyard, gaining insight into the island's personalities. The tombs are often ornate, some even monumental. According to Dr. Johnson, the prominent wreath-encircled column once had a stone flame at its tip. A mother erected it for her son, paid $5,000 (the same as the portico and steeple of the church), and brought it from Italy. Others hold bits of inscribed verse or statement. Certain that he would lose a duel to a notorious outsider, one islander arrived with a mattress to bear his own body away. Instead, he won and paid for his opponent's stone—which warns, "Prepare to meet thy God." "Perished in the wreck of the steamboat Pulaski, which was lost by the explosion of her boilers," says another. "Left us in the full assurance of a seat in that Grand Lodge above," is inscribed for an entombed Mason. Far to the left, three stones give names and only the date "Christmas 1865." They were Union missionaries who drowned while crossing St. Pierre Creek after a Christmas Eve gathering. Their friends put them over there, as far from the secessionists as possible. A suicide denied burial was placed here anyway, and a substantial fence erected to guarantee he stayed.

38.3	**0.0**	*Continue on S.C. 174 South.*
38.9	**0.6**	*Turn left onto Steamboat Road / S-10-968.*
40.5	**1.6**	*Dirt road dead-ends at Steamboat Landing parking lot.*

❽ STEAMBOAT LANDING
Water always connected the island with Charleston, and most of the planters had their own craft. On the eve of the Civil War, the slave-rowed canoe *Nellie*

Fier or *Nullifier* (depending) carried off a young Mikell. By the 1820s, however, patriarch William Seabrook had begun a regular steamboat service to Edisto. That paddlewheeler, *The William Seabrook*, ended as a small but notorious blockade runner, and Seabrook's wharf wound up as the current public boat landing. The short, pretty, oak-shrouded drive offers a nice view of North Edisto.

40.5	**0.0**	*Retrace Steamboat Road / S-10-968.*
41.3	**0.8**	*Turn left onto Jenkins Hill Road.*
42.9	**1.6**	*Continue on the graded, dirt state road (unmarked).*
44.8	**1.9**	*At stop sign, on left is the Old First Baptist Church.*

❾ THE FIRST BAPTIST CHURCH, c. 1818
Not open to public.

Now the New First Missionary Baptist Church, this was one of the island's earliest Baptist churches, though not the first. (See Euhaw Baptist Church, Tour 7.) Locals tell the story of Hephzabah J. Townsend, who began her life under the most perilous of circumstances. She was born in the midst of the Revolution. Her mother died almost immediately and, fearing smallpox would get her as well, two faithful slaves smuggled the infant out of the blockaded city. From such a beginning grew a woman of conscience and resolve. Despite her husband's objections, she insisted on building this church in 1818, and eventually gave it to the Baptist slaves. Immediately after the war, the little Greek Revival meetinghouse was doubled in size and the portico added. The monument at the rear is Mrs. Townsend's. Her children wrote: "Her character was so strongly cast, and her impulses were so generous that she was an object of indifference to no one."

44.8	**0.0**	*Turn left onto S.C. 174 South.*
45.0	**0.2**	*On right is Trinity Episcopal Church.*

❿ TRINITY EPISCOPAL CHURCH, c. 1880
Grounds open to public.

Although among the parishes laid out by the Church Act of 1706, the first building here didn't come until 1774. After the Revolution, however, when other congregations floundered, this one remained active and in 1840 built an impressive new church—perhaps even grander than the Presbyterian. Inspired by St. Michael's of Charleston, it seated 200 people and had a steeple 100 feet high. It burned in 1879, and was replaced the following year with this little Gothic building. After hurricane damage in 1893, a former slave craftsman added the remarkable interior woodwork. Though it's usually locked, you can appreciate the Tiffany glass from the outside. The stones of the surrounding graveyard are far older than the present church, and though not so grand as those already visited, they still remind of the incredible mortality, especially among the young, on the island.

45.0	**0.0**	*Continue on S.C. 174 South.*
45.6	**0.6**	*On left, The Old Store.*

⓫ THE OLD STORE, (With These Hands), date unknown

Originally the bridge passed over Store Creek to the left of what is now the store With These Hands, so the building faced the road the other way. That wasn't its first move, though, for it was brought from Eddingville Beach and reassembled here. The present gallery specializes in fine handmade items, and beside it the old post office is now a restaurant.

45.6	**0.0**	*Continue on S.C. 174 South, crossing Store Creek.*
47.5	**1.9**	*Intersection of Oyster Factory Road. Freedman's Village.*

⑫ FREEDMAN'S VILLAGE
Unmarked

Most of the island's plantations were kept intact at the Civil War's end, but here one was broken up and sold to the newly freed slaves. The creek was always a ready source of food, and the new owners worked as tenants or

Spanish Moss
Spanish moss is not a parasite: It is attached to the tree but gets its nourishment from the rain and air. Settlers once used it to stuff mattresses and in baby diapers—an itchy proposition since it often contains bugs.

planted their own small patches in cotton until the boll weevil arrived. When they felt the plantation stores were getting the better of them, "midnight gin houses" ensured some of the cash went into their own pockets.

Within the slave community, religion was very important. Some of the old stories and spirituals have been recorded, which is good, because even if Freedman's Village and the other small communities survive, it seems inevitable that resort development will erode much of this island's Gullah culture.

47.5	**0.0**	*Continue on S.C. 174 South from intersection of Oyster Factory Road.*
51.3	**3.8**	*Turn right just past the sign for Edisto Beach State Park Nature Trail, onto State Cabin Road.*
52.2	**0.9**	*Park under the trees to enjoy the trails.*

⑬ EDISTO BEACH STATE PARK NATURE TRAIL and INDIAN MOUND
On this day, we join a naturalist who guides us through the park. Any mistakes contained below are mine, not hers. None of these trees appears ancient, so this was probably in cotton or even truck crops not too long ago. As we walk on toward the water, more typical Sea Island forest emerges—live oak, water oak, gum, and loblolly pine, with palmetto, magnolia, and hickory increasing toward the end. The yucca at the beginning is a rare one—note the blue-green leaves. We'll see the common variety at the Indian Mound, which is about a 4-mile walk round trip on the Spanish Mount Trail.

A marker points out a turn in the trail, where a small Virginia pine struggles. A saw palmetto, aptly named for its saw-like stem, grows close by. Sweet gum shed their prickly balls, spreading their seeds for the next generation. Sapsuckers have drilled their distinctive rows of small holes in the bark. Ferns show their wing-like fronds. From a blown-over oak, we observe the shallow road system typical of this moist area.

Animal signs abound, from where raccoons fed on grapes from a large

Edisto Indians

One ethnologist suggests this site once held the main village of the Edisto Indians. The Lord Proprietor's explorer, Sanford, visited in 1666 and was royally entertained. (The man-eating Westoes had driven the tribe here not long before Sanford's arrival.) The Englishman entered a "large house of Circular form," observed "fair forest" and "diverse fields of maize," and watched a ball game played with "bowle and six foot staves." The remnants of this tribe sided with the settlers in the Yemassee War, and a few may have remained on the north end of the island well into the 18th century.

ropelike vine to a dead tree so full of woodpecker holes that our guide calls it a "natural condominium." We see deer tracks and hear wrens call "cheerily" from the trees.

Upon crossing a narrow marsh slough via a boardwalk, we spy periwinkles on the tops of marsh stalks, poisonous coral bean (recognized by its bright red pea in a dark pod), and a "mitten tree." But now we've reached the mound. Below the sign saying, "Don't use metal detectors or remove artifacts," sweet bay grows and wild grasses are seeding up. We traverse the top of the shell mound and down. Unfortunately, Spanish Mount, as the shell midden is known, has eroded greatly in recent years, but what remains is still interesting.

We make our way home talking of copperhead snakes and fossil hunting.

53.1	**0.9**	*Return to S.C. 174 from parking lot, turn right (South).*
54.3	**1.2**	*Turn left into Edisto Beach State Park.*

⑭ EDISTO BEACH STATE PARK

Pleasant surprises await on these two miles of beach. First, it features several famous plantation houses, all private, but nice to look at nevertheless. The relatively new Edisto Environmental Learning Center (843-869-4430) holds exhibits that highlight the area's natural wonders, including the many fossils found here.

Though a few are found on Pawleys Island and Litchfield Beach, Edisto is a great place to look for Pleistocene relics. If you want to camp so your fossil hunting lasts longer than a day, the park offers more than 100 sites that usually require advance booking. Both day and overnight visitors benefit from picnic tables and restrooms.

Fossils

For at least the last million years the world has been going through a series of ice ages, which means that glaciers have spread and retreated across much of the Northern Hemisphere and the oceans have risen and fallen. (About 12,000 years ago, the ocean at Edisto started roughly six miles farther out, and has been moving inland ever since.) During this period, animals migrated many times between continents. Because of connections between land masses, there is evidence of all sorts of unexpected occupants—many of them extinct all over the world and others missing only from America. A

A *secluded beach on Edisto.*

glass display case in front of the main park office shows fossilized parts of tapir, sharks, parrotfish, mastadon, mammoth, horses, sloth, and armadillos, all found here. Some of these finds are quite large; you shouldn't expect anything so dramatic.

Along the normal high tide line, a fairly thick strip of mostly worn shell—oysters, clams, cockles, bulls eyes, and lettered olives (our state shell)—assembles. High up on the beach, a second strip marks where the storms reach. Along here, sea turtles nest. You may see their nests marked by flags.

For successful fossil-hunting, here's what you need to know:
1. For our purposes, a fossil can be defined as the mineral deposit where bone, tooth, cartilage, or shell has been. (We aren't likely to find vegetation, burrows, or imprints here.)
2. The color in fossils comes from the surrounding material—brown if the dead animal was buried in sand, black if the bone was in mud or vegetation. These are the two colors usually found on Edisto, but some shells turn grayish-white or even golden.
3. Fossils are normally heavier than bone, but if you're uncertain which you have, dry it and burn a corner. New bone has protein and will still smell when burned.
4. Look for the porous marrow part of the bone. This is an easy way to distinguish fossil from stone, but there are many exceptions: stingray plates, ear bones, ivory, and teeth. Pieces of clam and oyster shell can weather into strange shapes and colors and easily fool you.
5. Look for fossils at the ebbing tide or at low water, preferably after a storm. The bigger items will be thrown higher on the beach and are more quickly buried in the sand. The lighter ones drift back with the surf.
6. Watch the beach in front of you. In her fossil book, Thomas says don't talk to your companion, and wear a hat.

54.3	**0.0**	*From Edisto State Park Beach gate, turn right onto S.C. 174 North.*
72.0	**17.7**	*Turn right onto S.C. 164.*
74.2	**2.2**	*Junction with S.C. 162.*
75.0	**2.8**	*Town limit of Hollywood.*
81.8	**6.8**	*Town limit of Rantowles.*
83.1	**1.3**	*At yield sign, continue straight onto U.S. 17 North.*
94.7	**11.6**	*South side of Ashley River Bridge.*

END TOUR

Additional Day Trips from Charleston

MORE TOURS

ADDITIONAL DAY TRIPS FROM CHARLESTON

❶ SHELL ISLAND

Take a boat tour to a barrier island, complete with excellent shell collecting.
Available year-round, weather permitting. The tour lasts approximately four to five
hours. Starting time can be scheduled directly with Capt. Sandy and will be based
on the tide. Admission is charged, and the boat can accommodate groups
up to 16. This is one of the special tours available from Capt. Sandy's Tours,
343 Ida Drive, Georgetown, S.C. 843-527-4106.

0.0	**0.0**	*From Charleston, take U.S. 17 North; begin clocking mileage at north (Mount Pleasant) side of Cooper River Bridge.*
57.0	**57.0**	*Turn right onto Front Street and Georgetown County Chamber of Commerce Visitor Center (531 Front Street, Georgetown, S.C. 29440, 800-777-7705) will be on your right.*

❷ SOUTH ISLAND

Wildlife abounds, and bird watchers are particularly thrilled by "one of the
largest concentrations of waterfowl in the Southeast." To tour South Island, you
must register at least a year in advance and cross by ferry. A guide directs a bus
tour of a small portion of the 24,000 acres. Contact the Tom Yawkey Wildlife
Center at 843-546-6814.

0.0	**0.0**	*From Charleston, take U.S. 17 North; begin clocking mileage at north (Mount Pleasant) side of Cooper River Bridge.*
40.8	**40.8**	*Cross over the Santee River.*
44.0	**3.2**	*Turn right onto North Santee River Road.*
48.8	**4.8**	*Turn left onto Estherville Road.*
51.6	**2.8**	*Turn right onto South Island Road / SC-18.*
52.3	**0.7**	*Road ends at South Island Ferry boat landing. Visitation must be pre-scheduled.*

❸ BULL ISLAND

"Certainly one of the wildest and most beautiful of the barrier islands," was the
original description I gave of Bulls Island. Hurricane Hugo took a toll on the
island's tropical forest, but natural beauty remains—it's just a different sort than
it was before the storm.

The *Carolina*, bringing the first settlers to this colony in 1670, made landfall
here and slipped in behind the island to take on fresh water. It was here that those
early settlers first conversed with the Indians. The years since weren't always idle
ones. "Live oakers" cut many of the ribs for our first Navy ships here, and cultivation
and livestock herding were intensive. In 1936, however, the island became a part
of the Cape Romain National Wildlife Refuge, and nature was quick to reclaim

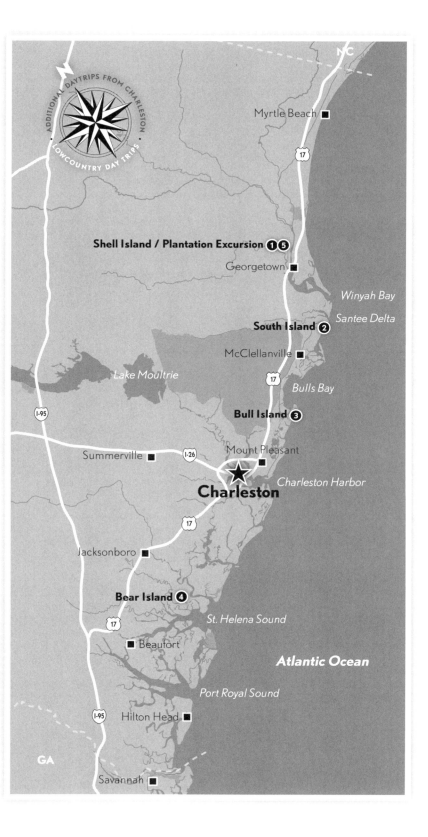

Snowy egrets near Bulls Island.

her own: The island grew thick with oaks, palmettos, and magnolias. Hugo greatly reduced the oak and magnolia population. Sixteen miles of winding roads and trails crisscross the island, passing by and over ponds and savannahs, and out onto a beach famed for its "boneyard" of driftwood stumps. Wildlife is still in evidence— deer, raccoons, fox squirrels, alligators. Bird watching can still be enjoyed; Peterson did work here, as did South Carolina's own Chamberlain and Sprunt, and more than 277 species have been reported. The island also offers saltwater fishing, an "Old Fort," and photography opportunities. The biggest drawback remains the bugs. During the summer, the mosquitoes can be bad except along the beachfront, and the ticks are the worst in the world. Carry repellant and don't wander too far off the trails.

The trip over from Garris Landing is an adventure in itself, as the ferry twists and turns through a maze of saltwater channels. Remember that you're there for the whole day and are responsible for bringing your own lunch, water, and bug spray.

0.0	**0.0**	*From Charleston, take U.S. 17 North. Begin clocking mileage at the north side of the Cooper River Bridge (Mount Pleasant side).*
14.6	**14.6**	*Turn right onto Seewee Road / S-10-584.*
17.9	**3.3**	*Turn right onto Bulls Island Road / S-10-1170.*
19.4	**1.5**	*Arrive at Garris Landing pier parking lot.*

❹ BEAR ISLAND

Bear Island Wildlife Management Area, located between the Ashepoo and Edisto rivers, consists of more than 12,000 acres of varied coastal habitat. Marsh impoundments of 5,385 acres (some are former rice fields), tidal marshes, maritime-influenced woodlands, and managed agricultural lands provide refuge for game species ranging from bobwhite quail to white-tailed deer. In the fall and winter, the area hosts thousands of waterfowl. Hunting is allowed by special annual drawings and permits. Bear Island is also home to numerous non-game and endangered species, including alligators and bald eagles. February through March is the recommended season for visitors interested in bird watching and general wildlife observation and photography. Incidentally, this is the cornerstone of the ACE Basin conservation project. Presentations by South Carolina Department of Natural Resources personnel on wildlife natural history and management techniques can be prearranged. For more information, call 843-844-8957.

0.0	**0.0**	*From Charleston, take U.S. 17 South; begin clocking mileage from south side of Ashley River Bridge.*
37.7	**37.7**	*Turn left onto S-15-26.*
50.5	**12.8**	*Turn left into Bear Island W.M. Area.*

❺ PLANTATION EXCURSION

You will enjoy this boat cruise that highlights beautiful plantations and nature's treasures on Lowcountry rivers. This is one of the special tours available year-round, weather permitting, from Capt. Sandy's Tours, 343 Ida Drive, Georgetown, S.C. 843-527-4106. Starting time can be scheduled directly with Capt. Sandy and will be based on the tide. Tour lasts for approximately three hours.

0.0	**0.0**	*From Charleston, take U.S. 17 North; begin clocking mileage at north (Mount Pleasant) side of Cooper River Bridge.*
57.0	**57.0**	*Turn right onto Front Street and Georgetown County Chamber of Commerce Visitor Center will be on your right.*

INDEX

Adams Run — **204**
All Saints Parish Waccamaw Church — **121**
Ashley River Bridge — **28**
Atalaya — **137**
Audubon Swamp Garden — **36**
Bacon's Bridge — **44**
Baptist Church of Beaufort — **92**
Bear Island — **219**
Beaufort — **83**
Beaufort National Cemetery — **84**
Beaufort Visitors Center — **91**
Bethel Presbyterian Church — **173**
Biggin Church Ruins — **196**
Bluffton — **149**
Boone Hall Plantation — **70**
Brabant Plantation — **190**
Brookgreen Gardens — **122**
Bull Hill Methodist Church — **154**
Bull Island — **216**
Cainhoy — **190**
Charles Pinckney National Historic Site — **72**
Charles Towne Landing State Historic Site — **31**
Charleston Harbor — **62**
Christ Episcopal Church — **68**
Church of the Holy Trinity — **145**
Colleton State Park — **167**
Colonel Isaac Hayne's Tomb — **173**
Colonial Dorchester State Historic Site — **44**
Cordesville — **192**
Cypress Gardens — **183**
Dennis Wildlife Center — **197**
Detyens Shipyards — **188**
Drayton Hall — **34**
Edisto Island — **207**
Edisto Beach State Park — **212**
Edisto Beach State Park Nature Trail and Indian Mound — **211**
Edisto Nature Trail — **174**
Euhaw Baptist Church — **145**
Fort Moultrie — **75**
Fort Palmetto — **70**
Francis Beidler Forest — **162**
Francis Marion — **195**
Francis Marion's Grave — **200**
Freedman's Village — **211**
French Quarter Creek — **191**
Garris Landing — **102**
George Parsons Elliott House — **85**
Georgetown — **111**
Georgetown County Visitors' Center — **111**
Georgetown Tours — **115**
Hampton Plantation State Historic Site — **107**
Henry C. Chambers Waterfront Park — **85**
Hobcaw Barony Discovery Center — **120**
Hopsewee Plantation — **109**
Huger — **192**
Hunting Island State Park — **97**
Huntington Beach State Park — **134**
Indian Field Campground — **166**

Indigo Vats **181**
Jacksonboro **173**
Jefferies Generating Plant and Pinopolis Dam **196**
Magnolia Plantation and Gardens **36**
McClellanville **103**
Mepkin Abbey **193**
Middleburg Plantation **191**
Middleton Place **40**
Moncks Corner **184**
Mount Pleasant **65**
Mount Pleasant Presbyterian Church **66**
Murrells Inlet **139**
Naval Weapons Station **180**
Nesbitt House **183**
Newington Plantation **45**
Old St. Andrew's Parish Church **33**
Old Santee Canal Park (Stony Landing) **200**
Palmetto Islands County Park **71**
Parker's Ferry Battle Site **172**
Patriots Point Naval and Maritime Museum **62**
Pawleys Island **120**
Penn Center **94**
Pinckney Island Wildlife Refuge **148**
Pineville **199**
Pinopolis Methodist Church **184**
Pompion Hill Chapel **191**
Pon Pon Chapel of Ease Ruins **172**
Presbyterian Church on Edisto Island **209**
Quinby Bridge **192**
Rice Hope Plantation **193**
River Road **33**
Rose Hill Plantation **146**
St. George **165**
St. Helena's Episcopal Church **92**
St. James–Goose Creek Church **180**
St. John's Baptist Church **185**
St. Stephen's Episcopal Church **198**
St. Thomas Church **190**
Santee Coastal Reserve-Washo Reserve **108**
Savannah National Wildlife Refuge **154**
Sheldon Church Ruins **83, 142**
Shell Island Tour **216**
Silk Hope Plantation **192**
Snee Farm **72**
South Island **216**
Stallsville **46**
Steamboat Landing **209**
Strawberry Chapel **192**
Sullivan's Island **72**
Summerville **46**
Sweetgrass Basket Stands **68**
Taveau Church **193**
Trinity Episcopal Church **210**
Victoria Bluff Heritage Preserve **147**
Walterboro **167**
Wappetaw Burial Ground **102**
Willtown Church (Christ St. Paul's Church) **206**
Windsor Plantation **208**

William P. Baldwin, III is a lifelong resident of the South Carolina Lowcountry. He graduated from Clemson University with a B.A. in History in 1966 and an M.A. in English in 1968. He and his wife, Lil, have two grown sons. Over the years, he's worked as a shrimper, builder, contractor, and most importantly, as a writer. He's done numerous articles on local subjects, is author if the well-received novel, *The Hard to Catch Mercy*, and wrote the text for N. Jane Iseley's perennial favorite, *Plantations of the Lowcountry.*

N. Jane Iseley is a graduate of Radford College and the New York Institute of Photography. As a staff photographer for Colonial Williamsburg for nine years, she was the photographic author of six books. As a freelance photographer, she has 23 more books to her credit, including *Charleston, Charleston Entertains, Plantations of the Low Country: South Carolina 1697-1865, The Charleston Interior, Savannah Tour of Homes and Gardens*, and *Savannah Secret and Public Gardens*. She is the president of Legacy Publications. Her home is on a family farm in Burlington, North Carolina.